HOW TO PUBLISH

YOUR CHILDREN'S BOOK

LIZA N. BURBY

SQUAREONE
WRITERS GUIDES

Cover Designer: Phaedra Mastrocola
In-House Editor: Joanne Abrams
Typesetter: Gary A. Rosenberg

Square One Publishers
115 Herricks Road
Garden City Park, NY 11040
(516) 535-2010 • (877) 900-BOOK
www.squareonepublishers.com

Publisher's Cataloging-in-Publication Data

Burby, Liza N.
    How to publish your children's book : a complete guide to making
the right publisher say yes / Liza N. Burby.
        p. cm. — (Square One writer's guide)
    Includes index.
    ISBN 0-7570-0036-3 (pbk.)
1. Children's literature—Publishing. 2. Children's literature—Marketing.
3. Books—Marketing—Handbooks, manuals, etc. I. Title. II. Series.
Z286.C48B87   2004
070.5—dc22

Printed in the United States of America

10   9   8   7   6   5   4   3   2   1

CONTENTS

*This book is dedicated to
my own budding writers,
Danielle and Laura.*

ACKNOWLEDGMENTS

Special thanks to my family, Steve, Danielle, and Laura, without whose patience and love I would never meet a deadline. Also, to Rudy Shur, my publisher, for giving me the opportunity to write this guide; to Joanne Abrams, my editor, for her insightful guidance; and to my agent, Grace Freedson, for making the match.

Numerous people answered my many questions while writing this book. They include authors Laura Backes, Johanna Hurwitz, Eoin Colfer, Marcia Byalick, Louise Borden, Annette Griessman, Joanne Di Napoli, Paula Danziger, Gordon Cormier, Ellen Levine, Gail Carson Levine, and Lee Better Hopkins; editors Susan Eddy at Mondo Publishing, Amy Griffen of Orchard Books, Rahel Lerner of Viz LLC, Louise May and Jennifer Frantz of Lee & Low, Laura Hornik and Lori Benton of Henry Holt, Phoebe Yeh of Harper, and Jodi Kreitzman of Knopf Delacourte Dell; and agents Jenne Dunham of Dunham Agency, Tracey Adams of Adams Literary, and Tema Siegel. I would also like to thank children's book editor Jill Jarnow for her careful review of the final version. I had help in my own community as well, from children's librarians Janet Scherer and Lynn Vitters of the South Huntington Library, and Jim Sullivan, assistant superintendent of South Huntington Public Schools.

Finally, I thank Laura Backes and Jon Bard for allowing me to draw from "In Their Own Words: The Best of CBI's Interviews," and reprint the words of authors Elizabeth-Ann Sachs, Jane Yolen, Dandi Daley Mackall, and Kathleen Duey.

PREFACE

How many times have you felt just the tiniest bit envious of *Harry Potter* author J.K. Rowling, even as you read her words with admiration? How about the talented Marc Brown, author of the *Arthur* books? How many times have you told yourself that you, too, have a tale or nonfiction topic to share with children? Surely you've asked yourself: How can I get *my* work published?

It takes a lot of effort to turn your written words into a published book, but it's also an enjoyable process. Whether you're describing the life of a basketball star like Sheryl Swoopes or telling the tale of a magical land, writing for children is fun. After all, how many of us aren't writing just for our young readers, but also for the pure pleasure of immersing ourselves in the world of children? That's why we owe our words the dedication it takes to see them in print. Nevertheless, in the process of pursuing a publishing contract, most of us can use some help to get the work from our computers to the bookstore and library shelves.

I'm the author of biographies, history, science, health, and social issue books for readers from elementary through high school. In fact, I've seen my name on the cover of thirty-eight children's books. I've also been a book editor. I know the most common mistakes writers make, the ones that get their work rejected. And I know what makes editors reach for the phone with excitement to say, "I want to publish your book."

How to Publish Your Children's Book offers practical information based on my own experience, as well as advice from agents, editors, publishers, and published authors. Throughout these pages, you'll find many helpful hints that will give you an extra edge as you pursue your first publishing contract. For instance, the best way to stay at the top of your game, so to speak, is to read children's books. How is that for agreeable "homework"?

Your dream of being a published children's book author can come true, and this book can help you make it happen. In Chapter 1, you'll be introduced to the world of children's book publishing, and to the Square One System for getting your children's book into print. This chapter also presents the first of many rules that you must learn and follow to get your book published. These rules will pop up now and then throughout the book, helping to steer you toward your goal.

One crucial difference between success and failure is having a clear understanding of where your book fits in the market. Chapter 2 therefore explains what book categories are, and introduces the Square One Book Classification System—a system that will help you easily and accurately identify the category in which your book belongs. This important chapter also acquaints you with the marketplace and explains the importance of identifying your audience, all with the goal of pinpointing the best companies for your book.

Chapter 3 discusses the business side of publishing, so you'll know what actually happens when you send your manuscript to a publishing house. This chapter will also help you determine the type of company that would be most likely to consider your work.

Since locating potential publishers is a crucial component of the Square One System, Chapter 4 familiarizes you with the best resources for zeroing in on just the right market. The world of publishing can be overwhelming, and the books designed as guides to this world can be equally intimidating. How, then, will you find the data you need on the companies you want to contact? Chapter 4 will lead you through the process, making it simple to both locate and understand the information you want.

Just like a resumé, a submission package must be carefully prepared if it's going to make a great first impression. Chapter 5 will work with you on a paragraph-by-paragraph basis, guiding you through the writing of a submission package that will get results. Because children's book writers often ask, "Should I include illustrations?" this chapter provides special sections for the writer who is also an artist, as well as for the person who is primarily an illustrator or photographer. Whether you've created a picture book for toddlers or a novel for young adults, this chapter will tell you just what you must include in your package—and what should be left out.

Once your package is ready to go, you'll want to turn to Chapter 6. Here, you'll find step-by-step instructions for sending out your package in a way that will maximize your chance of success; minimize your effort, time, and costs; and even allow you to fine-tune your submission package along the way. Is there a right way and a wrong way to send in your submission? There is, and this chapter will help you do it right from start to finish.

If all goes well, you may soon receive a contract in the mail. A joyful event? Sure. But the receipt of a publishing agreement can also be daunting. Just what does all that legalese mean? Chapter 7 not only explains all the terms, but also helps you make informed decisions throughout the negotiations process.

Despite your careful attention to the Square One System, there will probably be occasions on which your work just isn't what a publisher wants. Chapter 8 helps you pinpoint the possible cause of the problem, and presents a variety of ways in which it can be solved. And if there are still no bites, this chapter fills you in on some fascinating alternatives, including self-publishing.

Although this book is packed with information and tips to send your words on their way into the publishing world, it is not designed to overwhelm you. The information is broken down into clearly labeled sections, the advice is realistic, and the steps are simple to follow. So with your children's manuscript in hand, let's begin the journey that all children's book writers must take—the journey to being a published author.

—Liza N. Burby

A Note on Gender

To avoid long and awkward phrasing within sentences, the publisher has chosen to alternate the use of male and female pronouns according to chapter. Therefore, when referring to the third-person writer or editor, odd-numbered chapters use male pronouns, while even-numbered chapters employ female pronouns, to give acknowledgement to writers and editors of both genders.

CHAPTER 1

An Introduction

It's 9:00 A.M. on a Monday morning. The editor sits down with his cup of coffee, prepared to get through the pile of manuscript submissions on his desk. He knows that somewhere within that mountain of paper is one of the dozen or so manuscripts his house is hoping to publish that year. So he takes a sip of java and starts sifting through the envelopes. Sadly, though, just as the pile of manuscripts on his desk is slowly being whittled down, another pile is growing on the floor. It's the rejection pile, filled with the optimistic submissions of people like you and me.

It may seem that this caffeine-hyped editor has no more method to his mountain offensive than to move the pile from one place to another. But I assure you that he's using a very simple system—one that's been employed throughout publishing history by all editors, regardless of the publishing house in which their desk is found. Although it may seem a mysterious process to hopeful writers, the guidelines haven't changed over the years. When reviewing a submission, every editor asks the same question: Does it fit our house? If your manuscript submission doesn't, there's really nothing an editor can do about it, because it's his job to find the manuscript that matches his house's genre, reading level, and subject matter. And your job? To make sure you provide the perfect match. That's what *How to Publish Your Children's Book* is all about.

The book you are about to read presents a proven system of submissions that will (1) avoid the common mistakes that turn editors off, (2) save you valuable time and money, (3) allow you to find those houses best suited to your title, and (4) increase the odds of having your manuscript proposal accepted. Let's look at each of these points in turn.

AVOIDING MISTAKES THAT TURN EDITORS OFF

It's vital to remember that editors are busy people who can devote very little time to each proposal they receive. That's why it's so important to create an effective but concise submission package that avoids taxing the editor's patience.

Many authors unknowingly sprinkle their proposals with words and phrases that are almost guaranteed to trigger negative reactions on the part of an editor. Always remember that editors are busy people. If they see something in a proposal that tries their patience or raises questions about the abilities of the writer or the marketability of a book, they will instantly reject the proposal. I will show you how to clear your submission package of all unintentional land mines.

SAVING TIME AND MONEY

It takes a great deal of time to put together an elaborate submission package. And it takes a great deal of money to send it out. But the fact is that a good submission package doesn't have to be elaborate. In most cases, in fact, an effective proposal is fairly simple and light in weight, but is carefully crafted to hit its mark. This book will show you how to create a package that doesn't take hours to put together, that doesn't cost an arm and a leg to mail, and that is right on target.

FINDING THE HOUSES BEST SUITED TO YOUR TITLE

Most writers in search of a publisher pay little attention to the fine points of choosing a house that would best serve their needs. Instead, they select houses whose names are familiar to them, or they randomly send out proposals to all "legitimate" companies, hoping that someone somewhere will take an interest in their work. Remember the time and money mentioned above? You don't want to waste it by sending your carefully crafted submission package to publishers who would never even consider your proposal, or that are not a good fit for your title. This book will explain what you should be looking for, and what the right publisher should offer based upon your needs.

INCREASING YOUR ODDS OF ACCEPTANCE

While I may have painted editors as a fairly cranky group, nothing could be further from the truth. Recently, I attended a conference at which children's book editors discussed the types of books for which they're looking. At first, I was surprised that they genuinely seemed to want to reach out to us. But then I realized that they need us as much as we need them. To do their job, they require great manuscripts from people like you and me. Editors *want* to like our proposals, but they can base their response only on what we give them. And if we give them a bad submission package, chances are, they'll reject it.

Just as there are many ways to kill an editor's interest in your proposal, there are many ways to turn an editor on to your project. Some of them are relatively simple, while others require more preparation. In this book, you will find out how it's done.

RULE # 1

Sometimes, you just get lucky

Before I begin to detail the many steps that should be followed on the road to publishing success, I have to get one thing out of the way. Sometimes, it seems as though a writer simply rises out of the submissions pile to become an international star. At least that's what's been on the minds of all potential children's authors ever since J.K. Rowling wowed the publishing world with her *Harry Potter* books. Then there's Gordon Korman, author of over forty-five children's books, who sold his initial novel on his first try—when he was in the seventh grade. The problem is that when viewed from outside the industry, these seeming lucky breaks may be considered the norm. But the fact is that for most writers, rejection is part of the business. Even celebrated author Madeleine L'Engle experienced rejection. In fact, *A Wrinkle in Time* was rejected twenty times before a publisher took a chance on it!

Sure, publishing success will take some luck. And talent will certainly be required. But success will also necessitate a certain amount of publishing savvy. And how can you get that? Read on.

While an element of luck is involved in getting a book into print, you can greatly improve your odds of success by following a few simple rules.

WHAT'S IN THIS BOOK?

I have designed *How to Publish Your Children's Book* to provide the information you need to put my system into practice and get that longed-for positive response from children's book editors. For clarity, I have attempted to use nontechnical language throughout this book. Whenever I do include a technical term that's commonly used *in-house*—within a publishing company, that is—it's explained the first time it appears. And if you missed it the first time, you can always refer to the handy glossary in the back of the book.

Following this introductory chapter, the book is divided into seven chapters, each of which contains an important piece of the publishing puzzle. My aim throughout is to help you understand what goes on behind closed doors at a publishing house. We all read and hear about the huge advances some well-known writers receive, and about the book turned TV series or movie. But these success stories, while exciting, have nothing to do with the everyday workings of a publishing house, nor will they increase your chances of getting published. This book, however, was designed to show you exactly *what* to do and *why* you should do it.

Unless you know where your book fits in the market, you're going to have a hard time convincing an editor to buy it. That's why Chapter 2, "Where Does Your Book Fit In?," explains what book categories are, and what they mean to an editor and the marketplace. The chapter then presents the Square One Book Classification System, which will guide you in determining the specific book category into which your project falls. In addition, Chapter 2 will help you understand your audience and your marketplace—information that will be critical when you create your submission package.

Chapter 3, "The Business of Children's Book Publishing," continues our exploration of the book business, first by presenting the fascinating history of the children's book publishing industry. It then goes on to explain the publishing process as it is determined by different-sized companies, all with an eye to understanding how each type of company selects its books from the hundreds of submissions that pour in each year. And it helps steer you to the type of house that is most likely to accept your book proposal.

By the time you reach Chapter 4, "Choosing the Right Publisher," you will have determined the category into which your manuscript falls, and you will have learned a good deal about the publishing industry. The time will be right, then, to put your information to work and begin selecting the right publisher for your project. First, the chapter asks you some basic questions about your personal goals as a writer. Then, it provides a step-by-step system for creating a list of the best publishers—publishers that are right for your book and, just as important, right for you.

As the opening of this chapter indicates, editors are busy people who can spend only a very short time deciding whether any particular proposal is worth pursuing. This means that your submission package has to provide exactly what the editor is looking for in exactly the right form. If this task sounds a bit daunting, relax. Chapter 5, "Preparing the Package," provides a simple step-by-step system for creating each component of your submission. By following these steps, you'll be able to create an effective proposal that includes all the basic information the editor is looking for, and—just as important—avoids the pitfalls that keep so many writers from realizing their dream of publication. This chapter also offers special guidelines for the writer who is also an artist, and for the artist or photographer who is interested in illustrating children's book.

Once you've created your submission package, you may be tempted to print out a slew of proposals and send them to every publisher on your list. While this might *feel* good, there is a far more effective way to handle this part of the submissions process. Chapter 6, "Using the Square One System," will guide you in sending out your letter-perfect package so that you maximize your chance of success while minimizing your effort, time, and costs. You'll even have the opportunity to fine-tune your proposal along the way.

If you're like most authors—including yours truly—once your first group of proposals goes out, you'll be waiting for responses the way a child waits for his birthday gifts. The problem is that when a publishing contract does arrive, it's likely to be a bit more confusing than your average present. Terms like "indemnities" and "force majeure" can be intimidating. Add the fact that you need to understand not only what the publishing agreement *says*, but also what it *implies*, and your work is cut out for you. That's what Chapter 7, "The Deal," is all about. It sorts through the legal mumbo-jumbo, explaining all the standard terms used in a publishing contract. It also provides guidelines for negotiation, and helps you decide if you

It is important to understand what you hope to gain by getting your book into print. Do you want additional income? Enhanced status? Knowledge of your personal goals will help you choose the best publisher for your project.

want to handle the negotiation process on your own, or enlist the aid of a lawyer or literary agent.

Certainly, rejection isn't a favorite topic among writers. But because few published authors haven't suffered disappointment before their first success—and sometimes even afterwards—Chapter 8, "When It Doesn't Happen," looks at the many reasons why publishers may fail to show an interest in your proposal. Most important, it helps you both identify the problem and solve it. And if that hoped-for contract still proves elusive, the chapter fills you in on some great options such as self-publishing—options that may allow you to get your manuscript out of the desk drawer and into the bookstore.

Do you need to read every chapter of this book to get your own book into print? Not necessarily. You can always jump to the chapters that seem to best meet your specific needs. But do keep in mind that the Square One System is based on a steppingstone approach. By reading all of the chapters, you'll equip yourself with all the tools you need to become the type of author that editors seek. Of course, this will take some effort on your part. Once you learn what you need to do, you'll have to invest the time and do the work necessary to make it happen. This book doesn't offer any guarantees that you'll get your work published. But if you utilize all you learn in these pages, you'll greatly increase your chances of seeing your name on a publisher's contract—and on a book cover.

CHAPTER 2

WHERE DOES YOUR BOOK FIT IN?

I've been writing professionally for over twenty years, and in that time I've communicated with many editors. I've also sat on the other side of the desk and had many writers contact me. One thing I learned early in my career is that if you're lucky enough to get an editor's attention, you'd better get straight to the point. In order to do so, you have to be able to tell her the category into which your book belongs, the audience for which it's intended, and the book's marketplace—and all in about ten words. Here's an example: *My book is a middle-grade fantasy for the trade market.* In order to make a pronouncement like this, you need to know a lot more about your book than its characters and settings.

This chapter will help you pinpoint your book's category, audience, and marketplace. When you're able to define these three elements, it will be easier for you to find a publisher who produces the books you want to write. Further, you'll be able to convince the publisher that your book does, indeed, have an existing audience that can readily be reached.

RULE #2

Know your book's category

Why do you have to know where your book belongs? There are three

Knowing the category into which your book falls will help you:

❏ Create a list of publishing houses that are best suited to accept and market your work.

❏ Send your manuscript proposal to the appropriate editor within the company.

❏ Identify and analyze competing books in the marketplace.

important reasons for determining this information. First, you must know your book's category if you are to create a list of those publishing houses that are best positioned to accept and market your book. Second, in many cases, you have to know your book's category to address your manuscript proposal to the right editor. If you don't, you'll be sending your proposal into the dark abyss of the publishing house mailroom, from which it may never emerge. Third, pinpointing your book's category will enable you to identify and analyze your competition—other similar books that have already been published. By following the Square One Book Classification System, you'll be able to easily and accurately identify where your book belongs.

WHAT ARE BOOK CATEGORIES?

Book categories were created to help writers, publishers, bookstore owners, and librarians organize and locate books. It's not easy for the average writer to understand book categories. That's because there are actually several different book classification systems in use today. When I asked my local librarian for a breakdown of book categories, she assumed I meant the library system, based on either the Library of Congress or Dewey decimal systems, both of which are used to keep track of thousands of books. But there's also the system used by bookstores, which is a promotional tool that enables consumers to find the books they want. And there are the categories created by publishers to identify the types of titles in which they specialize, and in some cases, to indicate the outlets through which their books will be sold.

Clearly, many of the book categories created by these systems overlap. They have many of the same names, and often use the same criteria to arrange titles. For instance, your library has a young adult fiction section, as do both your local bookstore and the publishers who specialize in that category. But each of these systems has also created book categories that are unique to their needs. While in the children's section of my local bookstore, for example, I'm drawn to the "Newbery Honor Books" section because, as a parent, I'm always interested in finding good literature for my daughters. But as an author, would I ever send a proposal to a publisher in which I referred to my book as a future Newbery winner? If I did, you can imagine how she might react! Similarly, some children's books become supplemental education material. But in your proposal to a publisher, would you describe your book as such? I hope not, as decisions such as this are made by individual school districts. Moreover, if you did portray your book using one of these labels, the description would fail to tell the publisher anything she needs to know about your book.

Where does that leave you? It leaves you in search of a classification system that meets your specific needs. Fortunately, there is one—the Square One Book Classification System.

THE SQUARE ONE BOOK CLASSIFICATION SYSTEM

The Square One Book Classification System was specifically designed to help authors explain their projects to publishers. It presents book categories that editors can understand because it tells them what they want to know. Just as important, the system avoids all those categories that only confuse and bewilder editors—and make you look as if you don't have a clue about your own book.

The Square One system for children's books, both fiction and nonfiction, is composed of twelve categories, each of which is further divided into levels. As you will see, most of the categories are age-determined and format-related. The categories include:

> The Square One Book Classification System is composed of twelve categories, most of which are age- and format-related. This system was specifically designed to help authors explain their projects to children's book publishers.

1. Baby Books
2. Toddler Books
3. Early Picture Books
4. Picture Books for Older Readers
5. Easy Readers
6. Chapter Books
7. Middle Grade Books
8. Young Adult Books
9. Hi-Lo Books
10. Juvenile Series Books
11. Elementary and Secondary School Textbooks
12. Religious Books

Below you'll find a detailed description of each of the Square One system's basic categories. As an author, you must choose only one of the twelve categories for your project. As you learn more about these categories, keep in mind that while some publishing houses produce books in all of the different categories, most produce books in only one or a few categories—only books for young adults, for instance, or only books for children who are school-aged and older. In the latter case, within the publishing house, there will most likely be a separate division for each type of book, making it even more important that you know where your manuscript belongs.

Note that under most of the main categories, you will find three different subcategories, or levels. Each of these levels will help you further refine the classification of your book, and will therefore help you further narrow your search for an appropriate publishing house. Usually, level one categorizes your book as fiction or nonfiction; level two pinpoints the book's genre, if fiction, and the book's topic, whether fiction or nonfiction; and level three further clarifies the nature of your book by providing a succinct description that shows how you develop your topic and/or genre. The only categories that do not follow this pattern are Categories 11 and 12.

After the explanation of each category—under the heading "To Learn More"—I mention published works that can give you a clearer idea of what that category of books is all about. To better familiarize you with the types of children's books produced by the different publishing houses, I have included the publisher's name in each case.

Remember the puzzle pieces I mentioned in Chapter 1? Now is the time to gather them up and put them together so you can begin to target your manuscript to the right editor.

Although this book is designed chiefly for writers, many talented illustrators have ideas for various types of children's books. Chapter 5 offers special sections for people who are primarily illustrators and for writers who are also illustrators. (See pages 153 to 156.)

1. Baby Books

Baby books are picture books designed for infants and young toddlers from newborn to about twelve months of age. These books may have no words at all, and rely on just photos or illustrations to tell the story; may have a word or two on each page; or may provide larger amounts of text.

In addition to regular paper, baby books may be produced as almost indestructible thick cardboard or "board" books, may be

Is It Fiction or Nonfiction?

As part of the Square One Book Classification System, you are asked to determine whether your book is fiction or nonfiction. Although you may find this an easy task, in some cases, it can be a little tricky.

To begin, we can define *fiction* as a literary work created by the imagination, rather than being based strictly on facts. Therefore, if your toddler book or early picture book tells the story of make-believe characters, you know that you have created a work of fiction. As you move into books for older children—middle grade and young adult books—you'll note that a variety of familiar fiction genres, or forms, appear. These include:

Action and Adventure	Mystery
Contemporary (stories about family, friends, and school)	Novels
	Romance
Fantasy	Science Fiction
Historical	Short Stories
Horror	Sports
Humor	Westerns

While reading the above list, you might notice a certain overlap between fiction and fact in the genre of historical fiction—a form in which the story takes place in a historical setting, such as the Revolutionary War. While these books are often carefully researched, contain numerous factual details, and may even feature historical figures, the main characters and events are generally invented, which is why this is regarded as fiction. Similarly, many fiction books about science are also based on fact, but, to be entertaining, the information is presented through fictional characters. For instance, the picture book *Scrambled States of America* by Laurie Keller sneaks a geography lesson into an amusing tale of states that, bored with their locations, decide to switch places to get a different perspective. That's why when you categorize a work of fiction, you should often specify not only genre, but also topic.

Works of *nonfiction,* on the other hand, are based on fact, and are designed to convey information, present activities or experiments, or recount historical events with little or no embellishment. In children's books intended for very young children, nonfiction works are generally concept books, which use illustrations and simple words to explore basic ideas such as colors, numbers, or the alphabet. As you move onto more advanced children's books, however, a vast variety of topics can be addressed, including:

Action and Adventure	Cooking
Animals	Crafts and Hobbies
Antiques and Collectibles	Drama
Architecture	Economics
Art	Etiquette
Biography and Autobiography	Fables, Fairy Tales, Folklore, and Mythology
Business and Economics	Family
Careers	Games and Activities
Computers	Gardening
Concepts	Geography
	Health and Beauty

History

Holidays and Festivals

How-To

Humor

Inspiration

Language Arts

Law and Crime

Lifestyles

Lullabies

Mathematics

Metaphysics

Music

Nature

Nursery Rhymes

People and Places

Performing Arts

Philosophy

Poetry Collections

Psychology

Reference

Religion

School and Education

Science and
Technology

Self-Help

Social Science

Social Situations

Sports and Recreation

Study Aids

Toys

Transportation

Travel

Again, you may be struck by the overlap between fiction and nonfiction in the above list—

especially in poetry and in fables, fairy tales, folklore, and mythology. While poetry is definitely a product of the imagination, collections of poems are considered works of nonfiction. Fables, fairy tales, folklore, and mythology are regarded as nonfiction because they're based on tradition, even when the story has been modernized. Lullabies are considered nonfiction because they're music, which is a nonfiction topic.

If you are not sure whether your book should be categorized as fiction or nonfiction, a visit to your local bookstore or library may be helpful. There, you'll see hundreds of books—possibly one like yours. If this doesn't answer your question, talk to your local children's librarian, who should be able to guide you in making this determination. One final tip: Take a look at the copyright page of the book in question and pay particular attention to the Library of Congress information. Fiction books will simply state the word "fiction" and then the topic, like "fiction—contemporary." If the book is nonfiction, you'll often find the words "juvenile literature."

made of cloth for easy washing, or may be made of a squishy washable plastic material that's just right for a teething infant. Some books in this category are touch-and-feel books; some are scratch-and-sniff; some make noises, like crackles and squeaks; and some are lift-the-flap books, in which a baby (with a parent's help) lifts a small cardboard flap to reveal the hidden picture beneath it. Because these interactive books require a certain amount of coordination, they are more typical of toddler books than baby books. However, since parents are taught that it's never too early to introduce books to children, publishers are keen to produce books that appeal to babies—and their parents.

The manuscripts for baby books generally don't exceed a half-page to a page in length, or about 250 words. There are exceptions, though. A book of lullabies or nursery rhymes can be more than 250 words in length, and some baby books include no words at all. Printed books are usually 8 to 12 pages in length. Keep in mind, however, that these are only guidelines, and that length and format vary from publisher to publisher. That's why it's so important to obtain the writer's guidelines from every publisher of interest, and to make sure that your manuscript matches the publisher's specifications. (You'll learn more about this in Chapter 4.)

Of the twelve categories, is this the most appropriate for your title?

Level One

Because of their limited content, most baby books are nonfiction, but there are a number of simple fiction books as well. *Select one classification only for your title.*

Level Two

This level helps you pinpoint the genre of your book, if appropriate, as well its specific subject or theme. A very popular genre for this age group is the *concept book*, which presents basic information—in the form of photographs or other illustrations and one- or two-word explanations—on various subjects, which include but are not limited to people, places, foods, nature, religion, animals, moods, colors, sizes and shapes, senses, and other concepts that children at this developmental level are just beginning to grasp. Still other baby books present collections of lullabies, nursery rhymes, and *fingerplays*—verses accompanied by finger movements, like the classic "Itsy Bitsy Spider." Counting books and alphabet books are also popular.

Works of baby book fiction consist of simple stories that focus either on events in a baby's daily life, like bath time, playtime, mealtime, and bedtime; or on objects that are of interest to babies, such as toys, clothing, animals, and family. Remember that, whether fiction or nonfiction, the key word for baby books is *simplicity*.

Select one genre (if appropriate) and one subject area for your title.

Level Three

Once you have defined the subject of your book, level three explains how you intend to develop the topic. For example, you might write:

SAMPLE

Mommy and Me
by Neil Ricklen

(Little Simon)

Category # 1

Baby Books

Level One

Nonfiction

Level Two

Concept book/Mothers and babies

Level Three

This concept book uses winsome photographs of babies and their moms to illustrate simple ideas like "dancing."

To Learn More About Baby Books . . .

To learn more about baby books, look for these great titles on the shelves of your local library or bookstore.

☐ *Baby Einstein: Babies Board Book* by Julie Aigner-Clark, published by the Baby Einstein Company, is one of a series of popular books aimed at babies one month and up. This book contains adorable photos of babies from all over the world.

☐ *Spot Goes Splash!* by Eric Hill, published by Putnam Publishing Group Juvenile, is one of many Spot books. Using sentences that are three words at most in length, this book shows which toys can and cannot go in the bath.

☐ *Where Is Baby's Belly Button?* by Karen Katz, published by Little Simon, is an illustrated lift-the-flap book in which babies play peekaboo.

"This baby book introduces colors to infants and toddlers. Vivid photographs of fruits and vegetables are accompanied by two-word explanations, such as 'purple grapes.'" *Try to keep your description within one to four sentences in length.*

2. Toddler Books

Toddler books are designed for children of one to three years of age. Some toddler books tell a story or present concepts completely in pictures, without any words. Others include simple text.

Even though toddler books are read to the young child by parents, grandparents, baby sitters, older siblings, and the like, it's important to realize that this is the age at which children begin to pick up books that appeal to them and pretend to read them, or bring them over to an adult with whom they want to share reading time. These, in fact, are the books that adults will be asked to read again and again.

Toddler books come in a variety of formats, including regular paper books and various types of novelty books, such as pop-up books, touch-and-feel books, lift-the-flap books, and scratch-and-sniff books. The manuscripts for toddler books are usually no more than a page or two in length, with a total of about 300 words, although many have as few as 10 words. Printed toddler books are generally about 12 pages long, but length and format do vary from publisher to publisher so, again, you'll want to pay attention to each company's writer's guidelines.

Of the twelve categories, is this the most appropriate for your title?

Level One

Toddler books can be either fiction or nonfiction. *Select one classification only for your title.*

Level Two

This level helps you pinpoint the genre of your book, if appropriate, as well its specific subject or theme. Fiction toddler books often present simple stories that reflect scenes familiar in a child's everyday life, such as bath time or mealtime. These books can be written in prose form or in simple verse, or can have just one word or phrase per page, as with baby books.

Nonfiction toddler books are generally concept books. Like their baby book counterparts, these works teach colors, numbers, letters, animals, and so on through the use of illustrations and simple words. Another popular topic among this age group—or among their parents, anyway—is potty training, so quite a number of books for toddlers deal with this subject. While these books may be written as made-up stories about a child learning to use the potty, they are usually found in the nonfiction section because they focus on a behavior-related topic and often include advice for parents. Similarly, there are nonfiction toddler books about cooking items, tools, transportation, houses, lifestyles, and other subjects of interest to a toddler. And, of course, a staple for this age group are the rhymes of Mother Goose, which, you may remember from the inset on pages 11 to 12, are considered nonfiction, along with lullabies and fingerplays.

Select the genre (if appropriate) and subject area for your title.

Level Three

Once you have defined the subject of your book, level three explains how you intend to develop it. If in level two you determined that you're writing a simple story about the wind, for instance, you might state: "Three-year-old Lois is reassured by her mother that the wind

---

SAMPLE

Once Upon a Potty
by Alona Frankel

(HarperFestival)

Category # 2

Toddler Books

Level One

Nonfiction

Level Two

Potty training

Level Three

This toddler book uses words and illustrations to explain toilet training in a frank, open way. Available in two formats—one for girls and one for boys—it helps motivate the leap from diaper to potty.

To Learn More About Toddler Books . . .

To learn more about the toddler books category, look for these great titles on the shelves of your local library or bookstore.

☐ *Goodnight Moon* by Margaret Wise Brown, published by HarperFestival, is a short, beloved poem of goodnight wishes from a young rabbit. Adults recognize that the rabbit is trying to delay bedtime, but young children simply enjoy the poem's rhythm.

☐ *Pat the Bunny* is a touch-and-feel book by Dorothy Kunhardt, published by Golden Books. It contains things to touch, things to move, things to smell, and hidden surprises.

☐ *The Very Hungry Caterpillar Board Book* by Eric Carle, published by Scott Foresman, uses colors, shapes, sizes, sounds, and early counting ideas to teach the life cycle of a caterpillar. It's considered fiction instead of nonfiction because the caterpillar eats such human foods as pizza. Even toddlers know that's silly.

isn't as mean as it sounds. Through photographic images, toddlers learn, along with Lois, about all the things the wind helps us to do." *Try to keep your description within one to four sentences in length.*

3. Early Picture Books

Early picture books, also called storybooks, are geared for children of three to five years of age—preschoolers and slightly older children. As the name of this category implies, these books are heavily illustrated. An illustration appears on every page or every other page, and plays a significant role in telling the story. The plots of these books are simple, and usually include one main character who personalizes the child's viewpoint. This character is changed by the events of the story and thus learns, for instance, to overcome a fear, adjust to a new sibling, or appreciate a child from a different culture. Usually, text accompanies the illustrations, but in some cases, the story is told solely through pictures.

Although in most cases, the book will be read to the child by a parent or other caregiver, many children in this age group have the ability to recognize letters as well as some simple words, which makes "reading" the book far more thrilling for them. The drawings, of course, also help the children read, and inspire their imagination as well. Put an early picture book in the hands of an articulate three-year-old child and watch her make up a story to go along with the illustrations!

Early picture book manuscripts are 2 to 3 pages long, with about 500 words of text. The printed book is usually 32 pages in length, but even this isn't an ironclad rule; some books are as short as 16 pages. As is true of the previous two categories, length and format do vary according to the publisher, so remember to send for those writer's guidelines and to give each company exactly what it wants.

Of the twelve categories, is this the most appropriate for your title?

Level One

Early picture books can be either fiction or nonfiction. *Select one classification only for your title.*

Level Two

This level helps you pinpoint the genre of the book, if appropriate, as well as its specific subject. Within the realm of fiction, simple stories can be provided in prose or verse form in the following genres: action and adventure, contemporary, fantasy, historical, humor, mystery, sports, and Westerns. In these genres, a variety of topics can be explored, including celebrations and holidays, ethnic themes, etiquette, family, health, history, lifestyles (like living in the country), nature, people, places, the performing arts, science, sports and recreation, toys, and transportation.

Nonfiction early picture book topics include action and adventure, animals, architecture, art, biography and autobiography, careers, computers, concepts, cooking, crafts and hobbies, etiquette, fables and legends, family, games and activities, gardening, geography, health, history, holidays and festivals, how-to, humor, language arts, lifestyles, mathematics, music, nature, nursery rhymes, people and places, performing arts, poetry collections, religion, school and education, science and technology, social situations, sports and recreation, toys, transportation, and travel.

There is also a new format, influenced largely by television, the *photo essay*. This type of early picture book uses simple text and

SAMPLE
Where the Wild Things Are
by Maurice Sendak

(HarperCollins Juvenile Books)

Category # 3
Early Picture Books

Level One
Fiction

Level Two
Prose/Fantasy

Level Three
This fantasy book uses illustrations and words to tell the story of Max, a young boy who misbehaves and gets sent to bed without his supper. Once in his room, Max imagines he'll run away to where the wild things live and show his mom a thing or two. But Max eventually learns that he'd rather be at home, where people love him.

To Learn More About Early Picture Books . . .

To learn more about early picture books, look for these great titles on the shelves of your local library or bookstore.

☐ Gene Zion's *Harry the Dirty Dog*, published by HarperCollins Juvenile Books, relates the messy adventures of a bath-hating dog and his transformation from a white dog with black spots to a black dog with white spots.

☐ In *Officer Buckle and Gloria* by Peggy Rath-mann—a 1996 Caldecott Medal Book published by Putnam Publishing Group—Gloria the police dog inspires students to listen to Officer Buckle's boring safety lessons by pantomiming his words behind his back, causing the children to roar with laughter.

☐ *Noah's Ark* by Jerry Pinkney, published by Sea Star Books, was a 2003 Caldecott Honor Book. It tells the familiar Bible story through the use of detailed watercolor illustrations.

dramatic photographs to explore a variety of topics, especially nature subjects.

Select one genre (if appropriate) and subject area for your title.

Level Three

Once you know the genre or subject matter of your book, level three explains how you intend to develop your theme. For example, you might write: "This early picture book explores the complexities of first friendships through the character of Janey. When Janey's best friend moves away, the five-year-old believes she'll never have another—that is, until the Crumpetts and their five-year-old quintuplets move next door. Then Janey has so many best friends, she doesn't know what to do." *Try to keep your description within one to four sentences in length.*

4. Picture Books for Older Readers

Designed for kids between ages six and ten, picture books for older readers are enjoyed both by younger children who are good readers and by older children with weaker reading skills.

Picture books for the older reader are designed for children of ages six to ten. Like early picture books, works in this category tell their stories largely through illustrations, although text is included as well. However, these works deal with more complex subject matter—interracial friendships, for instance—than do early picture books, even though the reading level and vocabulary are still aimed at the young reader.

Children in this age range often have their own library cards, and seek out books that are of interest to them. Younger children who are good readers often prefer this category of books to early picture books because of their more sophisticated characters and subject matter. At the upper end of the age range, children with weaker reading abilities often prefer these books to, say, chapter books, because the picture book format—which uses illustrations to break the text into small "chunks"—permits them to read with greater ease. Note that in both publishers' catalogues and libraries, these books are categorized simply as picture books, although specific grade and age designations are included to help determine the reading level.

The manuscripts for picture books for older readers can range from 1,000 words to 1,500 words, or about 4 to 6 manuscript pages. When printed, these books are generally 32 to 64 pages in length. As usual, guidelines vary from publisher to publisher, so you'll want to send for the writer's guidelines and follow them to a T.

Of the twelve categories, is this the most appropriate for your title?

Level One

Picture books for older readers can be fiction or nonfiction. *Select one classification only for your title.*

Level Two

In this category, the sky's the limit when it comes to genre and topic. Within the realm of fiction, the older crowd loves historical fiction. Contemporary stories are also popular, though—especially when they involve strong children who overcome a challenge in their lives. Other possible genres include action and adventure, fantasy, horror (ghost stories), humor, mystery, science fiction, sports, and Westerns. Picture book stories can focus on a range of topics, including animals, celebrations and holidays, ethnic themes, etiquette, family, health, history, lifestyles (like living in the country), nature, people and places, the performing arts, science, sports and recreation, and toys.

Nonfiction topics include action and adventure, animals, architecture, art, biography and autobiography, careers, computers, con-

---

SAMPLE
Tornadoes
by Liza N. Burby

(Rosen Publishers)

Category # 4
Picture Books for Older Readers

Level One

Nonfiction

Level Two

Science and Nature/Tornadoes

Level Four

Through text and photos, this picture book teaches children what tornadoes actually are, where they come from, and how they act, as well as what we can do to keep safe when tornadoes occur.

To Learn More About Picture Books for Older Readers . . .

To learn more about picture books for older readers, look for these great titles on the shelves of your local library or bookstore.

☐ *Pink and Say* by Patricia Polacco, published by Philomel Books, uses the author's own family story to discuss interracial friendship during the Civil War.

☐ Tomie de Paola's *Oliver Button Is a Sissy*, published by Harcourt, gently explores the issue of gender stereotypes through Oliver, who'd rather dance and read than participate in sports—even though the other kids pick on him.

☐ *The Glorious Flight: Across the Channel With Louis Bleriot* by Alice and Martin Provensen, published by Puffin, won the 1984 Caldecott for its illustrations. This story of a Frenchman who built a flying machine to cross the English Channel is still popular with children.

cepts, cooking, crafts and hobbies, drama, etiquette, family, games and activities, gardening, geography, health, history, holidays and festivals, how-to, humor, language arts, lifestyles, mathematics, music, nature, people and places, performing arts, poetry collections, religion, school and education, science and technology, social situations, sports and recreation, toys, transportation, and travel.

Select the genre (if appropriate) and topic for your title.

Level Three

Once you know the genre or subject matter of your book, level three explains how you intend to develop your theme. For example, you might write: "This book provides step-by-step instructions for building birdhouses, while also teaching children about birds that are native to North America." *Try to keep your description within one to four sentences in length.*

5. Easy Readers

Laura Backes, editor of *Children's Book Insider,* a newsletter that reports on the industry, says that easy readers are the trickiest category to define because their format varies so much from publisher to publisher. Some publishers have easy readers aimed only at children up to the second grade. Others include short chapter books for grades two through four. Each company has its own length requirements.

Regardless of the publishing house, however, easy readers are generally designed for pre-readers, children who are just starting to read on their own, and children who have been reading for only a short time, usually up to third graders. In fact, all students now learn to read with easy readers because the plots are simple and somewhat predictable, and the language utilizes the reading vocabulary of designated grades. So you may see one easy reader for kindergarten through grade one, and another for second and third grade. Rhyming patterns are often used because when children know that the last words of certain lines will rhyme, they have an easier time identifying the words. Illustrations—often in color—appear on every page.

Publishers usually have their own specifications for the length of easy readers, making it necessary to study each company's writer's guidelines. Manuscripts range anywhere from 350 to 1,500 words, or $2\frac{1}{2}$ to 6 manuscript pages. When printed, easy readers are generally 48 to 64 pages in length.

Of the twelve categories, is this the most appropriate for your title?

Level One

Easy readers can be either fiction or nonfiction. *Select one classification only for your title.*

Level Two

Like level two in other categories, this level helps you pinpoint the genre and/or specific subject of your book. In the case of easy readers, however, you must also specify the book's reading level.

The majority of fiction easy readers are contemporary in genre, covering topics such as sibling rivalry, school, friendship, and family issues. In fact, to reflect the reader's own experience, most plots take place at either school or home, and

Starting with easy readers, books tend to be designed for either girls or boys, as the latter group usually has no interest in books that have primarily female characters. This is also the reading level at which series books appear. (To learn more about series books, see page 33.)

WORDS FROM A PRO

Elizabeth-Ann Sachs

Author of *I Love You, Janie Tannenbaum*
(Aladdin Library)

Elizabeth-Ann Sachs says that a writer has to work in the genre that is most appealing to her, rather than catering to the market. However, writers must also understand how the market works. "You have to know that children's books are broken into categories, and if you're starting out, you have to fit into one of those established categories," Sachs advises.

may involve pets, sports, toys, or other familiar subjects. Other popular genres include action and adventure, fantasy, horror (ghost stories), historical fiction, humor, mystery, science fiction, sports, and Westerns.

Popular nonfiction topics include action and adventure, animals, architecture, art, biography and autobiography, careers, computers, concepts, cooking, crafts and hobbies, etiquette, fables and fairy tales, family, games and activities, gardening, geography, health, history, holidays and festivals, how-to, humor, language arts, lifestyles, mathematics, myths, music, nature, people and places, performing arts, poetry collections, religion, school and education, science and technology, self-help, social situations, sports and recreation, study aids, toys, transportation, and travel. Often these books explore a single topic, so rather than looking at animals in general, for instance, the book may focus on only elephants or tigers.

Most publishers of easy readers produce different levels for children of different ages and reading abilities. For instance, Level One books may be designed for preschoolers through first graders, and have one to three sentences on a page, each with no more than ten words. The type is usually large, and the text repetitious. A Level Two book, designed for grades one to two, might have thirteen lines on a page with sentences broken into phrases and slightly smaller type. Often, the ending punctuation doesn't come until the bottom of the page, making for short lines and long sentences. This structure gives the reader an opportunity to read a line and then get a visual break before tackling the next section of the sentence. A Level Three book might be aimed at the second and third grader, and reflect slightly more advanced vocabulary than the other two. It may even be formatted as two- to three-page chapters.

Select one genre and/or topic only for your title, as well as one reading level.

Level Three

Once you have defined the genre of your book, if appropriate; have pinpointed the topic; and know the reading level, level three explains how you intend to develop the subject or use the genre. For example, you might write: "This humorous story for children from preschool through kindergarten uses rhyme to tell the story of a sleepy bear

To Learn More About Easy Readers . . .

To learn more about easy readers, look for these great titles on the shelves of your local library or bookstore.

☐ *The Cat in the Hat* by Dr. Seuss, published by Random House, is a classic easy reader, as are all other Dr. Seuss books.

☐ Prolific writer Cynthia Rylant has created many books in this category. A favorite among easy readers is the *Henry and Mudge* series, published by Aladdin Readers, featuring Henry and his lovable 180-pound dog, Mudge.

☐ *Our Earth* by Anne Rockwell, published by Harcourt Brace, is one of Rockwell's many books that teach children about science and animals through easy-to-understand vocabulary.

who doesn't want to get up for school—until his parents get some funny ideas that make him change his mind." *Try to keep your description within one to four sentences in length.*

6. Chapter Books

Once children are comfortable reading on their own, they can usually handle chapter books, which are designed for the seven-to-ten-year-old reader. As the name of this category implies, these books are divided into separate chapters, rather than being one continuous narrative. Some chapter books resolve a separate episode in each chapter. In other books, the chapter ends in the middle of the action to keep the reader turning pages.

The sentences in chapter books are more complex than those in easy readers to reflect the child's higher reading level. But paragraphs are short—not more than two to four sentences in length. While these books are usually illustrated, the drawings are often in black and white and appear only sporadically throughout the chapters. In fact, readers of chapter books now view picture books as "babyish," and are no longer satisfied with easy readers. These children feel that reading books with chapters makes them older and more sophisticated.

The manuscripts for chapter books usually contain about 1,500 to 10,000 words, or 6 to 40 pages. The printed books are generally 64 to

128 pages long, with chapters of 3 or 4 pages each. But as with easy readers, most publishers have their own specifications regarding book length, making it vital to research each publisher's guidelines.

Of the twelve categories, is this the most appropriate for your title?

Level One

Chapter books can be fiction or nonfiction. *Select one classification only for your title.*

Level Two

This level helps you pinpoint the genre and/or specific subject matter of your chapter book—which generally parallel the genres and topics used in easy readers. Mysteries and horror stories are both popular fiction genres, as are action and adventure, fantasy books, short stories, historical fiction, science fiction, and Westerns. Often, the books are contemporary in genre and focus on subjects and conflicts familiar to children—sibling rivalry, school, friendships, family issues, and the like. Animals stories are common, as well.

Nonfiction chapter books, too, are much like easy readers in terms of content—although, of course, the treatment is more sophisticated and developed. Popular nonfiction topics include action and adventure, animals, architecture, art, biography and autobiography, careers, computers, concepts, cooking, crafts and hobbies, etiquette, fables and fairy tales, family, games and activities, gardening, geography, health, history, holidays and festivals, how-to, humor, language arts, lifestyles, mathematics, myths, music, nature, people and places, performing arts, poetry collections, religion, school and education, science and technology, self-help, social situations, sports and recreation, study aids, toys, transportation, travel, and other subjects that appeal to children of that age.

Select one genre and/or topic only for your title.

Level Three

Once you know the genre or subject matter of your book, level three explains how you intend to develop your theme. If in level two you determined that you're writing a fantasy chapter book, you might

To Learn More About Chapter Books . . .

To learn more about chapter books, look for these great titles on the shelves of your local library or bookstore.

☐ *Henry Huggins* by Beverly Cleary, published by Avon Books, tells the story of Henry, whose life is dull until he meets up with a stray dog named Ribsy. Suddenly, Henry's days are action-packed.

☐ *Horrible Harry's Secret* by Suzy Kline, published by Puffin, relates the tale of Harry, who falls in love with classmate Song Lee. Harry's best friend Doug is disgusted, and wonders when Harry will return to his horrible self.

☐ *Seabirds* by Beth Wagner Brust, published by Creative Education, is filled with scientific facts, striking photography, and unique activities that teach children about seabirds and their habitats.

write: "This fantasy chapter book tells the story of spoiled Prince Peter, who meets his match in fairy princess Tanya. When Princess Tanya vows to take over his kingdom by teaching the subjects to dance, the prince—who clearly hates dancing—struggles to maintain control." *Try to keep your description within one to four sentences in length.*

7. Middle Grade Books

Ah, the golden age of reading. At least that's what those who publish books for children call the middle grade book level, since by the ages of eight to twelve, most children are reading well on their own. That makes middle grade books a popular selection in bookstores and libraries.

The standard middle grade book is divided into eight to sixteen chapters. In the case of fiction, the plots are more complicated than those in chapter books, and for the first time, subplots are also used. The text is more descriptive, as well, with numerous details included about the characters—what they look like and how they act. Secondary characters also usually appear in middle grade books. At this point, readers want to be able to visualize the action, so these books are also rich in details about the story's setting.

By the time children are ready for middle grade books, they have developed an enthusiasm for reading and have begun selecting

Most children are reading well by ages eight to twelve, and are ready for more challenging material. That's why middle grade books feature more complicated plots and fuller main characters, along with subplots and secondary characters.

their own books. Adults may still give their children advice about what to read, but clearly they no longer have control over their kids' selections. The children talk about the books they like with friends, share them in book swaps, and make recommendations to one another.

The word count for middle grade fiction manuscripts ranges from 10,000 to 30,000 words, or about 40 to 120 pages. Printed books are anywhere from 96 to 168 pages in length. Printed nonfiction books tend to be a bit shorter—64 to 100 pages. Some middle grade books include illustrations, but you'll find fewer here than in previous categories. As always, though, you'll want to send for writer's guidelines and be sure to meet the requirements of each publisher of interest.

Of the twelve categories, is this the most appropriate for your title?

Level One

Middle grade books can be fiction or nonfiction. *Select one classification only for your title.*

Level Two

The genres and topics explored by middle grade books are much like those that are typical of easy readers and chapter books. Within the realm of fiction, you'll find mysteries, horror stories, fantasy books, science fiction, short stories, historical fiction, Westerns, and more. Nonfiction middle grade topics include action and adventure, animals, architecture, art, biography and autobiography, careers, computers, concepts, cooking, crafts and hobbies, etiquette, fables and fairy tales, family, games and activities, gardening, geography, health, history, holidays and festivals, how-to, humor, language arts, lifestyles, mathematics, myths, music, nature, people and places, performing arts, poetry collections, religion, school and education, science and technology, self-help, social situations, sports and recreation, study aids, toys, transportation, and travel.

Within both the fiction and the nonfiction categories, there tends to be a separation along gender lines. This means that while many books still appeal to both girls and boys, children of this age usually seek out books of interest based on their gender. You can probably guess, for instance, that middle grade boys want both fiction and nonfiction books that feature sports, science, or horror, while girls look for books about friends, ballet, sports like gymnastics, and horses. Of course, this isn't a hard-and-fast rule, as a number of books have crossed the gender lines and appealed to both boys and girls. (Just think of the *Harry Potter* phenomenon.) But it's important to keep the gender distinctions in mind, as publishers certainly consider this before adding a book to their seasonal list.

Select one genre and/or topic only for your title.

Level Three

Once you know the genre or subject matter of your book, level three explains how you intend to develop your theme, and, if appropriate, states the gender for which is was designed. For instance, if you're writing a work of fiction about a girl who's starting junior high school, you might write: "This book tells the story of Jessica, who enters junior high school hoping that she won't be labelled 'a weirdo,' as she was in her previous school. Girls will enjoy Jessica's journey of discovery as she finds hidden talents in her new dance class, and ultimately wins acceptance and respect among her peers." *Try to keep your description within one to four sentences in length.*

To Learn More About Middle Grade Books . . .

To learn more about middle grade books, look for these great titles on the shelves of your local library or bookstore.

☐ *Ella Enchanted* by Gail Carson Levine, published by Harper Trophy, was a debut novel that earned the author the Newbery Honor Medal in 1998. A clever twist on the Cinderella story—and a fascinating look at traditional female roles in fairy tales—the novel tells of strong-willed Ella, who receives an unfortunate gift: obedience.

☐ *Out of the Dust* by Karen Hesse, published by Scholastic, Inc., offers a series of prose poems that tell the mournful story of a mother's accidental death, a father's disintegration, and the 14-year-old narrator who watches her life unravel in the Oklahoma dust bowl. This work of fiction won a Newbery Medal in 1998.

☐ *A Joyful Noise: Poems for Two Voices* by Paul Fleischman, published by Harper Collins, won the 1989 Newbery Award. A book of poetry about insects, it was designed for two readers to enjoy together.

8. Young Adult Books

By the time most readers are twelve years of age, they are developmentally ready to tackle challenging text. They don't see themselves as kids anymore, so they're looking for sophisticated stories that relate to their lives and the world they learn about in the media. That's what young adult books are all about. Designed for preteens and teenagers, these books provide a segue between children's books and adult works—and sometimes are so mature in content and style that the same title can be found in both the young adult and the adult sections of the library.

The young adult reader may be reading for pleasure, reading assigned books for school reports, or looking for useful information that can help her solve a personal problem, such as difficulties with a teacher or friend. Parents rarely make purchases for their children at this point, as a child's taste in books is as individual as her taste in clothes.

As you might expect, young adult books are the longest of all the books in the juvenile category. Manuscripts generally run from 30,000 to 56,000 words in length, or about 120 to 225 pages. Finished books range from 168 to 250 pages in length. But these numbers vary so widely from publisher to publisher, and even from one type of book to another, that you really have to follow writer's guidelines to determine if the length of your manuscript is appropriate for the company in question.

Of the twelve categories, is this the most appropriate for your title?

Level One

Young adult books can be fiction or nonfiction. *Select one classification only for your title.*

Level Two

The genres and topics explored by young adult books are as numerous and wide-ranging as those found in adult works. Other than novels, the fiction category includes, but certainly is not limited to, historical fiction, mysteries, fantasies, science fiction, horror, and

Westerns. Short stories are well received, action and adventure books are popular with boys, and romance is highly popular with girls. And, of course, many works of young adult fiction deal with topics that are of interest to today's teenagers, including tough themes such as sexuality, racism, feminism, addiction, and violence.

Young adult nonfiction topics include action and adventure, animals, antiques and collectibles, architecture, art, biography and autobiography, business and economics, careers, computers, cooking, crafts and hobbies, drama, etiquette, fables and fairy tales, family, games and activities, gardening, geography, health and beauty, history, holidays and festivals, how-to, humor, inspiration, language arts, law and crime, lifestyles, mathematics, myths, music, nature, people and places, performing arts, poetry collections, psychology, reference, religion, school, science and technology, social sciences, social situations, sports and recreation, study aids, transportation, and travel. Self-help books are also very popular, as teens try to cope with difficult issues.

Finally, you'll want to be aware of a new genre, the *graphic novel*, which, despite its name, can be either fiction or nonfiction. Based on animation and comics, the graphic novel has been garnering a lot of interest in recent years—so much so that librarians are now making

Basically comics printed in book form, graphic novels tell a story in sequential panels.

To Learn More About Young Adult Books . . .

To learn more about young adult books, look for these great titles on the shelves of your local library or bookstore.

☐ *Chicken Soup for the Teenage Soul* by Jack Canfeld, published by Health Communications, is immensely popular with young adults. This book presents stories, poems, and cartoons that relate to the troubles that affect all teenagers.

☐ *Holes* by Louis Sacher, published by Dell Yearling, is a tall tale reminiscent of Mark Twain's *Huckleberry Finn*. Stanley Yelnats finds himself at Camp

Green Lake because it seemed a better option than jail for a conviction based on a case of mistaken identity. The Yelnats family has become accustomed to a long history of bad luck, thanks to their "no-good-dirty-rotten-pig-stealing-great-great-grandfather!"

☐ *The Outsiders* by S.E. Hinton, published by Prentice Hall, was a groundbreaking novel in 1967 in that it examined gang life. Written by the author when she was only sixteen years of age, it has become a classic.

sure that these books are available in their young adult sections. (See the inset on page 31 for more information.)

Select one genre and/or topic only for your title.

Level Three

Once you know the genre and/or subject matter of your book, level three explains how you intend to develop the topic or use the genre. If in level two you determined that you're writing a nonfiction self-help book for teens, you might write: "This self-help book guides preteen girls in identifying the warning signs of eating disorders, and offers steps to bring readers back to physical, psychological, and emotional health. Clear text is interwoven with first-person accounts to provide girls with the information they need in an easy-to-read and approachable format." *Try to keep your description within one to four sentences in length.*

9. Hi-Lo Books

Hi-lo books—high interest, low reading level—are designed for readers who need help developing their reading skills, but want information that's age-appropriate. These children have advanced to the upper grades—middle school and beyond—but their reading level is actually several steps below their grade level, anywhere from grade two through grade six. So a book could be written to appeal to a fifteen-year-old who reads at the level of a fourth grader.

Although not all children's publishers produce hi-lo books, educators—particularly special education teachers and English as a second language (ESL) instructors—recognize a need for them. In fact, it is these teachers, and not the kids themselves, who generally purchase hi-lo books. However, most libraries have selections of hi-lo books for readers who need them for homework assignments or who want to read on their own.

Hi-lo books tend to be broken into short chapters, each of which is only about five pages long. The vocabulary is simple and the sentence structure is short, with works of fiction having brief dialogue and only single plot lines. Manuscript pages are similar to those of an easy reader, with about 350 to 1,500 words, or $2\frac{1}{2}$ to 6 manuscript

Graphic Novels

The term *graphic novel* describes stories that are written and illustrated in comic-book style, yet published in book form, in either a hardcover or a paperback format. In the comic book industry, these works are actually called *trade comics* and are divided into three main categories: graphic novels, trade paperbacks, and comic strip collections.

Graphic novels represent original book-length stories or collections of related short stories that have never before been published in comic-book form, such as *JLA: League of One* by Craig Lemon (DC Comics). *Trade paperbacks* are collections of stories previously published in comic-book form, like reprinted consecutive issues of an ongoing or limited series. These collections, like *Batman: The Dark Night Strikes Again* by Frank Miller (DC Comics), usually include additional materials, such as unused sketches or an introduction. *Comic strip collections,* like *The Revenge of the Baby-Sat* by Bill Watterson (Andrew McMeels Publishing), present serialized newspaper strips that don't necessarily tell a continuing story. In this book, of course, we're most interested in the book-length graphic novel.

While graphic novels have been available since the eighties, appealing mostly to adolescent males who were reluctant readers, in recent years, there has been a growing popularity among pre-teen and adolescent girls. Although there are several types of graphic novels, of particular interest to girls is *manga,* which means "comic" in Japanese. Manga reflects a certain type of artistic style, complete with characters with large eyes. Many of these works, like the widely popular Inu-Yashi (VIZ Communications), are also based on *anime shows*—Japanese animation.

In all graphic novels, the pictures and narrative are interdependent. Unlike traditional text-based books, the story unfolds in panels from the upper left corner to the lower right—just like a comic book. Despite the use of the word "novel," these books may be either fiction or nonfiction. Fiction genres include action and adventure, crime and mystery, fantasy, historical, horror and supernatural, humor, martial arts, romance, science fiction, sports, and superhero. Many are written as part of a series, either as a story arc—which means that each book has a self-contained story—or, in the case of manga, as story lines that flow from one book in the series to the next. Some graphic novels are even adaptations of classic literary works, such as *Moby Dick.* Nonfiction topics include art, autobiography, history, myths, legends and fairy tales, poetry, and sports. Note that many, but not all, have mature content, including violence, sexuality, and profanity.

Most completed graphic novels are 112 pages long, although they can range from 32 to over 400 pages. Both black-and-white and color versions are available. The writer who likes to illustrate comics would find this an appealing market, but because the narrative is so closely integrated with the art, publishers accept only those submissions that contain both. Thus, the writer who can't illustrate her own book must have an artist do so before submitting her work to a publisher.

You can find graphic novels in collector stores, bookstores, and libraries. There are over 150 comic book publishers, including DC Comics, Dark Horse, and Marvel. Some traditional trade publishers, like Pantheon, a division of Random House, also produce graphic novels. To find a complete list of publishers that specialize in graphic novels, visit the www.comiclist.com website and click on "publishers and distributors."

SAMPLE

Amazing True Stories

by Don L. Wulffson

(Scholastic)

Category # 9

Hi-Lo Books

Level One

Nonfiction

Level Two

Law and Crime

Level Three

Fifty-four unbelievable but
true stories, arranged in
nine categories, deal with
such high-interest topics
as crime and punishment,
accidents and disasters,
and the unknown and
mysterious.

pages. When printed, hi-lo books are generally 48 to 64 pages in length, but this varies a good deal from publisher to publisher and according to the book's format. Often, illustrations are included to increase appeal.

Of the twelve categories, is this the most appropriate for your title?

Level One

Hi-lo books can be fiction or nonfiction. *Select one classification only for your title.*

Level Two

Hi-lo fiction genres include adventure, contemporary, fantasy, ghost stories, graphic novels, historical fiction, romance, mystery, science fiction, short stories, and sports. Stories often focus on peer pressure, challenges, relationships, and values.

Nonfiction hi-lo books cover topics such as action and adventure, animals, antiques and collectibles, architecture, art, biography and autobiography, business and economics, careers, computers, cooking, crafts and hobbies, drama, etiquette, family, games and activities, gardening, geography, health and beauty, history, holidays and festivals, how-to, humor, inspiration, language arts, law and crime, lifestyles, mathematics, myths, music, nature, people and places, performing arts, psychology, reference, religion, school, science and technology, social sciences, social situations, sports and recreation, transportation, and travel.

Select one genre and/or topic only for your title.

Level Three

Once you know the genre and/or subject matter of your book, level three explains how you intend to develop the subject or use the genre. If in level two you determined that you're writing a nonfiction how-to book, you might write: "This how-to book explains how girls and boys can repair their own computers. Step-by-step instructions are provided through both easy-to-understand text and clear illustrations." *Try to keep your description within one to four sentences in length.*

To Learn More About Hi-Lo Books . . .

To learn more about hi-lo books, look for these great titles on the shelves of your local library or bookstore.

☐ *Making Heaven: The Koreans* by Tana Reiff, published by Globe Fearon, is the story of a family adjusting to life in New York in the seventies. Reiff is considered a pioneering author of hi-lo books.

☐ *Inhalants and Your Nasal Passages: The Incredibly*

Disgusting Story by Kerri O'Donnell, published by Rosen Publishing, uses a nonpreachy voice to educate teens about the dangers of drugs.

☐ *Odd Jobs: True Stories About Real Work* by John Diconsiglio, published by Scholastic, portrays people who have chosen unusual work environments. Included is a profile of a window washer at the World Trade Center, written before his death in the September 11, 2001 terrorist attacks.

10. Juvenile Series Books

Anyone who grew up reading Nancy Drew, the Hardy Boys, or the Bobbsey Twins understands the attraction of the series book. Each book presents a new and exciting plot, but brings back a familiar format and theme, as well as characters that the reader knows and loves. That's why the juvenile series book has been thriving since 1900, and now exists for all categories from easy readers through young adult books.

While the primary market for series books has long been middle grade readers—children of ages eight to twelve—publishers are now expanding their easy reader selections in both fiction and nonfiction categories. It appears that once a child can read reasonably well on her own, the publishing industry offers a wide selection of books to suit her tastes. Most juvenile series books are paperbacks and therefore sensibly priced. This makes them perfect purchases for the child who may now be receiving her first disposable income, an allowance. Since teen romances are very popular, teenage girls also constitute a large audience for the juvenile series. And, of course, parents often buy favorite series books for their kids because they're thrilled to see them reading.

In each of the categories, the page count of a series book loosely parallels that of other books in that category. In other words, a mid-

Although you may hope that your book will be part of a series, you should write it as a complete story. Young readers will be disappointed if your story is open-ended. Instead, try to develop strong characters who have the *potential* to carry on their adventures, but who manage to triumph at the end of the current book.

SAMPLE

Dear America Series

*Christmas After All:
The Great Depression
Diary of Minnie Swift*

by Kathryn Lasky

(Scholastic)

Category # 10

Juvenile Series Books

Level One

Fiction

Level Two

*Historical Journal/
Middle Grade*

Level Three

*In her fictionalized journal,
eleven-year-old Minnie
Swift recounts how her
family dealt with difficult
times during the
Depression, and how
the arrival of an orphan
from Texas, just before
Christmas 1932, changed
their lives.*

dle grade series book could be anywhere between 100 and 160 pages when printed. But because each series has its own parameters, it's crucial to study series similar to the one you hope to write to establish the appropriate manuscript length.

Of the twelve categories, is this the most appropriate for your title?

Level One

Juvenile series books can be fiction or nonfiction. *Select one classification only for your title.*

Level Two

The fiction genres featured in this category particularly lend themselves to series treatment. Thus, you'll find adventures, fantasies, horror (ghost stories), historical fiction, historical diaries, mysteries, and romances. Most of these series fall on either one side or the other of the gender line. Mysteries for boys have male protagonists who save the day, while mysteries for girls almost always feature heroines. Interestingly, though, librarians say that once children begin selecting and reading books on their own, girls are usually willing to read about male protagonists, but boys aren't willing to read about girls. Some series, however—like R.L. Stine's *Goosebumps* series from Scholastic—manage to attract both genders by involving a boy-and-girl team.

Series books are also written as nonfiction, with science (planets, weather, and disasters) and the arts (famous painters and musicians) being the most popular topics. But nearly all nonfiction subjects are available in this category, including action and adventure, animals, architecture, art, biography and autobiography, business and economics, careers, computers, concepts, cooking, crafts and hobbies, drama, etiquette, fables and fairy tales, family, games and activities, gardening, geography, health and beauty, history, holidays and festivals, how-to, humor, inspiration, language arts, law and crime, lifestyles, mathematics, myths, music, nature, people and places, performing arts, poetry collections, psychology, reference, religion, school and education, science and technology, self-help, social science, social situations, sports and recreation, study aids, toys, transportation, and travel.

To Learn More About Juvenile Series Books . . .

To learn more about juvenile series books, look for these great titles on the shelves of your local library or bookstore.

☐ *Amelia Bedelia* by Peggy Parrish, published by Harper Trophy, is an easy reader series that always gets children laughing as maid Amelia Bedelia follows her instructions literally, creating hilarious situations as she sows seeds with a needle or dusts furniture with dusting powder.

☐ *The Chronicles of Narnia* by C. S. Lewis (Harper Trophy) is a series of seven fantasies aimed at the middle grade reader, but loved by the young adult and adult reader as well.

☐ The *America the Beautiful* series (Children's Press) includes fifty different nonfiction books for middle school readers, covering the geography, history, government, economy, industry, arts, leisure activities, and historic sites of each state.

Select one genre and/or topic only for your title, as well as one age-related category.

Level Three

Once you know the genre or subject matter of your book, level three explains how you intend to develop it. If in level three you determined that you were writing a fantasy, for instance, you might write: "This fantasy tells the story of sisters Ann and Alice, who lose their way while walking to school together, and find that they have accidentally entered the magical land of Purple Mountain. They want to go home, but to do so, they must first help to free the unicorns who've been trapped by the evil ruler of the Purple Kingdom." *Try to keep your description within one to four sentences in length.*

II. Elementary and Secondary School Textbooks

This category is different from most of those that preceded it because rather than being an age-related grouping, it encompasses books for all school-age children. The books in this category are designed for use as learning materials in elementary schools, intermediate schools, middle schools (also called junior high schools), and high schools. Commonly called *el-hi books,* they include hardcover and

SAMPLE

*A History of the Republic,
Volume 2: The United
States From 1865*
by James West Davidson
and Mark H. Lytle

(Prentice Hall)

Category # 11

*Elementary and Secondary
School Textbooks*

Level One

Eighth Grade

Level Two

Standard textbook

Level Three

American History

Level Four

*This textbook for eighth-
grade students presents
a history of the United
States from the Western
Frontier through the 1980s,
with special features like
skill lessons, maps, and
selected readings.*

softcover publications that can be ordered by an individual teacher, a local or regional curriculum committee, or a statewide textbook adoption committee. Because this category is very different from the previous ten, be aware that the levels are different as well. *Of the twelve categories, is this the most appropriate for your title?*

Level One

Level one of this category defines the specific grade or grades at which the work is aimed. Within elementary schools, you can label a book for use in kindergarten, first grade, second grade, third grade, and so on. In middle schools, the grades may include sixth, seventh, and eighth—although these grades vary from one school district to another. In high schools, level-one categories may cover ninth, tenth, eleventh, and twelve grades. In certain cases, an editor may define a project in terms of its reading level. For instance, a textbook may be described as having a third-grade reading level. In almost all cases, the publisher monitors and adjusts the reading level as necessary. *Select one classification from the following four: (1) elementary school, (2) intermediate school, (3) middle school, or (4) high school. Include the grade level(s) where applicable.*

Level Two

Level two of this category specifies the format of your book. In the case of elementary school books, your book may borrow a format from one of the earlier classifications. It may, for instance, use a picture book format to teach children about a topic such as time. However, as you might expect, many el-hi books are formatted as standard textbooks, workbooks, manuals, or maps. *Select one format only for this level.*

Level Three

Level three classifies el-hi books according to general subject matter. At the elementary school level, this could include art; computer science; health; language arts such as grammar, literature, reading, and writing; mathematics; music; science; and social studies, including current events, economics, geography, history, and government. At the middle and high school levels, the classifications could include art; business subjects such as accounting, advertising, finance, and marketing; career training; computer science; English; foreign language; health; history; home economics courses such as family and consumer sciences; mathematics; music; the sciences, such as biology, chemistry, earth science, and physics; technology; and social studies, such as economics, geography, government, and history. *Select one subject classification only.*

Level Four

If your book is designed for elementary school use, level four should define the specific curriculum. For example, your book may cover local history, an integral part of your state's social studies curriculum. Make sure to include a description that details the material in your proposed work. If your book is written for middle or high schools, it should specify the course—trigonometry, for example. Because some course titles do not clearly define the actual topic covered, you should avoid these titles if they do not specify the subject of your work. For instance, if your project is an economics

Children's trade books often cross over to the el-hi market. A high school teacher, for instance, may adopt a young adult novel that takes place in India for use in her social studies course. However, true el-hi books are designed for a specific course of study, and rarely if ever cross into the trade market.

To Learn More About El-Hi Books . . .

To learn more about elementary and secondary school textbooks, look for these great titles in an online textbook publisher's catalogue, or visit a bookstore that specializes in textbooks.

☐ *World Literature: An Anthology of Great Short Stories, Poetry, and Drama* by Donna Rosenberg, published by Glencoe, is a textbook for high school seniors that explores literature from around the world, including the Mediterranean, Continental Europe, Africa, Asia and the South Pacific, South and Central America, North America, and Great Britain. The goal is to show the joys and sorrows that connect people across all cultures.

☐ *The 100+ Series: Using the Standards—Number & Operations, Grade 4,* published by McGraw-Hill Companies, is one of a series of elementary school math textbooks in paperback format. The text includes reproducible worksheets that focus on numbers and operations.

☐ *Spectrum Reading: Grade 5,* published by McGraw-Hill Companies, is designed to engage reluctant readers and enhance the skills of children who have gained proficiency. Part of a complete reading series geared for children being home-schooled, it includes full-color illustrations that provide cues for comprehension.

text for high school students, you might write: "This introductory text, geared for high school juniors and seniors, presents all of the basic concepts of economics, including budget and trade deficits, inflation, interest rates, and unemployment. It also explains how economics influences world events, and how it affects our daily lives." *Try to keep your description within two to four sentences in length.*

12. Religious Books

Like the el-hi texts discussed above, the category of religious books is not an age-related grouping. Instead, religious books can fall into any of the previously discussed categories, including the el-hi category. What all religious books have in common is that they are designed to pass on information specific to that faith—instructions for First Confessions, for instance—or to instill moral values important to that religion.

If you read the inset "Is It Fiction or Nonfiction?" (see pages 11 to 12), you know that some of the books that fall into earlier categories, such as young adult, focus on religious topics. The books we are referring to in Category 12, however, are produced by religious publishers rather than secular trade publishers, and are generally designed for people who have a personal involvement in a specific religion.

Of the twelve categories, is this the most appropriate for your title?

Level One

Above, you learned that religious books can fall into any of the previously discussed categories. Thus, level one of the religious books category should first define the age- or education-related category into which this book falls. In other words, level one classifications include baby books, toddler books, early picture books, picture books for older readers, easy readers, chapter books, middle grade books, young adult books, hi-lo books, juvenile series books, and elementary and secondary school textbooks—Categories 1 through 11 of the Square One Book Classification System. In the case of elementary and secondary school texts, level one should also state the grade for which the book was designed.

In addition, this level should define the specific religion, if any, that the book addresses. At this level, then, you might describe your work as being a Baptist picture book, a Jewish juvenile series book, or—in the case of a title that embraces general Christian beliefs—a Christian easy reader.

Select one classification only from this level. In the case of a textbook, also specify the grade level. Make sure to include a religious affiliation when appropriate.

Level Two

Level two specifies whether the book is fiction or nonfiction. *Select one classification for your title.*

Level Three

This level helps you pinpoint the genre of your book, if fiction, and/or the specific subject or theme of your book. Because religious books run the gamut of age-related categories, they can be on a wide range of subjects and cover a wide range of genres, all of which were discussed in the earlier sections on Categories 1 through 11. *Select one genre and/or topic for your title.*

Level Four

Level four explains how you intend to develop your chosen subject or genre. If you have determined that your work is a Christian young adult work of fiction, you might say, "This Christian young adult novel shows how 16-year-old Cathy, a new girl in town, copes with the desire to fit in at her new school, and the sometimes conflicting need to remain true to her own moral values." *Try to keep your description within one to four sentences in length.*

If You Haven't Found the Perfect Fit

By now, I hope you have a clear understanding of the Square One Book Classification System. If, at this point, you feel that your book doesn't fit into one of the twelve categories, don't panic. It's true that some books simply defy classification. But before you send out your

---

SAMPLE

Children's Book of Classic Catholic Prayers
by Bishop Robert F. Morneau

(Paulist Press)

Category # 12

Religious Books

Level One

Catholic Early Picture Book

Level Two

Nonfiction

Level Three

Prayers

Level Four

This book brings together twenty classic Catholic prayers in a child-friendly package designed to help little ones develop a rich spiritual life. Included are the Lord's Prayer, the Hail Mary, and many more well-loved prayers.

To Learn More About Religious Books . . .

To learn more about the religious books category, look for these great titles on the shelves of your local library, in a regular or religious bookstore, or in an online catalogue of religious books.

☐ *What Does God Look Like?* by Lawrence and Karen Kushner, published by Skylight Paths, uses a baby book format to invite young children to explore things that, like God, are all around us.

☐ The picture book *Shalom, Salaam, Peace* by Howard I. Bogot, published by the Central Conference of American Rabbis, presents an illustrated poem that calls for peace in the Middle East.

☐ The easy reader *Young Cousins Mysteries* series by Elspeth Campbell Murphy, published by Bethany House, follows cousins Titus, Timothy, and Sarah-Jane as they solve various mysteries around their neighborhood. The theme of each book is based on a biblical verse.

manuscript, hoping that your impossible-to-define work will somehow find an editor to champion it, take the time to reevaluate your manuscript. This can best be done by working the three-level category system backwards.

For level three, within one to four sentences, write down what your book is about, being as descriptive and accurate as possible.

For level two, try to determine your book's genre or topic. Is it a mystery story? Is it a book on dogs?

For level one, determine whether it's a fiction or nonfiction book. There can only be one answer to this. It's either a fact-based book—nonfiction, in other words—or one that's purely a work of the imagination. If you're not sure, reread the inset on page 11.

Finally, to determine the book's category, you'll have to decide the reader for whom your book is intended. At this point, many writers find a conflict between one of their levels and their category. For instance, if you've written a novel with lengthy paragraphs in which each chapter is a continuation of the story, but you've pegged your book as a chapter book (a common confusion), you have found your problem. Chapter books, as I explained earlier in this chapter, tend to contain short but complete chapters and brief paragraphs, all aimed at the child who has recently become comfortable reading books on her own. In this particular case, I would advise you to rework your book into a young adult novel by using more complex sentences and sophisticated vocabulary. It may require some research about basic reading levels, but if the story is one you're intent upon selling, you'll have to compromise to make it work. Or, if you have your heart set on the chapter book market, you'll have to rewrite your book to be sure it more closely matches other works in that category.

Yes, an editor does occasionally fall in love with a topic or a story, and finds a way to make the book fit her product line. But remember that your goal in reading this book is to increase your chances of being published. So why not make it easier on yourself and create a book that fits into an existing category with a defined market?

RULE #3

Know your book's audience

While it's important for any writer to know her audience, this knowledge is particularly crucial when you're writing a book for children. Children's ability to comprehend written material and handle various concepts increases dramatically as they mature. Their interests, too, change over time. Editors know this, and you must understand it, as well, if you are to convince an editor that your work is appropriate for its readers. Moreover, especially if your readers are quite young, you must acknowledge the importance of your secondary audience—the parents, teachers, and other adults who will buy your book and read it to the children in their life.

THE IMPORTANCE OF UNDERSTANDING YOUR PRIMARY AUDIENCE

If you've successfully categorized your book according to the Square One Book Classification System, you know whether you're writing for toddlers or preschoolers, for ten-year-olds or teens. But now that you've narrowed your audience down, consider how well you *really* understand your readers. In order to write a book that appeals to a certain group of children, you have to know those children pretty well. While you can—and should—read every available book in the category into which your book falls, there's no substitute for getting to know your audience firsthand. So even if you have to borrow

Publishers—and bookstore buyers, too—know that every book must be designed and marketed for one clearly defined audience. While this is true in all areas of publishing, it is especially true in the world of juvenile literature, as children's ability to comprehend written material and handle different concepts changes dramatically as they mature.

Once you've pinpointed your audience, try to get to know it firsthand—even if that means volunteering in a school or library. This will enable you to learn about your audience's interests, problems, and reading level.

someone else's kids, do everything you can to learn what they think, how they talk, and how they perceive the world. If you want to write young adult fiction, spend time with some teenagers. If you prefer picture books, volunteer in a school or library so you can observe what books draw children again and again. During your research, you'll want to focus on three basic areas—your audience's interests and problems, the world in which your audience lives, and your audience's reading level. Let's look at each of these in turn.

Your Audience's Interests and Problems

Understandably, it's vital to have a clear idea of your audience's interests and problems. If the kids aren't interested in your book's topic, they won't read it. In fact, the book will probably never make it to the shelves of a bookstore or library, because children's editors will know that it won't appeal to your intended audience.

Certain topics—that of horses, for instance—are of interest to children of a wide variety of ages, but a good many subjects and problems are keyed to age and maturity. For instance, while pre-schoolers want answers to the "why" questions—Why does it rain? Why do the seasons change?—teenagers are more likely to be interested in solving relationship problems or dealing with issues such as drugs or sex. Moreover, older children often have to write school reports on topics such as world hunger or racism. If your nonfiction book is on such a topic, it could fill the bill.

While you're considering topics of interest, you'll want to consider the gender of your audience, as after a certain age, it has a marked impact on the reader's concerns. Be aware that as much as you may want to keep your story gender neutral, it often won't work. You need to know the difference between girls' and boys' developmental characteristics. For instance, the middle grade female reader is probably just becoming interested in boys, so if it's applicable to your plot, your character can notice her male classmates in a new way. Most boys of that age, however, still think that girls have cooties, so make sure that your character development reflects that as well. In fact, that particular difference alone has guided many a plot structure in children's literature.

While we're discussing characters, it's important to be aware that because most kids are always striving to be "more grownup," they usually like to read about someone who is slightly older than they are. This means that the main character in your middle grade book can be thirteen years old even though the reader is only eleven. But this isn't a hard-and-fast rule. Strong, realistic characters—characters who aren't saints or predictable stereotypes, but believable people—appeal to readers regardless of age. After all, how many adults are avidly following the story of young Harry Potter?

The World in Which Your Audience Lives

While you may have no interest in the latest fashion trends or technology, be assured that most kids—especially preteens and teens—are very much attuned to the world around them. They know which clothes are in and which are out. They know which bicycles are the coolest. And they're often better than their parents at using electronic devices such as VCRs, DVDs, and computers.

The stories I read as a child may have referred to banana bicycle seats and eight-track tape players. Today, most young readers don't have a clue about those items. That's why it's so important to be aware of the world in which your audience is living, and to notice the details. That doesn't mean, of course, that your work of fiction should refer to passing fads that will soon go the way of the dinosaur. However, it does mean that you should take care to avoid items that will confuse or turn off your readers. A good rule of thumb is to not be so specific that you date your book. In other words, it's okay to say that one of your characters is working at her computer, but it's not a good idea to refer to a *specific* computer that may soon be off the market.

What if you're writing a historical novel? Naturally, you'll want the clothes and other objects to be appropriate to the time about which you're writing. Just keep in mind that your readers may not have the experience needed to understand items that are no longer in use. It's your job, therefore, to fill them in.

Your Audience's Reading Level

Your characters may be engaging, and your plot, riveting. But if your book doesn't match your audience's reading level, it will not appeal to your readers.

Although you may not be aware of the latest fashion trends and the newest technology, most kids are. So unless you're writing a historical novel, make sure that your references to clothes, bicycles, computers, and the like are all up-to-date.

Many computer programs now include a feature that assesses the suitability of text for children of a specific age or grade by evaluating factors such as sentence and word length. While these programs may be helpful in alerting you a reading-level problem, they are not foolproof. If you think a problem exists, check with a children's librarian or teacher, or refer to Alijandra Mogilner's *Children's Writer's Word Book*.

To a degree, you'll be able to gear your book to the correct reading level by paying careful attention to the vocabulary you use. Here, again, knowledge of actual children in the target age group is invaluable. By talking with kids, you'll soon get a feel for the words they use on an everyday basis. You'll also be able to learn about appropriate vocabulary by looking at existing books in your chosen category. You can even get word lists from school teachers. But if you still need help in this regard, and if you're writing for relatively young kids, you'll want to get a copy of the *Children's Writer's Word Book* by Alijandra Mogilner. This helpful resource provides word lists for each grade through the sixth, and offers alternative words based on grade. I have used it many times to simplify my language while writing about complex nonfiction topics for elementary school students. For instance, the meaning of the adjective "bedraggled" will be understood by the average fifth grader, but you'll have to change it to "worn" for third graders and "messy" or "dirty" for first graders.

Of course, reading level is determined by more than just vocabulary. The younger the reader, the shorter you'll want to make each sentence, each page of type, and each chapter. Existing books in your category can help you determine if your sentences are too complex or your chapters too long.

THE IMPORTANCE OF UNDERSTANDING YOUR SECONDARY AUDIENCE

Recently, I attended a fascinating lecture presented by Australian educator Tony Stead. He discussed a study in which he had asked elementary school children and their teachers, "What makes a good picture book?" The results from children, he said, were the same all over the world, as were the results from teachers. But when he compared the two, the children and teachers did *not* have the same opinions.

For children, in order of importance, a good picture book:

1. Makes them laugh.

2. Has naughty characters.

3. Has justice in the end. (The bad character needs to learn a lesson, and children don't mind at all if that character winds up dead.)

4. Has simple illustrations, with bright colors and funny or scary elements.

5. Rhymes—especially if the book is for preschoolers and younger children.

6. Has special features like foldouts and pop-ups.

For teachers, in order of importance, a good picture book:

1. Teaches children an important moral lesson.

2. Has well-structured language that is pleasing to the ear.

3. Is well paced.

4. Includes interesting and unusual art.

5. Is not too long.

6. Is read again and again because the children request it.

What does that mean to you, the writer? It means that you have to satisfy not only your primary audience, the children, but also your secondary audience, the adults who buy the book and perhaps read the book to the children.

To begin, when children are young, you want the books to have repeat appeal so that parents and other adults don't lose patience with your story. You want them to be happy—not exasperated—about the tenth request to read the book aloud.

You also want adults to feel good about the messages that children are getting from your story. Those who live and work with children are constantly fighting to protect them from the violent and graphic images that bombard us all from the media. The struggle to preserve their child's innocence in a changing world sometimes feels like a losing battle. At the same time, these images and the issues they represent are the very same ones that most caring adults understand they have no choice but to address. Your children's book can make that easier for them, and the characters you create in your stories can become helpful companions to adults, as well as friends to the children they care about. Take a moment to think back to the fictional book characters who influenced your childhood. Didn't they often demonstrate the importance of love, friendship, loyalty, honesty, and other qualities that we would all like to instill in our children?

Unlike an adult book, a children's book—and especially a book for young children—has to please two audiences. Both the child for whom the book is intended and the adult who buys the book must find the story appealing.

Further, because we live in competitive times, when educational standards for our children are continually under scrutiny—and often found lacking—teachers, librarians, and parents are always searching for ways to increase children's knowledge about areas ranging from basic life skills to academic subjects. That makes nonfiction a staple in every library. Maybe you didn't realize the important role you were taking on!

To get a better understanding of your audience, both young and old, you may find it helpful to interview educators, librarians, and parents about what they view as appropriate topics for your target age group. In fact, performing your own informal poll among the adults in your life can be a real eye opener!

HOW BIG IS YOUR AUDIENCE?

Initially, it may seem that the larger the audience, the greater the interest on the part of the publishing house. However, that is not always true. While some publishers are equipped to market to large audiences, others are better equipped to market to smaller audiences.

Before most editors select a book for publication, they want to consider two important pieces of information: the size of the book's audience, and the past performance of similar titles.

Audience size refers to the number of people potentially interested in a book's subject. In most cases, you will not be able to determine the *exact* number of possible readers, but you should be able to demonstrate the fact that your book will have a sizeable audience.

Fortunately for the fiction writer, children's fiction editors already know much about their potential audience. Children's interests are influenced in large part by their developmental stages, as outlined in the Square One Book Classification System, and these interests don't tend to shift dramatically over time. However, the interests of young readers are influenced at least temporarily by trends. When events occur in our world, editors want to provide books that discuss these occurrences and satisfy their readers' thirst for information. For instance, war-related books and books about Middle Eastern culture and religion became more popular in the wake of the September 11, 2001 terrorist attacks on America.

Approach trends very carefully, though. You won't be the only one rushing out to write a book on a hot topic, and it won't be long before editors say, "Enough!" Trends are also a tricky business because publishing houses determine their book offerings several months before the books actually hit the shelves. This means that what's all the rage in fall 2005 may no longer be on the radar when the book comes out in spring 2006. You'll want to get your proposal out while both readers and editors have an interest in your topic.

Whether your work is fiction or nonfiction, one of the best steps you can take to determine if you have an audience is to look at *Subject Guide to Children's Books in Print*, which you'll find in the reference section of your library. This book will allow you to track down children's books on nearly any subject imaginable. If you find a number of books written about a topic that is similar to your own, take those books out of the library and determine what, if anything, is different about yours. This will allow you to show the editor you've done your homework, and will quickly prove that your book has an audience, ready and waiting. (You'll read more about this in Chapter 5.)

Another great research tool is the Amazon.com website. Simply type in a topic under "children's books," and see how many books on your subject come up. A long list of titles will demonstrate audience interest.

If you've written a nonfiction book, you can sometimes determine your audience size by contacting organizations that gather statistics on the relevant subject. Let's say you have written a book on electric model sailboats. First, locate the *Encyclopedia of Associations* by Gale Research, a multivolume source found in the reference section of the library. If you find an association that pertains to your topic, make a call and ask if they know how many children in the United States have such a collection. If you can tell an editor that one million children under the age of fifteen are electric model sailboat collectors, in effect, you'll be telling her that she has one million potential readers. Related magazines may also be able to provide you with this important information.

It's important to let editors know that you understand how well books of a particular genre or type are selling. In some cases, you can determine this information by looking at your library's copy of *Publishers Weekly*, which prints lists of best-selling picture books and children's fiction. (These lists can also be found on the *Publishers Weekly* website.) Also talk to school and public librarians about the books

WORDS FROM A PRO

Jane Yolen

Author of *How Do Dinosaurs Say Goodnight?* (Scholastic)

Jane Yolen says that a writer who wants to break into children's books can maximize her chance of success by belonging to a writer's group and performing market research. Most important, she should never take "No" for an answer.

that children of a particular age tend to ask for. Above all, watch the world around you. If you see that teen romances are flying off the bookshelves, and if every teenage girl you know is talking about them, you can safely refer to this genre as being popular, and thereby help convince the editor that your book has an audience. She will be able to further check sales numbers by reviewing internal sales figures supplied by her marketing department; by reviewing trade journals such as *School Library Journal*; and by speaking to other editors, authors, and salespeople. If past sales were adequately large, the editor will give serious consideration to a similar project.

RULE # 4

Know your marketplace

At this point, you should know your book's category and be familiar with your audience. Now you need to understand how your book will reach its intended audience—in other words, the marketplace. Without a clear understanding of where your book is going to sell, you can't select an appropriate publisher—a publisher who is equipped to promote and distribute your book properly.

THE IMPORTANCE OF UNDERSTANDING YOUR MARKETPLACE

When people hear that I'm a children's book author, they immediately ask me where they can buy my books. I have to tell them they're not available in bookstores, although they can be ordered through Internet stores such as Amazon.com. That's because my nonfiction books were written for the school and library marketplace, and therefore are sold almost exclusively through school and library sales catalogues, rather than the traditional retail bookstore marketplace. I knew that when I approached the editors with my proposals. What should you know about marketplaces? You should know that a marketplace is the means through which a publisher is able to sell your book to its audience. If a publisher has no way of accessing the appropriate marketplace for your book, your book will never reach your readers. Just as important, if no marketplace is geared to sell your book, your project will have very little chance of finding an interested commercial publisher. That's why you must know the basics of marketplaces: what they are, what they carry, and how they're reached.

THE MARKETPLACES

A *marketplace* is simply any place or system that sells books to consumers. As you'll see, a marketplace can assume numerous shapes and sizes. In the early part of the twentieth century, the marketplace for books was both limited and uncomplicated. The vast reading audience was generally reached through bookstores and libraries. Publishing firms had salesmen who promoted their company's lines throughout their territories. Books were then directly sold and distributed by the book publishers to bookstores and libraries. But as time went on, and an ever-growing audience became even more eager to buy books, the number and types of marketplaces increased. Now, any one book may be sold through a host of different outlets. That's why my books now have a broader market than they used to.

Let's look at some of the standard marketplaces that serve today's book-buying public. After reading this section, you'll better understand how your particular book can reach its audience.

Traditional Retail Bookstores

Traditional retail bookstores are those whose stock is composed primarily of books. For our purposes, the children's section is the most important. There, you'll find both fiction and nonfiction works in all the categories discussed earlier in the chapter. You'll also find toys, stuffed animals, games, puzzles, tapes, and so on. This marketplace includes chain stores like Barnes & Noble and Borders, as well as independent bookstores.

Most of the books sold in these stores are published by trade publishers. However, retail bookstores may also offer religious trade books. Their stock includes hardbacks, paperbacks, and mass market paperbacks.

Trade publishers promote their books through sales calls made by either their own sales force or the sales force of a distributor

Many authors mistakenly think that the term marketplace refers to a book's audience. This is understandable, because the term *market*—which is often used as a synonym for marketplace—has two separate meanings. A market can be a place or system through which books are sold to consumers (a marketplace, in other words), or a segment of the population considered buyers for a particular type of book (an audience). For clarity, in this book, we will attempt to use the term marketplace only when referring to bookstores, libraries, and other book outlets.

A number of years ago, terms like *distributor,* wholesaler, and jobber had very specific meanings in the book business. A *distributor* was a company that inventoried and sold books for publishers, usually on an exclusive basis. Based on their agreement, distributors could sell titles to wholesalers, bookstores, libraries, and nontraditional outlets. A *wholesaler* was a company that inventoried and sold books to bookstores on a nonexclusive basis—sometimes within a local vicinity, sometimes within a regional area, and sometimes on a national basis. A *jobber* was a wholesaler who specialized in selling mass market books to bookstores and supermarkets. Today, in spite of the fact that distributors may still have exclusive agreements with certain publishers, the three terms are used interchangeably.

employed by the publisher. They also advertise in trade journals such as *Publishers Weekly,* and through mailings of brochures and seasonal catalogues. A number of the larger trade houses promote their books in newspapers and popular magazines. And many present their new season's titles at annual trade shows, attended by distributors. The stores purchase their books either directly from the publisher or through a distributor.

Unsold books that are held by bookstores can be returned to the distributor and/or ultimately the publisher for full credit, generally for up to one year. This returns policy—which is so different from that used in many other businesses—creates a risky financial situation for the publisher, who sometimes has to refund thousands of dollars for returned books.

Specialized Retail Bookstores

Specialized retail bookstores primarily sell books that focus on a specific subject. Many of these stores sell related products, as well—science experiments, toys, videos, CDs, and computer games, for instance.

Some specialized bookstores are devoted entirely to children's books, and offer a children's theater, author visits, crafts, and story hours. A few clever storeowners have created shops just for women and children, and offer feminist- and parenting-related books, as well as all manner of products beyond books.

A number of religious bookstores have cropped up over the last few years. In fact, nearly every community now boasts a Christian bookstore. In addition to adult books, these stores often carry religious children's books, such as picture Bibles and devotionals geared for kids.

In general, most of the books sold in these stores are published by trade publishers, although in the case of religious bookstores, of course, many are produced by religious book companies. Their stock includes hardbacks and paperbacks. Publishers promote their books in this marketplace just as they do in the traditional trade retail marketplace. The stores purchase books either directly from the publisher or through a distributor, and unsold books can be returned to the distributor and/or ultimately the publisher for full credit for usually up to one year.

Nontraditional Book Retailers

A nontraditional book retailer is any specialized retail store that carries books as a sideline. You will, for instance, find educational and craft supply stores like L.L. Weans, which carries activity books, how-to books, biographies, nature and science titles, early picture books, and easy readers; educational toy shops like Imaginarium, which carries many of the same types of books; gift stores that offer a variety of inspirational books for children—and so on. This is an ever-expanding market.

While this overall marketplace has grown steadily in the last decade, it's important to understand that it's made up of many separate and distinct submarkets. Each of these marketplaces has its own system of marketing, sales, and distribution. Over the years, the publishers that produce books appropriate for these retailers have learned to access the various outlets. In most instances, books are sold to retailers on a nonreturnable basis.

Online Retailers

With the emergence of the Internet has come a new way of selling just about anything. E-commerce, as it's called, is composed of Internet stores that allow web browsers to buy products from the comfort of their home or office at any time of the day or night. While there are a number of sites that specialize in books, such as Amazon.com and Barnesandnoble.com, literally hundreds of other sites sell thousands of products, including books.

The majority of children's books sold on these websites are trade books, but online stores also carry books for the school and religious markets. Their stock includes hardbacks, paperbacks, and mass market paperbacks.

To date, rather than advertise their books through a website promotion, most trade publishers rely on media exposure of a title to result in increased Internet sales. All it takes is for a book to win the Caldecott or Newbery Medal, or to gain exposure through TV and movies, and online sales soar. Online retailers purchase their inventory directly from the publisher or through a distributor. Most online retailers keep a limited supply of books on hand. At the moment, sales through websites may represent up to 5 percent of a given pub-

When researching publishers for your book, by all means visit any appropriate nontraditional book retailers and look at the books they offer for sale. If, for instance, you are writing a how-to book on building model ships, stop by the craft stores in your area and see who publishes the books they stock. Write down the names of all the companies, but place an asterisk next to the names of those whose books you find particularly attractive and high in quality. It's very likely that these companies should be on your A List of prospective publishers.

lisher's sales. Like traditional bookstore retailers, online retailers can return unsold books to the distributor for up to one year.

Mass Market Outlets

Mass market paperbacks are $4\frac{1}{2}$ x 7-inch softcover editions that sometimes are reprints of hardcover trade books, like the *Harry Potter* series, and sometimes are written specifically for paperback publication. While mass market outlets include traditional bookstores, the term *mass market outlets* really refers to book outlets that can be found in high-traffic areas such as airport stores, newsstands, drugstores, discount retailers like Kmart and Wal-Mart, and supermarket chains. These outlets can reach the "mass" audience rather than the general bookstore's trade audience.

Few publishers sell their titles directly to mass market outlets. Most books that reach these outlets are sold through wholesalers known as independent distributors, or IDs.

Instead of returning unsold mass market books to publishers for credit, IDs rip the covers off the unsold books. They do this because the freight costs involved in returning these books to the publisher can't be recouped. Unlike hardbacks, these books cannot be resold by the publisher. To keep the IDs in business, mass market publishers have agreed to accept a verification sheet stating that the covers of unsold books have been stripped off, and that the remaining inventory has been destroyed. In turn, the unsold inventory is deducted from the publisher's bill. Publishers may have to refund money up to 70 percent of their books.

Elementary and Secondary School Markets

To understand how books are sold to elementary and high school (el-hi) markets, you first have to realize how these books are purchased at the school level. First, you must understand that every school district has a budget, and of that budget, a certain amount is set aside for textbook purchases. Although individual policies about purchasing textbooks can vary among school districts, the following procedures are widely used.

At the elementary school level, committees consisting of teachers, administrators, and often parents are formed to pick textbooks, always keeping in mind the curriculum requirements of that state. These committees generally contact various publishers, who send representatives to formally present their texts. Gradually, the field is narrowed down until the books are chosen and presented to the district's board of education for final approval.

At the secondary level, the acquisitions process is a good deal simpler. New texts are usually reviewed by the relevant department—the English Department, for instance—which makes recommendations to the school superintendent. Ultimately, again, the texts must be approved by the board of education.

It is worth noting that some states, such as Texas, have state-wide adoption procedures in which committees are formed to adopt texts for, say, every high school in the state. Clearly, publishers vie for such adoptions, and are sometimes even willing to customize books in order to follow state guidelines.

Individual supplementary materials—novels, for instance—are usually handled at the department level and do not require a formal adoption process. An effort is often made to keep these materials consistent from one classroom to the next, so that everyone in a specific grade is reading the same novel or other supplementary material. However, it's not unusual for one fifth grade class to read one novel while a second class reads a different novel.

When a textbook adoption takes place, publishers routinely supply large amounts of supplementary materials, such as teachers' editions and workbooks, at no cost to the school. It's not uncommon, for instance, for a school district to purchase a reading series and receive thousands of dollars of free materials. This is a good investment for the publisher, as once a school district adopts a textbook, it is likely to continue ordering the text for several years. Books are sold directly from the publisher to the schools, and any unused books cannot be returned to the publisher.

Library Markets

Books are sold to a wide variety of libraries, including public, state, county, and regional libraries; federally sponsored libraries; educational libraries, such as those found in public schools; and specialized libraries that serve the needs of specific readers, such as medical researchers. Although a public library carries all types of books,

In some states, texts are adopted not for a single school, but for every appropriate school in that state. Naturally, publishers vie for such adoptions and are often willing to create customized editions to meet the state's needs.

including trade and educational books, the collections of educational and specialized libraries are geared specifically to the needs of their patrons.

Publishers promote their books to libraries via sales calls, catalogues, brochures, and attendance at library conventions and meetings. Libraries are also reached through trade publications such as *Publishers Weekly, Library Journal, School Library Journal, Choice, Booklist,* and *Kirkus Reviews.* Wholesale distributors also often recommend specific titles to libraries based on the profile of the library's patrons. In fact, the majority of library sales are channeled through these distributors, who give larger discounts than those provided by the publishers, and also simplify the ordering process by enabling the library to contact one business rather than a myriad of separate publishing houses.

Book Clubs

School-based book clubs represent a win-win-win situation. Children and their parents receive substantial discounts on their purchases; teachers earn bonus points for their classrooms, enabling them to buy additional materials; and publishers reach children who might not otherwise read their books.

Did you order books from clubs when you were in school? I remember the excitement of choosing from among a four-page selection of TAB Books. These still exist in schools, although the market has expanded tremendously. The books—and other merchandise, including stickers, videos, cassettes, and software—are offered at substantial discounts directly from the publisher.

In the world of school-based book clubs, Scholastic Books rules. Teachers earn bonus points for their classrooms with every order placed with the clubs, which can then be used to obtain a range of free teaching materials and classroom resources. Scholastic's five book clubs are Firefly, SeeSaw, Lucky, Arrow, and TAB. Teachers distribute the catalogues to their students, and then place the orders online or by phone, fax, or mail. Scholastic then delivers the items straight to the classroom.

Not all book clubs are school-based, of course. The Children's Book-of-the-Month Club, now owned by Bookspan, offers substantial savings to parents. Members first pay an enrollment fee. Then every three weeks or so, they receive a catalogue from which they can choose a book for their child. A minimum number of books must be ordered each year, either by mail or online, to maintain the membership. Other children's book clubs, such as one offered by Disney, are also available.

School Book Fairs

School book fairs provide publishers with another way to sell books directly to children, parents, and teachers. In fact, many publishers—Scholastic included—have their own book fair department.

Book fairs are generally organized by either the Parents Teachers Association (PTA) or school librarians, and are annual events in most schools. Interested PTA members or librarians follow step-by-step online ordering instructions provided by the publisher, and order the books at a deep discount, which is passed on to the parents and kids. The school then earns bonus points, most of which are used to purchase more books for the school library.

Like book clubs, school book fairs allow parents and kids to buy books at a deep discount. In return for hosting the fairs, schools earn bonus points that they can use to purchase more books for the school library.

Special Sales

Yet another marketplace is the *special sale*—a catchall phrase that represents creative ways for publishers and authors to sell their books to audiences that are beyond the reach of standard sales channels. Technically speaking, a special sale refers to the sale of books on a deep discount, on a nonreturnable basis, to a marketplace that does not interfere with any of the marketplaces previously discussed in this chapter. You have probably already seen many books sold on this basis. Some examples include:

☐ A cereal company has a promotion in which it packs a best-selling picture book in each box of cereal.

☐ A salesman known as a display marketer drops by your office and leaves a children's book for people to thumb through. In a week, he returns to pick up the book and take orders.

☐ When a children's book author visits a school, the PTA buys copies of one of her titles and distributes them to the students free of charge.

☐ Children's camps, after-school programs, and the like purchase books as prizes for children.

☐ Medical offices that cater to children, from the dentist and orthodontist to the pediatrician or surgeon, purchase books to give to children as "get well" gifts or as a means of providing them with important information.

☐ Ads on the back of food products, like macaroni and cheese, promote a children's book that you can buy by enclosing shipping and handling costs along with proof of purchase.

☐ A children's show gives books to the first hundred children to purchase tickets to the show.

For publishers, authors, and book buyers, these are win-win situations. They also open the door for authors to get certain hard-to-distribute books into print. And if an author has the ability to create such sales opportunities, it definitely gets the attention of editors.

CONCLUSION

At the beginning of this chapter, I explained that if you want to get an editor's attention, you have to be able to pinpoint your book's category, audience, and marketplace. If you've read this chapter, you've taken an important first step toward turning your manuscript into a published book. The next chapter will take you further on your journey by explaining the business of publishing and guiding you toward publishers who can help you meet your goals.

CHAPTER 3

THE BUSINESS OF CHILDREN'S BOOK PUBLISHING

For those of us who sit in front of our computers spinning stories and dreaming of bestsellers, the publishing industry can easily be perceived as a hurdle to be surmounted before we can move on to greatness. After all, it's the people in that industry who are the gatekeepers—who have the power to make our words available to our audience, or to stuff them in an envelope and send them back to us. The fact is, though, that just as you need the editor to like your work, he needs you to provide quality material for his readers. The two of you are not enemies, but potential partners in the business of providing good books for children.

When you view the children's book industry more as a business into which you can fit, rather than an omnipotent barrier, you can begin to analyze how best to approach it. That means taking the information you compiled about your book in Chapter 2—your category, audience, genre, and topic—and finding a market in which it will be the perfect fit. That's what Chapter 3 is all about.

This chapter first provides a brief history of children's book publishing so that you can understand how the industry evolved into what it is today. It then describes the different types of children's book publishing houses, presents their general editorial structures, and explains the basic criteria they use to review and determine the fate—the acceptance or rejection—of each book proposal they receive. This chapter also points out the advantages and disadvantages of each type of house for prospective authors, and clearly illustrates what happens to a proposal once it's in the hands of those gatekeepers—I mean, editors.

IB   Run for it

C   Cut it.

S   Snatched it

D   Divided it.

From *The Tragic Death of an Apple-Pie*

Artist Unknown

THE HISTORY OF CHILDREN'S BOOKS

One of the best ways to understand an industry is to look at its history. By learning why and how children's literature was first introduced, and how the business of children's books has evolved over the years, you'll be better able to understand the industry as it exists today.

The Early Years

Once upon a time, there was the oral tradition—the passing down of tales and myths from one generation to another through the spoken word. In the Middle Ages, stories like *Beowulf* were repeated around campfires and in castles. Hence, they were called castle or cottage stories. There were many storytellers, called bards or minstrels, who, for payment of food and lodging, told their tales to people of all ages as entertainment.

In the 1400s, the *hornbook* was introduced—a printed sheet of text glued onto a small wooden paddle and covered with a very thin protective sheet of cow's horn. Usually the text included the alphabet and numbers, and was used as instructional material for children and adults. The Lord's Prayer was also common, as most children knew it already, which made reading easier. Other books of the time were manuscripts that were hand-lettered by monks or scribes, and used to teach those children privileged enough to attend monastery schools.

In 1450, when Johann Gutenberg (c. 1400–1468) invented the first printing press, it finally became possible to mass-produce books. Then in 1476, when William Caxton (1422–1491) established a printing press in England, the first book-publishing business was born. Caxton published *Aesop's Fables* in 1484, and followed this with Thomas Malory's *Morte d'Arthur (The Death of Arthur)* in 1485. These early books were written for adults, but were often shared with those children lucky enough to have parents who were both literate and able to afford the luxury of Caxton's expensive printed material. Reading beside the fire was family entertainment.

In the early 1500s, legends and fairy tales became available through a less expensive means, *chapbooks*—small penny books that were generally printed on one large sheet of paper, which was then folded into a book of sixteen to sixty-four pages. These books were of poor quality, but they were readily available through peddlers (known as chapmen) and printers. Although intended for adults, chapbooks were also popular with children, who enjoyed their tales of adventure.

One of the reasons that books weren't originally written specifically for children is that adults saw children as miniature adults who were expected to act like grownups at all times. The subjects of child psychology and child development would have been greeted with peals of laughter. Of course, adults did acknowledge that it was their duty to instill in children a sense of morality and obedience. As a result, by the late seventeenth century, when some astute printers realized that they could publish books with children in mind, most of the stories told tales of children who suffered terrible consequences for their unruly behavior. Some books even threatened children with hell and damnation to get them to behave properly. James Janeway's 1672 *A Token for Children,* for instance, described thirteen little children who spent their days converting all whom they met in their own efforts to stay out of hell. Other books were more palatable, however. Despite its moral themes, for example, John Bunyan's 1678 *Pilgrim's Progress* appealed to its young readers because the hero, Christian, experiences many entertaining adventures along the road to salvation. Indeed, *Pilgrim's Progress* became required reading for Colonial children.

Fortunately, at least one book was not only written for children, but had an entirely new goal—that of education and enlightenment. Written in 1658, *Orbis Pictus,* or *The World in Pictures,* used simple language and woodcuts to explain almost two thousand words and notions. Often described as the first picture book, it must have been a welcome relief to the young people of the time.

Little by little, the Western view of both children and children's literature changed. In the late 1600s, political and educational philosopher John Locke (1632–1704) began to present the revolutionary concept that children were not miniature adults, but beings with their own ideas, which must be formed by careful adult influences. Locke believed in the value of learning through both play and education. Taking his words to heart, many writers began creating stories in which fictitious children learned social lessons and subjects such as mathematics. While the stories were no longer designed to frighten, each one of them had a deliberate lesson.

Since the beginning of printed literature, many stories intended for adults have become crossover titles, appealing to children as well as their parents. Included among the long list of these titles are *Robinson Crusoe* (Daniel Defoe, 1719), *Gulliver's Travels* (Jonathan Swift, 1726), *Grimm's Fairy Tales* (Brothers Grimm, 1812), *Little Women* (Louisa May Alcott, 1868), *The Adventures of Tom Sawyer* (Mark Twain, 1876), and *The Hobbit* (JRR Tolkien, 1937). But it wasn't until 1997, with the publication of JK Rowling's *Harry Potter and the Sorcerer's Stone,* that a children's book crossed over into the adult market, consistently appearing on *The New York Times* Best-Seller List for adults.

Even as some books began to be especially conceived for children, many of the books written for adults continued to be well received by youngsters. *Robinson Crusoe* by Daniel Defoe (1719) and *Gulliver's Travels* by Jonathan Swift (1726) delighted adults and children alike. But perhaps the adult book that drew the most enthusiastic young audience was the French-published *Contes de ma Mere l'Oye*, or *Tales of Mother Goose*. First published in 1697, this collection of stories about Sleeping Beauty, Blue Beard, and Little Red Riding Hood soon became the rage.

Through the ages, children would continue to adopt certain adult books as their own. But soon a man of vision would begin producing a new type of children's book—and would change the face of children's publishing forever. That man was John Newbery.

Children's Books Become a "Delight"

Bookseller, publisher, and author, John Newbery (1713–1767) is said to be one of the first to recognize that books intended for children could be something more than an extension of an adult's lectures. His first children's book, *A Little Pretty Pocket Book*, published in 1744, included rhymes, games, a ball for boys, and a pincushion for girls. On the frontispiece was the Latin motto *Delectando Monemus*, or *Instruction with Delight*. Newbery's goal was to raise the standards of children's publications in every way, from the level of the writing to the quality of the illustrations, and to provide books that would give children real pleasure as well as instruction. During his lifetime, he developed a large list of children's titles, establishing juvenile literature as an important branch of the publishing business.

John Newbery's contributions to the world of children's literature are acknowledged annually, when the Newbery Medal is awarded to the most distinguished children's book of the year. Named after the British bookseller, the medal was presented for the first time in 1922, becoming the first children's book award in the world.

By the early nineteenth century, the children's book business was growing by leaps and bounds. Juvenile books now offered fairy tales, fantasy, humor, and realism. One famous children's work arrived on the scene in a particularly interesting way. In 1812, brothers Jakob and Wilhelm Grimm published a collection of eighty-five German folktales, including the now-familiar stories of Hansel and Gretel and Rapunzel. The first edition was largely scholarly, with plenty of commentary by the Brothers Grimm. The brothers had really not intended to produce a children's book, but merely to preserve the folktales of their native country. But because children responded so well to the original book, the brothers soon produced a second edition, which featured no commentary, but did have illustrations contributed by another brother, Ludwig. By 1823, the collected tales had been translated into English and published under the title *German Popular Stories*. Along the way, the brothers, catering to their young audience, made the originally cruel tales a little softer and sweeter.

While the Grimms' stories were collections of tales that had been passed down for generations, it was Hans Christian Andersen who is usually credited as being the first to write an original fairy tale. His *Fairy Tales and Stories*, written between 1835 and 1872, was said to enrich children's imaginations, and was certainly far less horrifying than those of the Grimm brothers.

Many other authors now well-known to us began writing for children during this time as well. Clement Moore's *The Night Before Christmas* (1823) made children laugh. And in 1865, Lewis Carroll introduced the world of fantasy in *Alice's Adventures in Wonderland*, in which Alice neither learns a lesson nor converts a soul. Of course, not everyone was able to leave behind the moralizing of earlier times. In 1848, *Struwwelpeter* by Heinrich Hoffman was published in Germany. In it were nonsense poems with cautionary tales, like the one about a boy who wouldn't stop sucking his thumb. What better way to deal with the tyke's stubbornness than to chop off the offending digit? Apparently, children loved it!

The Changing World of Topics

The world of children's books had been forever changed, and into this atmosphere stepped authors like Nathaniel Hawthorne, William Makepeace Thackeray, Charles Dickens, Rudyard Kipling, Beatrix Potter, Jules Verne, and Kenneth Grahame. In 1868, family life became a legitimate storyline with the publication of Louisa May Alcott's *Little Women*. In 1876, Mark Twain's *The Adventures of Tom Sawyer* presented characters who were not exactly up to society's standards, but were likeable anyway. And in 1921, the children's nonfiction market was established in the United States with the publication of Hendrik van Loon's *The Story of Mankind*, a fascinating view of world history created just for children.

All of these authors turned children's literature away from the morbid to provide youngsters with a cheerful escape into books. Reading became a pleasant pastime, rather than a pedantic task

**From *Alice's Adventures
in Wonderland*
by Lewis Carroll**

Illustration by John Tenniel

imposed by adults. Now when parents sat around a fire with their children, it was to share a bedtime story.

Over time, as the country struggled through two world wars, children's books began to better reflect the world around them. By the 1960s and '70s, juvenile literature began to help children understand the various social issues that concerned them, from civil rights and crime to divorce and foster parenting. In fact, it was during this period that publishers seemed to realize for the first time that not all children were white, and produced books that featured black protagonists or multiethnic characters. By the late 1970s, however, the publishing world had recognized that the *problem novel*—a book in which the main character deals with issues like death and addiction—was, in its own way, as preachy as the books that had been published centuries earlier. By the 1980s, editors and writers seemed to realize that children just want to read about strong characters involved in interesting plots, regardless of any moral lesson being conveyed.

The Changing Marketplace

At the start of the twentieth century, children most often looked for books in a library rather than a store, and relied on children's librarians to help them with their selections. Eventually, many of these librarians became editors in the children's divisions of publishing houses.

At the dawn of the twentieth century, libraries constituted the chief marketplace for children's books, with most parents leaving the selection of their youngsters' books in the hands of librarians. In the years after World War One, several publishing houses established separate editorial departments for the genre, with Macmillan in the lead with its Department of Books for Boys and Girls, created in 1919. Most of the people who headed these departments were former librarians who already knew what children liked best. The companies marketed their children's books to consumers by utilizing radio time, during which they read from new titles. They also established Children's Book Week as a means of launching the winter holiday buying season.

By the 1930s, spring had been established as the second publishing season, which allowed for Easter tie-ins with department stores. Department stores, in fact, were then the most popular place to purchase children's books, and all manner of promotional tools were used, such as the 1944 stunt in which a real elephant appeared in Chicago's Marshall Field's to promote *The Elegant Elephant* by Susanne Suba.

By the end of World War Two, publishing companies no longer viewed their juvenile book departments as mere adjuncts of their

The Importance of Illustrations

Today we know that illustrations are a significant component of children's books. But even with the influence of John Newbury, most books that appeared before the 1800s contained only crude woodcuts. By 1865, however, illustrators like Kate Greenaway (1846–1901), Walter Crane (1845–1915), and Randolph Caldecott (1846–1886) were using detailed drawings and vibrant colors to make children's books livelier and more attractive. These gifted artists were widely admired, with the children of the time eagerly awaiting every publication in which their work appeared.

By the 1930s, picture books had become a staple of every children's book department in department stores, with works by Ludwig Bemelmans (*Madeline*), Wanda Gag (*Millions of Cats*), and Robert Lawson (*The Story of Ferdinand*) making juvenile literature more popular than ever. The picture book genre became so important, in fact, that in 1938, the Caldecott Medal, named after English illustrator Randolph Caldecott, was created to honor the most distinguished American picture book of the year.

Over the years, many fine illustrators have striven to bring children's stories to life, with some artists having a profound effect on the industry. In 1963, for instance, Maurice Sendak received international acclaim for his book *Where the Wild Things Are*. Believing that an illustration should not just clarify text but also add to the mystery of the work, Sendak created inviting images that seemed to be full of action. He designed the double-page spread and was able to create art that needed no words at all, yet still managed to keep the story moving. Consequently, his work influenced all children's book illustrators who came after him.

Today, children's titles compete not only with one another but also with other media, including television and computer games. Therefore, the brighter the art and the more clever the doodads, from pop-ups to flip pages, the more likely they are to sell well. But strong art that captures the world as children either know it or imagine it is still the most powerful and the most popular.

adult divisions. Little Golden Books and Western Printing Company made low-priced picture books available in five-and-dimes and drugstores. And by the 1950s, children's books were being promoted not only on the radio, but through television as well.

The industry's second growth spurt occurred in the mid-1960s with the Johnson era, during which school and public libraries received substantial government funding. But by the 1970s, that funding had ended, and libraries were hard hit. At the same time, Macmillan introduced picture book reprints in paperback form. Previously, paperback children's books had been shunned by book publishers and librarians simply because it was thought that young hands would be too rough on them. But since hardcovers were expensive for most families, the availability of paperbacks opened a new door for the publishing industry. Within two years, in fact, these less-expensive editions accounted for a quarter of Macmillan's book sales.

With the birth of paperback children's books came the birth of children's book departments in bookstores. By the late 1970s and early 1980s, first independent children's bookstores and then the chains began to grow. Now children's book publishers had yet another marketplace for their product. Today, most publishers produce hardcover versions of books, followed about eighteen months later by paperback versions. Moreover, special library bound versions are created for schools and libraries.

The baby boom of the 1980s and early 1990s resulted in the largest retail market for children's books in the history of juvenile literature. Trade books were now used in schools as part of the Whole Language method of teaching, in which children develop language skills through reading, writing, and listening, rather than use of basic readers. (Remember, "This is Sally. See Sally run."?) Additionally, the new teaching method led to the development of new children's book categories. Instead of being able to choose between only picture books and novels, children could also select easy readers and chapter books, which became increasingly popular. The link between the publishing world and the world of education had become stronger, and students today are encouraged to read for pure pleasure, both in and out of school. Some state education departments, in fact, strongly suggest that students read a certain number of books on their own each year.

Because library and school markets remain so important for publishers, the financial health of the publishing industry today depends a great deal on federal funding for education. In lean times, publishers are hesitant to take chances on unknown authors. When government purse strings relax, though, publishers are more willing to gamble on a new name.

The Modern Publishing World

Since the 1980s, book publishers have been merging with one another at a frenzied pace, making it difficult for even insiders to keep track of all the players. Penguin and Putnam have become one, as have Simon & Schuster and Macmillan, Random House and Bantam Doubleday Dell, Harper Collins and William Morrow, and Scholastic and Grolier. These billion-dollar *megapublishers*, as they're called, dominate the children's book market, and except for Scholastic, Inc., which publishes only children's books, they also control the adult book industry. In addition, many publishing houses are owned by media conglomerates. Bertelsmann—which owns Random House,

Bantam Doubleday Dell, and more—is part of the AOL/Time Warner group. Liberty Media Corporation owns Houghton Mifflin. Simon & Schuster falls under the ownership of Viacom, Inc. And the Walt Disney Company owns Hyperion and Disney Children's Book Group. What exists of those earlier publishing houses are imprints, which means that they survive in name and logo only. As subsidiaries of the megapublisher, each imprint is responsible for a set number of books for each selling season—books that fit within the publisher's specific list.

On the plus side, once writers get a contract, they often are provided with more opportunities to earn money. Because of licensing, in which one company sells a brand to another company, a book character can become a TV show, a movie, or a doll. This becomes even easier when your book is published by a company such as Simon & Schuster, which is owned by Viacom, Inc., which also owns Nickelodeon.

In this multimedia atmosphere, it seems that the exploratory days of children's books have been forgotten. As you'll see later in this chapter, marketing plans for a book are carefully considered before any contract is offered to an author, and the company's sales staff has much to say about your manuscript as well. Whether or not you agree with that process, it's the industry into which you're sending your manuscript. And when it works, it works in your favor as much as the publisher's.

Of course, not all publishing houses were swallowed up by mergers. There are many medium-sized companies—like Running Press, which has a children's book division—that continue to compete successfully with the larger publishers. In addition, small independent publishers have been growing steadily, creating their own wish lists for topics, and developing niches in the marketplace. While the megahouses have been reporting decreased trade sales across both the adult and children's markets, sales for small presses have been growing.

Although J.K. Rowling's *Harry Potter* created a huge industry buzz when it stormed across the Atlantic to grab the readership of children and adults alike, when you look back at the history of children's book publishing, this should be no surprise. From the earliest book to catch children's attention—despite the fact that it was intended for their parents—it has been clear that children's books

Billion-dollar megapublishing companies such as the Bertelsmann Group from Germany now dominate both the United States and European book markets. Nevertheless, a good number of medium-sized and small publishers continue to produce excellent children's books.

have to appeal not only to kids, but also to adults. From the parents of generations ago who shared books with their offspring in front of a fire, to parents who read to their children at bedtime today, to children's librarians, to chain store bookbuyers, to editors, the one constant in this changing industry has been that the best, most successful children's books have universal appeal.

The remainder of this chapter will help you understand the workings of modern children's book publishers. But if you've learned anything from our brief look at the history of juvenile literature, it should be that the publishing world is not a stagnant one. The goals of children's books, the topics covered, the genres explored, the marketplace, and even the nature of the companies that produce the books are always changing. That's why any writer who hopes to not only see his book in print but also please his readers must stay informed of trends, and remain alert to changes in the industry.

RULE # 5

Know the differences between publishing houses

All publishers are not created equal. And if you intend to find the best company to represent you and your project, it's important to be aware of the major differences between them. Most basically, publishing houses are either commercial or noncommercial. The following discussion details the different kinds of publishers that fall under each of these main categories.

COMMERCIAL PUBLISHING HOUSES

Commercial publishing houses—companies that produce books for both general and specialized sales, primarily for profit—are of three types. First, there are trade publishers, who create books for the general reader, and market them chiefly to bookstores. Second, there are school and library publishers, who create books to meet the needs of the elementary-to-high school market and the library market. Finally, there are educational publishers, who produce the textbooks and supplementary materials used in schools, from the elementary school level through the high school level.

Trade Book Publishers

Traditional trade houses can be categorized as large, moderate-sized, or small. Each has its own internal dynamics based on the company's history, the company's goals, and the various personalities that determine if a book is signed on, as well as how it is produced and marketed. While a number of publishers have their own distinct company cultures, dictated in large part by their owners, the basic principles that underlie the day-to-day operations of these firms tend to be universal.

Many writers assume that large houses are the best places to send their manuscripts. After all, who wouldn't want the opportunity to have their characters become household names through licensing? It's usually the large houses whose books dominate the bestsellers lists. And when you hear of big money being offered in author advances, the larger firms are generally behind the offers. But it's also important to consider the hundreds of quality moderate-sized and small publishing houses that can provide a wonderful home for your book. Many, in fact, are more appropriate than larger firms for certain titles. Instead of picking companies by size and name, the wisest course of action is to gain a clear understanding of the wide diversity of existing publishers, and learn what each has to offer.

Although many writers insist on sending their manuscripts to only large publishing houses, small and mid-sized companies are often more appropriate for certain titles. Moreover, smaller houses are far more likely to consider the works of first-time authors.

Large Houses

What determines how "big" a house is? For the most part, it comes down to money. Usually, to be considered a large house, annual sales figures must reach $50 million or more. Moreover, between all their imprints, large companies generally publish over 500 titles a year, and usually well over that number.

Large publishing houses have highly defined organizational structures in which departmental roles as well as individual accountabilities are clearly established. Throughout every stage of a book's creation—from its acquisition and production, to its marketing and

In most large children's book publishing houses, and in many mid-sized ones as well, there are no "acquisitions editors"—no individuals whose sole task is to find and secure new titles. Instead people at almost every level—from the publisher to the editor-in-chief, senior editor, and associate editor—may be responsible for signing on new books. And in most cases, the person who acquires a title will also shape it, choose an illustrator, and see the project through to completion.

promotion—everyone involved knows the responsibility and parameters of his specific job.

Acquiring Manuscripts

Most large-sized publishers have spring and fall seasons, meaning that they introduce one list of new books before the spring holidays, and another list around back-to-school time. Editors are generally responsible for acquiring anywhere from one to five titles a season each, and—between paperback versions of last season's books, the current season's titles, and next season's books—are always working on several different seasons at a time.

When a manuscript attracts an editor's attention, he usually brings it to the next editorial meeting, which is attended by other editors in his *imprint*—the specific publishing division in which he works. There, he passes it on to another reader for a second opinion. If that person is also enthusiastic about the manuscript, the original editor talks to his publishing director or department head, who then reads it. Usually, the publisher or editor-in-chief reads it as well. In most houses, a marketing director is called in for his opinion, based on what he knows of the market. If all agree that it's a saleable manuscript, the editor approaches the author and makes an offer.

When analyzing a manuscript or book proposal for possible approval, two questions are considered carefully: Will the book sell enough copies to make money for the company? Is the manuscript right for the house? The following information explains how these criteria are regarded in a large firm.

■ *Will the Book Sell Enough Copies to Make Money for the Company?*
Since this is the primary question an editor considers when reviewing a manuscript, it's important to understand that editors do not make this determination in an arbitrary manner. Each editor is assigned a specific category—picture books, for instance—in which he is expected to find possible titles. Experienced editors know their markets. They are aware of the types of books within their particular category that have sold well in the past, as well as those that have failed. Conscientious editors keep up with trends in the marketplace, and can generally anticipate whether a book will be in demand or will perform poorly.

The editor is then expected to create a profit-and-loss statement. Based on what he understands of his market, the editor first comes up with an estimate of the size of the first printing, the number of books that would sell, and the price at which the book would be sold. Then the finance department considers these figures in light of the royalties the author would be paid, as well as the production costs, and determines if the profits would outweigh the losses. As you might imagine, the pressure to come up with realistic numbers is great. The books the editor selects have to earn enough money to show a predetermined profit percentage over the course of time. If too many of his picks fail to be profitable, the editor will be out of a job.

■ *Is the Manuscript Right for the House?*

When determining if a manuscript is right for his house, an editor considers several different factors. First, of course, the editor tries to determine how the book fits his list. In other words, does it fall into his specific category, and does it satisfy a niche the house has been trying to fill?

Editors also judge if the subject matter will be controversial, which may or may not be what they want at a given time. For instance, I once heard an editor say that he looks for "talkable" books—books that get the media and consumers buzzing about the topic. Other editors, however, may wish to avoid controversy.

Every editor must also consider the shape that the manuscript is in. For the most part, editors want books that require little work. But some have told me that they'll accept a manuscript that needs editing if the subject matter and the voice of the characters grab their interest. In other words, if your manuscript has potential, but isn't sparkling, a publishing house may still be willing to work with you. But don't rely on an editor's being so enchanted with your project that he's willing to fix sloppy prose. Besides, whenever an editor recognizes that time will have to be spent reworking a manuscript, the author's advance is decreased.

Another factor to be considered is author credibility. In trade book houses, an author who has a history of writing books that sell well is highly impressive. This doesn't help the first-timer, of course, but it is useful to keep in mind once you've broken into the business.

An editor also has to determine if the format you're proposing is one he can handle. If your proposal requires full-color photographs, but that publisher uses only line drawings, chances are he'll pass on it. That's why it makes sense to study the publisher's book catalogue before you send in your proposal.

Finally, never forget that editors are human, with personal likes and dislikes that affect their decision-making. One editor I know never accepts proposals for picture books that open with a question— "What would you do if your mother was an octopus?" for instance. He's simply seen this opening too often. Another told me that he once sent a contract to an author because he loved the first sentence of the proposal: "My parents made me move three times in one school year." Since this had been the editor's personal experience, it struck a chord with him. While you're probably not a mind reader, you can see that it pays to do your homework and learn as much as you can about each publisher's books.

How a Manuscript Reaches an Editor's Desk

Most large-sized houses acquire many *unsolicited* manuscripts each day—manuscripts that they have not specifically asked to see. However, the vast majority of big houses return these manuscripts unread. Those that do accept unrequested manuscripts generally place them in a *slush pile,* the term traditionally used to describe a stack of unsolicited materials. While these manuscripts are reviewed in time, they are less of a priority than proposals received from known sources.

In most instances, editors in large firms rely on their personal networks of literary agents and other contacts. Many literary agents have cultivated working relationships with editors, keep lists of each editor's interests, and pitch only those proposals that are appropriate. Manuscripts sent by agents who don't have a relationship with an editor are usually added to the slush pile, along with the submissions of unknown authors. (For more about working with literary agents, see page 72.)

Previously published authors are another important source of manuscripts. In fact, when a large house hires an editor today, he's expected to bring authors with him. Considering the pressure placed on trade editors to sign on books that will make money for the company, this is easy to understand. A manuscript produced by a proven author with an existing audience is a draw to almost any publishing house.

Some major publishing houses reach out to new writers through contests. Random House, for instance, runs the annual Marguerite de Angeli Contest for readers age eight to twelve, and the Delacourte Press Contest for a First Young Adult Novel. Both competitions offer the winner a publishing contract.

It's vital to understand that trade house editors are incredibly busy. Editors claim to read every manuscript that comes their way, because they never know where that new bestseller may be found. But the fact is that reading manuscript proposals, whether agented or unsolicited, is just one of the many tasks that face the average editor. Other responsibilities include, but are not limited to, negotiating contracts, editing manuscripts that are already under contract, finding illustrators for books under contract, writing jacket copy, checking on books in production, reviewing page proofs, handling publicity materials, and providing the company's sales force with information on upcoming titles. In fact, editors usually wind up reading slush pile manuscripts on their own time—on the train coming home from work, over dinner, during weekends, or even during vacations. The bottom line is that an editor's time is at a premium, which is why it's so important to create a proposal that will make a great immediate impression.

Things to Consider When Working With a Large House

Is bigger better when it comes to working with a publishing house? There certainly are advantages. For one thing, big houses usually have an experienced sales force with strong established systems of distribution, as well as the financial backing to perform extensive marketing through publicity, advertising, and promotion. They also have well-established connections that allow them to get large quantities of books into the right hands. And due to the high visibility that comes with name recognition, large firms are often contacted by big companies that can offer them special selling opportunities, such as book club sales. When these large marketing machines work, they work very well indeed, with an author quickly becoming a household name as the characters he's created become licensed.

As you might expect, large publishing houses also usually pay authors more substantial advances than do moderate-sized or small publishers. The purpose, of course, is to attract previously published, well-known authors. Contracting with a popular author can translate into a sizeable return on the company's investment.

The average author, though, neither gets the large advances offered to well-known writers, nor the same kind of sales and marketing exposure that a famous author does. Projects not considered

Because editors have to juggle so many titles and tasks, things sometimes fall through the cracks. For instance, *Duck on a Bike* by David Shannon was eliminated from the running for the 2003 Caldecott Medal because of a missed problem in continuity. The bicycle pictured in the book had a distinctive bell on the handlebars in every illustration but one. Children and librarians caught the mistake that the editor had missed, costing the illustrator his Caldecott.

Do You Need a Literary Agent?

If you are worried about the difficulty of penetrating the closed doors of publishing houses, you may feel that you need a literary agent to get your book into print. At the same time, you may have heard that you need to be published to get an agent. The good news it that neither of these statements is entirely true.

First of all, let's consider what an agent can and should do for the writer he represents. A literary agent is a dealmaker whose job is to make a connection with a publisher on the author's behalf. In exchange, he receives a commission, which is usually 10 to 15 percent of both the author's advance and his royalties. A good literary agent has connections with acquisitions editors throughout the publishing industry. He also keeps pace with developments and trends in the industry. He knows which companies have merged, and he understands what that means to the welfare of a particular imprint. He is aware of which editor is moving to which new house. He pays attention to the authors that each editor has acquired, and he knows what they've recently published. He knows what topics each editor is looking for. And, unlike a first-time author, he can call an editor up and tell him what he has to offer.

Typically, an agent is responsible for helping you shape your submissions package so that it will appeal to editors. He even knows which editors prefer to see an e-mail query, and which ones want a complete manuscript in hard copy only. And it is the agent—not the author—who sends out the book proposal to those publishers he feels will be interested, usually at his own expense.

Finally, when a publisher shows interest in a submission package, it's the literary agent's job to negotiate the best deal—particularly since what's good for the writer is also good for the agent. Expertise in the area of contract negotiations enables a good agent to troubleshoot any potential weaknesses in the deal. (See Chapter 7 for more information about literary agents and contracts.)

---

priorities are afforded limited exposure and a limited period of time in which to perform. If a book initially sells well, additional marketing may be developed. But if it fails to produce the expected sales figures, it will quickly disappear from the marketing department's radar. In fact, even some well-known authors have complained that their books were declared out-of-print after only a few seasons.

It's also important to understand that because the editor in a large publishing house handles so many titles at once, manuscripts often don't get the attention they need and deserve. That's not to say that books published by large houses are ultimately of poor quality. In fact, because these companies have the money to invest in good-quality production, chances are that your book will be quite attractive.

But it's not always necessary to have an agent. In my nonfiction career, I've sold thirty-eight books without an agent. The fact is that if you're writing school-related materials or you want to work with a small publisher, agents generally won't even be interested in helping you, as the area of nonfiction usually doesn't involve big money.

If you've written a work of fiction, the story is a little different. If you choose to work with a smaller house, chances are you will not need an agent, as these firms are usually open to unagented proposals. If you want to write for the moderate- or large-sized houses, most likely you will need to find an agent. The standard policy of most of these firms calls for the immediate rejection of any unagented manuscript.

So it *is* possible to get published in both nonfiction and fiction without a literary agent—especially if you choose to work with a smaller house. Smaller houses, in fact, would usually rather deal directly with an author, as they often feel that agents create an adversarial relationship between author and publisher. And here's more good news: Often when a larger publisher has an interest in an unagented manuscript, the publisher helps the writer find an agent who can assist the author in completing the deal. (Note that publishers do this not out of a sense of altruism, but to facilitate negotiations.) Moreover, once you have had a book published—even with a relatively small house—you will find it much easier to find an agent who wants to work with you. Agents know that it's easier to "sell" a published author than one who's never had a book in print.

If you do decide that you want to use an agent, you can get a list of established literary agents in *Literary Market Place* and *Children's Writer's & Illustrator's Market*. Another way to find a good agent is to look at the acknowledgments page of a favorite children's book. Authors often use their acknowledgments to thank their agents, whom they mention by name. You can then find contact information through a source like the *LMP*. Be leery of any agents who request a reading fee, though. A reputable agent works only for a percentage of the author's advance and royalty.

Large firms publish books using specific formulas. According to some formulas, approximately 10 percent of a company's new titles will generate enough revenue to pay for its entire list of new books; 20 percent will pay for themselves, plus make a reasonable profit; another 20 percent will just about break even; and the remaining books will lose money. If your book falls within the top 30 percent, it's doing well. If not, odds are that any sales will just about cover your advance. Furthermore, in approximately eighteen months from its date of publication, your book will likely be out of print. Don't expect a large company to give your book a second chance, either. This would go against the economic principles by which large publishing firms operate.

Moderate-Sized Houses

To be considered a moderate-sized publishing house, annual sales figures must fall between $10 and $50 million, and the house must produce over 100 titles a year. Like large commercial firms, they usually have well-defined organizational structures in which departmental and individual responsibilities are clear and specific. Unlike large houses, however, moderate-sized houses may not necessarily have a standard corporate structure.

Many mid-sized firms have developed their own unique operating systems based on the marketplaces they serve and/or the people who run them. Often they are managed by one or more individuals as private businesses; are run as overgrown family companies; or are treated as subsidiaries of other businesses, such as newspaper chains or media conglomerates. As a potential author in search of the right press for your book, be sure to learn as much as you can about the operating practices of the individual firms in which you are interested.

Acquiring Manuscripts

Just as in large houses, editors who acquire manuscripts at moderate-sized publishing companies are responsible for signing on a certain number of new titles each season while staying within a set budget. Typically, the editor doesn't have a team to help him make decisions about signing on books, as he would in a larger house. Instead, he brings potential titles to a department head, who oversees the acquisitions process. This person has the authority to approve or reject a project. If the project's estimated production cost exceeds its allotted budget—if, for instance, the book would include colorful pop-ups, and therefore require the use of an overseas printer—the editor or department head must seek approval from a supervisor, who may, in fact, be the publisher. This process usually runs smoothly because it involves only a few levels of administrative approval.

However, editors in medium-sized companies must base their decisions on the same criteria used in large companies. They must consider if the book will sell enough copies to make money for the house, and if the project is right for the house.

■ *Will the Book Sell Enough Copies to Make Money for the Company?*
While some editors in moderate-sized publishing houses are responsible for signing on books in a specific category, others are responsible for acquiring books for all publishing lines. Regardless, the editor has to know his market well. An experienced editor will be familiar with what the competition has published, will know which titles have done well and which have performed poorly, and will make decisions accordingly.

Generally, any editor who finds a book with potential will meet with his department head to create a profit-and-loss statement. Just as in the larger houses, the editor and department head will weigh potential profits (estimated sales) against losses (advances, royalties, and production costs). But unlike his counterpart in a big company, the editor in a moderate-sized firm will not be held solely responsible for the final decision.

■ *Is the Manuscript Right for the House?*
Editors in moderate-sized houses ask the same editorial questions posed in large firms to judge if a proposed book is right for their list. Does the book fit in with existing company titles? Is the subject matter or genre appropriate for the firm? Will the manuscript need significant editing? Is the author known? Is the format one that the publisher can handle? Once again, a thoughtful review of a publisher's book catalogue can help you determine the general editorial profile used by the company's editors.

A careful review of a publisher's book catalogue can help you determine the editorial profile used by the company's acquiring editors. This, in turn, can help you decide if the company might be interested in your project.

How a Manuscript Reaches an Editor's Desk

Just like large publishing houses, in which an editor is responsible for acquiring a set number of books per season and all the work that goes with it, many moderate-sized companies expect their editors to both acquire and edit books. But for some moderate-sized companies there is an *acquisitions editor* who is responsible only for acquiring new titles and negotiating contracts. Usually, these firms have several editors who work on other aspects of the book's production—editing, for instance—once the contract has been signed.

If you can imagine an office filled with towers of unread manuscripts, you can visualize the workplace of the acquisitions editor at a moderate-sized house. It's typical for a house to receive about 3,000 unsolicited manuscripts a year. Usually the acquisitions editor has an editorial assistant who scans the proposals. Unsolicited materials that don't meet the house's criteria are returned. The rest are sent to the appropriate editor, who reviews each proposal and either rejects it or considers it for publication.

In addition to acquiring books through unsolicited proposals, most editors in these firms have a network of agents from whom they accept manuscripts. They may also have authors among their contacts. In fact, more often than their large-company counterparts, these editors may actively seek authors to write a book for an existing series or line that the house wants to continue.

As mentioned earlier, each mid-sized house has its own organizational structure, which can make it either easier or more difficult for a first-time author to get his proposal considered. If one or two individuals dictate a rigid editorial policy, for example, the types of desired projects may be greatly limited. But if the company's editorial culture is more liberal, the editors may be more inclined to take calculated risks on new and interesting projects. That's why it's so important to become familiar with a company's books before sending in a proposal.

Things to Consider When Working With a Moderate-Sized House

When investigating publishers for your project, consider asking about each company's editorial process—a process that varies from house to house. For instance, some mid-sized companies work closely with their authors to create high-quality books, while others budget little time for editorial input.

Many moderate-sized houses have established solid names for themselves in the children's book industry, not only with consumers, but also with librarians. This could be a draw for you. But a number of other factors should also be considered when evaluating a publishing company of this size.

Some mid-sized publishing companies pay substantial advances. For the most part, though, the royalty advances tend to be modest—especially for first-time authors—so don't assume that your advance will be sizeable.

Many moderate-sized houses encourage editors to devote a good deal of attention to each of their projects. This is a major advantage, not only because it usually results in a high-quality book, but also because—especially if you are new to the editorial process—you are likely to learn a great deal along the way. Of course, not all moderate-sized publishing houses have enough staff to devote that much attention to each individual author. When asking for a company's writer's guidelines, it may be a good idea to also inquire about its editorial process.

Typically, moderate-sized houses have strong distribution systems. Over time, they've developed the relationships needed to get their books to the public. Like large houses, they often also have name recognition in certain marketplaces, which increases their chances of special selling opportunities.

Some moderate-sized houses have an in-house sales force. Others rely on outside sales representatives. Still others have both. Some mid-sized firms even use the sales force of large publishing houses that also carry additional lines. For the most part, though, companies that maintain their own sales force are likely to give their books the best representation.

Many companies that use outside representatives often try to further encourage sales through direct mailings, telemarketing, and other promotional tools—anything that will help their titles stand out in the marketplace. However, not all companies put forth this effort. As a potential author, you should always try to learn how a company sells its books.

Just as in large firms, a book published by a moderate-sized house will be given a limited amount of time and exposure in which to perform. If the book sells well initially, additional marketing may be added to further promote the book. But books that don't sell well are generally relegated to backlist status, meaning that although they remain in print, they receive no further promotion. Occasionally, though not often, a mid-sized company will give such titles a second marketing opportunity. This depends on the strength of the company's commitment to a particular book.

Many mid-sized firms publish books using the same formulas employed in large houses. Approximately 10 percent of a company's new titles will generate enough revenue to pay for its entire list of new books; 20 percent will pay for themselves, plus make a reasonable profit; another 20 percent will just about break even; and the remaining books will lose money. If your book falls within the top 30 percent, it's doing well. If not, odds are that you won't make much more money than your advance. Some moderate-sized firms, however, may keep a slow-moving book in print for years, which is an important factor for many authors.

Small Houses

Commercial houses with annual sales of less than $10 million are considered small publishers. These houses also publish far fewer books than larger companies, with some firms producing only two titles a year, while others release close to a hundred.

Few small houses have complicated organizational structures. Many are run like family-owned or small businesses, and employ only a small number of people—sometimes as few as one or two. As a result, in most cases, the company's vision strongly reflects that of its founders. Sometimes, former employees of other publishing houses—editors, salespeople, copywriters, marketers, or publishers—establish small companies because they believe they've gained enough knowledge of the industry to run a successful business themselves. Other houses are created by special-interest groups who want to get their message out to the public, or even as a hobby, a self-publishing venture, or a tax write-off. Motivations for ownership of small houses are diverse, and it's this diversity that allows for their wide range of organizational styles, marketing philosophies, and topic coverage.

Today, the term *independent publisher* refers to any publishing house that is managed by its owners, as opposed to being publicly held or owned by a large publisher or business entity. While this term could be used to describe many moderate-sized houses, the true spirit of independent publishing clearly exhibits itself in the form of small presses. Overwhelmingly, small independent publishers are the ones that allow first-time authors to establish themselves as writers. They also provide the forum for authors to break new ground in publishing. For instance, since its establishment in 1993, Lee & Low Books has published over fifty first-time authors and illustrators. Of those titles, many have focused on controversial topics, such as the Japanese internment camps discussed in Ken Mochizuki's *Baseball Saved Us*. Small publishers are often the risk-takers—the ones that give unknown authors the chance to pursue their visions.

Small publishing firms are also the products of their creators. While it's true that they may provide great opportunities for unpublished authors, small houses may reflect not only the strength and vision, but also the shortcomings and weaknesses of the person in charge of the company.

Acquiring Manuscripts

In a small publishing house, because the staff size is usually minimal, only one or two people will handle your submission, one of whom is often the owner. That person is also keenly aware of the company's financial limitations, so that the number of books produced by the company may change each year based on the success of last year's list. The acquisitions person may also be responsible for other aspects of the production process, from editing the manuscript to designing book covers, and quite possibly managing the publicity as well. Another employee might be in charge of sales and advertising, while the duties of another might include bookkeeping, order taking, and office management. In many cases, publishers may hire part-time employees or freelancers to handle some of these tasks.

The person or people making the decision about a manuscript submission in a small house follow the same guidelines employed by larger houses. They want to determine if the book will sell well and if the manuscript is right for their house.

◼ *Will the Book Sell Enough Copies to Make Money for the Company?*
Regardless of the size of the company, earning a profit is an important consideration. However, in most small companies, estimating the potential sales of each accepted book proposal does not involve a formal process as it does in a larger house. Ideally, each project selected should earn enough money to pay for itself and earn a profit. If it doesn't, the person who took the chance on that book obviously won't lose his job. A series of bad choices won't bode well for his company, of course, but if the funds are there to keep the company alive, a publisher may decide that maintaining that book on his company's list is worth the loss.

◼ *Is the Manuscript Right for the House?*
When evaluating a book's suitability, editors in small publishing firms ask precisely the same questions that big-company editors ask. Does the book fit the company's list? Is the manuscript in good shape? Is the material too controversial—or not controversial enough? Can the company handle the format? And, finally, is the author truly informed about his topic?

Although small publishers are often willing to take a chance on new authors and new topics, they still have to earn a profit in order to stay in business. So just like larger companies, they must examine each manuscript critically and accept only those that they feel are a good fit for their firm.

One of the beauties of small publishing firms is that they often are willing to expand into new markets—to take on projects that do not fit in their established publishing program.

While a small company may have strict criteria for the line of books it already publishes, it often has the freedom to include projects that do not fall within its established editorial guidelines. If, for instance, a book is on a topic not previously touched upon in the publisher's line, or if the author is using a genre that is new to that house, the publisher may nevertheless decide to take it on and expand into a new market. At large and moderate-sized houses, a decision to expand into a new area of interest is usually handled on a corporate, not an editorial, level. Typically, when a project doesn't fall within a larger company's area, it is rejected immediately. And in the rare event that a project like this *is* considered, it requires careful and lengthy review and analysis, and the input of several company employees before a decision can be made. One of the beauties of a small publishing firm is that it can make these decisions in a timely manner, largely because only one or two people are involved in the process.

While larger trade-house editors may pursue high-profile best-selling authors, small houses don't. To put it plainly, economic restraints make it difficult for small firms to compete for big names. The good news is that smaller companies—whether trade or educational in nature—are very happy to work with first-time and lesser-known authors.

How a Manuscript Reaches an Editor's Desk

Large or small, every publishing house receives hundreds of submissions a month, almost all unsolicited. Few agents will bother to send a writer's manuscript to a small house because they feel the work required to secure a contract may not be worth their time, considering the small amount of money they'll earn on the deal. And small press owners tend to stay away from agents, too, believing that they can find the right author without an agent's help.

In general, all manuscripts submitted to a small house are opened, which makes small houses an appealing option for authors who have never been published. Don't let this "open door policy" make you less careful about crafting your proposal, however. A good proposal that's addressed to the correct editor will make the best impression on the person who ultimately opens the envelope and makes the decision to accept or reject.

Things to Consider When Working With a Small House

For some authors and their agents, the idea of having a small house publish their work is unthinkable. They know that small firms do not pay huge advances, do not take out ads in *The New York Times,* and do not send authors on extensive publicity tours. However, especially when they are just starting out, it is extremely foolish of writers to limit themselves to big-name houses. It's true that a small publisher cannot provide some of the benefits that a larger company does, but it is able to offer many other benefits instead.

First and foremost, because a small publisher is willing to take chances on an unknown writer who has potential, it can provide that all-important opportunity to be published. As independent publishers grow in prestige in the publishing world, this can launch a long-term writing career. And when a writer makes a name for himself with a small company, it's pretty much guaranteed that the big guys will take notice.

Strangely enough, another advantage for first-time authors is that the small house simply doesn't pay large advances. Why is this a benefit? Small publishers keep their advances modest because they like to keep their limited funds available as working capital, which they use in the development and editing of projects. That's why editors in small companies are able to devote time and attention to each project, and to develop a close working relationship with their authors. Because of the attention paid to each project and the commitment made on the part of the publisher in terms of marketing and promotion, an author's royalties can more than make up for the small advance.

Once larger publishing houses announce their titles for the upcoming selling season, new titles are rarely added. Not so with most small houses, which have the ability to add titles to their list at the last minute. If a small press wants to take on a new project for publication in, say, two months, it has the freedom to do so even if its distributors have not been notified. This flexibility can be a big plus for authors—especially when a book's quick release date will have an impact in the marketplace.

Very few small firms have their own sales forces. Few offer direct-mail promotions. Most do not have in-house telemarketing departments. And only a handful provide viable publicity. So how

Small publishers can offer a variety of benefits to the author, from ready access to staff members, to the generous investment of editorial time, to the ability to add new titles to their lists at the last minute.

**From *The Wonderful Life
and Adventures
of Robinson Crusoe*
by Daniel Defoe**

Artist Unknown

do they sell their books? Some small firms have in-house sales directors, but most rely on outside systems of distribution and sales representatives for their titles. As discussed earlier, an outside sales force can be a group of independent salespeople who visit accounts on behalf of a company. It could also be an independent book distributor that sells books through its own catalogue and sales representatives. Some small houses utilize the sales force of a larger publisher that carries additional titles. And some rely solely on their own catalogues for sales. As an author, it is important to learn how effective the sales operation is of any small company.

Some small companies sell their titles to very specialized niches, examples of which include ethnic audiences, religious audiences, or even crafts audiences. These markets are relatively easy to reach. Others sell to hidden marketplaces—for example, a charity group or other nonprofit organization that buys outside traditional channels. Some firms sell their books through strategically placed ads in newspapers and magazines that target specific audiences. Others work directly with authors to promote sales through events and lectures. These days, virtually every company, no matter how small, also has a website through which it can sell and promote books. The little guys may have to be more creative in their approach, but when they get it right, they usually develop a long-lasting stronghold in their area of concentration.

In order to stay in business, most small companies develop their own personal systems of sales. Some systems work very well, others work marginally well, and some don't work well at all. The financial level of success for a small house, therefore, is determined by just how cash rich or cash poor it is. Traditionally, small houses have limited funding, which tends to be reflected in overall sales. Unlike larger houses, they do not produce books on a formula basis. As discussed earlier, each book must sell to some degree in order for the company to stay in business. However, a book that has not performed as well as expected is not quickly put out of print, as is the standard procedure in larger houses. In spite of slow sales, the book will be kept in print for many years.

In most cases, small houses are direct reflections of the individuals who run them. If these people know what they are doing, they can create excellent and exciting vehicles for books. On the other hand, those who do not understand how to operate publishing companies correctly can be a source of nightmarish embarrassment for their authors.

School and Library Book Publishers

School and library publishers produce and market their books specifically for schools and libraries. For the most part, these books are hardcover, usually with special library bindings to make them sturdier than the hardcover book you might buy in a bookstore. Largely, these books fall into the nonfiction category. When an educational or library publisher does product fiction, it tends to be in the hi-lo category.

It's important to understand that although these books are used by students, teachers, and librarians, these are not textbooks, but are used in classrooms as supplemental readings. For instance, if a teacher is presenting a lesson for Women's History Month, he may assign a series of biographies of famous women. Usually, the students can obtain these books from their school or public library, or from the teacher's own in-class collection. On rare occasions, the books may even be sold in retail stores, as Chelsea House books were for a short time some years ago. In most cases, though, students who are unable to get these books from their school or library can buy them from an online store, such as Amazon.com.

Acquiring Manuscripts

Depending on the size of the company, school and library book publishers are usually set up much like moderate-sized or small trade houses. Many have a small staff, with a publishing director who oversees the editors, each of whom handles his own series of books. The number of books produced may change each year based on the success of last year's list. As in most trade book companies, each editor who acquires books is also responsible for all aspects of the book's production, including editing. In many cases, these publishers have special staff to handle publicity and advertising, while in other cases, they use outside people for this purpose. But almost all of them have their own sales director.

The acquisitions process in school and library publishing houses is very different from that in trade houses, as the majority of book ideas come from the editors themselves, with very few ideas coming

In school and library publishing, company editors come up with most of the ideas for the books, and then search for authors to write them. However, a certain percentage of books do come from outside sources.

from author queries or unsolicited manuscripts. These publishers study their market very carefully. They get feedback from their sales representatives about the topics in which children's librarians are interested, and they stay abreast of state and national school curricula and study state education guidelines. Because the United States does not yet have national education standards, requirements are different in every state, although certain general topics such as geography, history, and science are taught everywhere. The editor's goal is to fill any existing gaps. Moreover, whenever they can, editors try to create a series: women in sports, weird weather, career books, or scientific discoveries, for instance.

Once an editor decides the type of book he wants to produce—a middle grade book on hurricanes, for instance—he seeks out an author to write it. Sometimes he picks an author who has worked for the publishing house previously, and sometimes he relies on referrals or queries. In other words, an author who wants to write for this market doesn't need to send a proposal. A solid resumé and writing sample usually suffice.

Does this mean that no school or library books have their origin in unsolicited submissions? No. A certain percentage of the books do come from outside sources. But if you have an idea for a series, most houses would consider an outline or synopsis, rather than a full proposal.

Things to Consider When Working With School and Library Book Publishers

An advantage to working with school and library publishers is that their books are often reviewed in prominent journals like *Publishers Weekly, Library Journal, Booklist,* and *Kirkus Reviews.* When these reviews are favorable, they will not only boost your status in the school and library market, but also serve as a calling card should you choose to explore other markets, such as trade publishing.

If you are an unpublished author, school and library houses offer a relatively easy way to get published. As long as you can reliably provide accurate nonfiction manuscripts for the requested reading level, you have a good chance of developing a long-term working relationship with a publisher. This will enable you to quickly build up a list of published books, all of which will bear your name. Just be aware that because their market is a very narrow one, publishers may not want the same author to write too many books in a given year, the feeling being that librarians might question the accuracy of a prolific author's work.

A great advantage to working with a school and library publisher is that their books get reviewed in prestigious journals like *Publishers*

Weekly, *Library Journal*, *School Library Journal*, *Choice*, *Booklist*, and *Kirkus Reviews*. When favorable, these reviews will make a great calling card if you choose to expand your submissions to other markets.

Yet another plus to producing school and library books is that teachers and librarians often invite authors to speak at special events—usually, with compensation. Children don't care whether you've written a best-selling fiction book or a library book. They simply love to meet anyone who's written a book about a topic they enjoy.

There is, however, a downside to school and library publishers. First, it's important to understand that authors of school and library books almost always work-for-hire. This means that rather than receiving royalties, most authors are paid a flat fee, and all the money the book earns belongs to the publisher—regardless of how well it sells. Some publishers are now moving to replace flat fees with royalty payments, but you'll find that the rates and advances are lower than those offered by even the smaller trade houses. Because of the low pay, agents generally have no interest in representing the writers of these books.

Another drawback is that once an author hands in his manuscript to the editor, with the exception of providing the editor with fact-checking information, the book is no longer the author's. The copyright is in the publisher's name, so the author can't use any part of the book without the company's permission. However, in most cases, the author's name does appear on the cover of the book. If the contract doesn't indicate this, it could be an important point of negotiation. (You'll read more on negotiations in Chapter 7, "The Deal.")

Despite any drawbacks, this market is a great means of getting your nonfiction books into print, along with your name. It can be an end in and of itself, or—if your goal is to write for a trade publisher—it can be a way to get your career as a children's book author off the ground.

> Although school and library publishing can be a great means of launching a writing career, be aware that most of these companies offer work-for-hire arrangements, meaning that authors are paid a flat fee rather than royalties.

Educational Publishers

Educational publishers produce both standard textbooks, which are used to meet curriculum requirements in subjects ranging from math to language arts; and ancillary materials, which include teachers' editions of textbooks, workbooks, study guides, test prep materials,

Supplementary educational publishing is a $2.5 billion business in the United States. These ancillary materials—which range from simple math flashcards to grade-specific guided instructional reading lesson kits and audio-visual tools—are produced by both imprints of big textbook companies and smaller companies that specialize in this area.

guided instructional lesson kits, flashcards, abridged versions of literature, music tapes and CDs, software, posters, maps, games, CD-ROMS, and many other materials that supplement textbooks and help students learn core information. While many of these materials are produced for mainstream courses in elementary, middle, and high schools, some are geared for home schoolers, special needs children, and students of specific religious backgrounds.

Most textbooks are produced by large textbook publishers, such as Macmillan/McGraw-Hill and Houghton Mifflin. Some ancillary materials are also produced by these textbook publishers, while others are produced by smaller publishing houses that specialize in this area.

Acquiring Manuscripts

Educational publishing houses are usually set up much like large houses, meaning they have highly defined organizational structures in which departmental roles as well as individual accountabilities are clearly established. Some educational publishers, however, are moderate or small in size, and are therefore structured like the smaller trade houses. In the case of the smaller houses, the editor who acquires books is also usually responsible for all aspects of the book's production. In many cases, these publishers have special staff to handle publicity and advertising, while in other cases, they use outside people for this purpose. Almost all educational publishers, however, have their own sales directors.

Regardless of the size of the company, the acquisitions process in educational publishing houses is different from that in trade houses. Although most of these companies do accept proposals from authors, and have specific guidelines for doing so, the majority of these publishers are much like school and library publishers in that they come up with their own ideas for textbooks and other materials, and then seek out authors to produce them. As you might expect, these publishers study their market very carefully, stay abreast of state and national school curricula and guidelines, and get feedback from their sales representatives about the topics in which federal and state education departments are interested. Their goal is to help satisfy any needs that exist. For instance, in the late 1990s, when national test scores indicated that American fourth graders were below standards in mathematics, textbook and supplemental material publishers took notice and produced materials that would better prepare students for standardized tests.

Most of the authors that educational publishers use are found through company-directed searches. In the case of textbooks in particular, a company may have regional editorial directors whose job is to visit local schools and find prospective authors for a specific topic. For example, an editorial director from a New York office may be told by the head office that the company wants to publish a new high school chemistry textbook, perhaps one that is written specifically for New York State curriculum requirements. The editorial director then needs to find the teacher who is considered to be the best in his area—perhaps someone who was named teacher of the year or whose students consistently win state or national science awards. The editor then interviews the teacher, asks for a proposal, and, if all goes well, offers a work-for-hire or royalties contract. Authors of supplemental materials are often located in the same way, although in some small houses, the editors create some of these materials themselves.

As in school and library book publishing, many authors come to the editor's attention through a resumé and writing samples. The editor will often then send the writer a project on speculation to see how he handles it. If the writer does a good job, he may then become part of a group that the editor calls on repeatedly.

Again, as in school and library book publishing, writers can approach the publisher with ideas for textbooks or other educational materials, but the writer must be an educator, must know the company's specific writer's guidelines, and must be familiar with both the subject matter and the grade level.

Usually, before an educational company publishes a textbook or supplemental material, the work is reviewed for accuracy not only by the editorial staff, but also by outside educators and administrators.

Things to Consider When Working With Educational Publishers

If you have the appropriate educational background and can prove yourself a strong writer, you may be able to establish a long and lucrative relationship with an educational publisher. Keep in mind that textbooks need to be frequently updated, and that the publisher is likely to call on the author of the book to produce the revised editions. Moreover, publishers tend to ask the author of the textbook to produce supplemental materials, such as workbooks and teachers' editions. Finally, educational publishers like to create sets of books rather than stand-alone titles, and often prefer to hire one person to write the entire set of books for, say, the third grade reading program. Thus, an affiliation with an educational publisher often leads to a steady stream of work.

One of the downsides to educational publishing is, of course, that it rules out many writers simply because they don't have the required educational background. Additionally, educational work often creates feast or famine situations in which a writer may have no work for a long period of time, and then be so inundated with assignments that he is forced to refuse some of the much-needed work.

The method of payment is also sometimes a negative. Although some publishers offer royalties, many writers are offered work-for-hire contracts in which they are paid only a flat fee for their work. On the other hand, a number of educational publishers pay by the page, with some paying as much as $50 dollars a page!

NONCOMMERCIAL PUBLISHING HOUSES

So far, this chapter has discussed only commercial publishers. These publishers are primarily focused on the bottom line—in other words, on making a profit. But not all children's books are produced by commercial companies. Some—albeit, a relatively small number—are produced by houses for whom the "message," and not the bottom-line profit, is the primary focus. These noncommercial houses include university presses and foundation presses.

University presses are affiliated with institutions of higher learning, and for many years, their primary market was the academic audience. Recently, however, some university presses have become interested in projects of wider appeal, and have expanded their lists to include a variety of children's books, including poetry collections and fiction, as well as dictionaries and other reference works.

Foundation presses, also known as association presses, are usually extensions of established foundations that champion specific causes. Often, these foundations produce books that fill specific needs. The Juvenile Diabetes Association, for instance, carries numerous books for children who have diabetes, and for the parents of these children. Some of these books are provided free of charge, while others are sold to help fund the work of the foundation.

Like educational publishers, most university presses develop ideas for books and then seek out their authors, who are usually scholars in a particular field. This does not mean that you have to be a scholar to write for a university press, but it does mean that you have to show a solid educational background that indicates your suitability to write for a press of this type. Foundation presses, on the other hand, often have limited resources. Thus, very few publish original works, preferring to purchase them from other publishers.

If your goal is to make money, chances are that noncommercial publishers are not for you. But if you have the educational background required by a university house, or if your goal is to help a specific cause, you should inquire about the acquisitions process of the publishing house of interest. This work could be an end in itself, or could be a means of establishing yourself as a legitimate author with the ultimate goal of landing a contract with a commercial publisher.

Although university and foundation presses may not be right for the author whose primary goal is to make money, if you have the necessary background, they can be a means of establishing a career in children's writing.

OTHER PUBLISHERS

This chapter has presented traditional commercial and noncommercial publishing houses. You may also be aware of other types of publishers, such as book packagers, vanity presses, and electronic publishers. Book packagers, who prepare print-ready manuscripts, are popular with publishers who want to market a number of books in a series in one season. Vanity presses have been around for years, but they're quite unlike the publishers discussed in this chapter, as they require substantial monetary investments from authors before publishing their books. As for the burgeoning world of e-publishers, they're all different. Some require payment from authors to place their books on a website; others charge to advertise the books online. These companies are all discussed in detail in Chapter 8.

CONCLUSION

This chapter has covered the wide world of children's book publishing. The majority of publishers follow the organizational structures and acquisition models presented here. Armed with this basic information, you can now move on to the next chapter, which will show you how to begin choosing those publishers that are suited to your project.

CHAPTER 4

CHOOSING THE
RIGHT PUBLISHER

Almost 3,500 publishers are listed in *Literary Market Place*, the bible of the publishing industry. Of these companies, nearly 800 are either children's divisions of a larger publishing house or independent publishers that produce children's books. Should you send your book proposal to all 800 of these companies? Of course not! Aside from being prohibitively expensive and almost impossible to keep track of, a mass mailing of this sort would not increase your chances of getting your book into print. As you've learned from earlier chapters, all publishers are different, with different lines of books and different ways of acquiring manuscripts. Some may not have any interest in a book of your type. They may, for instance, produce books for infants and toddlers, while your book is for young adults. Just as important, some may not be able to help you meet your personal goals. The trick is to zero in on those specific publishers that are right for you and your project—those that publish titles in your category and fit other requirements that are important to you.

This chapter will lay the foundation for selecting the most appropriate publishers for your work. The foundation will be laid in two steps. First, you will have to honestly assess your personal goals in getting your book into print, as well as your expectations regarding publishers. Once you've pinpointed both your motivation and your needs, you'll be able to move on to step two: creating that initial list of publishing houses. At that point, you'll find that an array of books, websites, and other resources are available to help you learn about the many companies that produce juvenile literature.

RULE # 6

Know why you want to be published

STEP ONE—KNOW WHAT YOU WANT

Be honest. What's really driving you to get your work published? Do you want fame and fortune? Do you long to make a contribution to the world? Do you just want to see your name in print? All of these goals are valid, but more important, they are keys to choosing the best publishers for your work—firms that are most likely to meet your expectations.

What Are Your Personal Goals?

Every writer in search of getting her work published is driven by different motivations. Status, income, and making a contribution are probably the most common, along with simply wanting to see your book in print. Of course, you may very well have more than one motivation. If that's the case, you'll have to consider which of them is more of a priority for you. Take a closer look at these aspirations to see which best matches your own.

I Want a Big-Name Company to Publish My Book

If you have your eye on a big-name publishing company, be aware that most high-profile firms are not receptive to first-time authors. While smaller publishers may seem less "glamorous," they offer the best opportunity to new writers.

For some writers, image is everything. Having their work published by a big-name company is their one and only goal. If a high-profile company is what you want, it certainly won't take you long to make up a list of potential publishers. Just keep in mind that these houses aren't usually receptive to first-time authors. There are exceptions, of course. But these days, even writers who have been previously published often have a difficult time getting their work produced by big-name firms. If you use the Square One System described in this book, you'll certainly improve your odds of winning a contract with a well-known publisher. However, as you learned in Chapter 3, this won't necessarily guarantee success, fame, and fortune.

It's important to recognize that in the long run, readers won't pay much attention to the name of the publisher on the title page and spine of your book. What will matter most to them is the substance between the covers. Remember, too, that there are thousands of publishers out there. Some are famous, and others are not. But just because a publishing house doesn't have a familiar-sounding name doesn't mean that it won't do justice to your work.

It's not my intention to discourage you from pursuing the prestige that may be associated with well-known companies. I merely want to point out that there are publishers of all sizes that can also offer a solid publishing program—particularly for first-time authors.

I Want to Make Money

At one time or another, every writer dreams of spending her days writing while royalties from her previously published books roll in. It certainly can happen. But at almost every writer's workshop I've ever attended, the guest author has startled the audience by saying, "If you want to write children's books, you'd better not give up your day job."

If you plan on writing a book to get rich, consider that most of the authors who get huge advances are writers of mainstream adult fiction. Even in that category, it's only the few, like John Grisham and Stephen King, who can demand six-figure-plus advances, largely because they've been able to consistently produce bestsellers for their publishers. Having said this, though, I recently read about a first-time young adult author in England who received a six-figure advance. So it can happen. Just don't count on it. As for royalties, since the average book published in the United States sells approximately 5,000 copies, the average author rarely sees any money beyond her advance.

Does that mean that the potential for making money in children's books is nonexistent? Not at all. First, remember that most of the current popular children's book authors started out writing in their spare time while they kept their jobs as teachers, social workers, and the like. As time went on, though, they were able to rely on royalties alone. Second, realize that if you know your market, write quality books, and sign on with a publisher who has a solid marketing program, you will increase the odds of generating good sales. As mentioned in the last chapter, a book backed by a large publishing house must sell well initially, producing reasonable profits, or it will most

The average book published in the United States sells about 5,000 copies, and the average author rarely sees more money than what is offered in the advance.

likely be put out of print quickly. On the other hand, smaller publishers with strong backlists continue to sell their titles for many years. That means you may be collecting royalty checks for a long time to come.

Finally, remember that the savvy writer is her own best publicist, and creates additional opportunities to generate income beyond royalties. Naturally, if you've produced a lovable character that lends itself well to merchandising and other media outlets—and you don't mind exploiting that character—endless income-producing opportunities could potentially come your way. Marc Brown's *Arthur* character generated a truly impressive line of products, including stuffed animals, computer games, coloring books, calendars, lunch boxes, the PBS TV show, music CDs, and so on.

But even if your characters don't seem suitable for marketing, or you're simply not interested in that type of venture, there are other ways to increase your income. If you're comfortable speaking to an audience, you can earn money as a guest speaker in schools. All across America, schools host author weeks during which they invite published authors to speak to the children. In most cases, copies of the book are ordered for the children, and the author signs the books after speaking about her life as a writer. If your book happens to touch on a topic represented by an organization—if one of your characters has cancer, for instance—you can even arrange to be a guest lecturer at an event that's related to that issue.

Your book can spawn hundreds of moneymaking opportunities, in some cases, with little effort on your part. The key is to be aware of them. A great little book that can help you boost your sales is *An Author's Guide to Children's Book Promotion* by Susan Salzman Raab. Other good resources can be found in the Resource List on page 249.

> The savvy writer is her own best publicist. If you are comfortable speaking in front of an audience, consider making author visits at local schools. In most cases, copies of your book will be ordered for the children, and you will be asked to sign the copies after speaking about your life as a writer.

I Want to Make a Contribution

Because I participate in many author visits, and see firsthand how a book can light up a child's face, this, perhaps, is the motivation that matters most to me. It's so rewarding when children ask questions which indicate that a book has captured their imagination and started them thinking about a new topic. In fact, I can safely say that of all the audiences for which you could choose to write, children are probably the most inspiring and responsive. Just take a moment to think

back to the books you enjoyed as a child, and remember the characters who came to life for you. As a writer, you have the chance to
touch other children's lives, just as a writer touched yours so many
years ago.

A book is also a great means of delivering information that can
help children understand the world around them. Today, many of the
works of juvenile fiction found on bookstore and library shelves deal
with some fairly tough topics, from adoption to sexuality. Through a
world of likeable characters, most of these books offer children a safe
way to explore issues that may be affecting them. The words you
write can easily become the first means by which a child is able to
comprehend her own feelings. In other words, you can truly make a
difference in a child's life. That's fairly heady stuff.

During your research, you might want to start with those companies that have already successfully published books on similar
topics. Depending on your subject, you may even choose to contact
appropriate organizations and associations that might be interested
in publishing your work.

I think there's a little of the messenger in all of us. And in the
hands of the right house, your message will get out.

I Just Want to Be Published

Some writers care about nothing more than seeing their work in
print—and this is certainly a valid and fairly common reason for
wanting to get published. However, if this is your attitude, think
about all of the time and effort you have put into writing your book.
Shouldn't you consider going to a publisher that can do more than
simply put your words into book form?

As discussed in Chapter 3, there are many different kinds of publishers out there. If you put forth some basic effort in researching the
most appropriate houses for your work, you will increase your
chances of seeing your book in print, as well as giving it an opportunity to sell in the appropriate marketplace.

What Do You Expect From a Publisher?

Not too long ago, I spoke to a published author of young adult fantasy novels. She told me that once her latest manuscript had become

If your primary goal in being published is to deliver specific information or a particular message, seek out those publishers that have already successfully produced books on similar topics. Depending on your subject, you may also want to contact appropriate organizations.

a bound book, the publisher failed to give it any attention beyond a mention in the catalogue. When the novel didn't sell well, it literally disappeared. In fact, the publishing house had it destroyed along with other unsold books. Now the author is buying up used copies of her own book online just so she can have a few editions of her own!

To avoid an unpleasant surprise such as this, you'll want to think about the following criteria when analyzing publishers. A clear and honest assessment will help you put your expectations into proper perspective.

The Publisher's Specialty

Lee & Low Books—a small publishing company—focuses solely on multicultural literature. But through its various imprints, Dutton Children's Books—a far larger company—handles both fiction and nonfiction on a range of subjects for all age levels.

No matter how big or how small, every publisher specializes in certain markets. Small and medium-sized companies usually have only one or a few areas of specialization, while large companies often publish in many areas through their various imprints.

It's vital to make sure that the publishers you place on your list print titles in your subject area. (I will show you how to do this later in the chapter.) This may seem like an obvious consideration, but the fact is that many first-time writers don't realize this, and waste time and money sending proposals to publishers who would never produce a book such as theirs.

The Age of the Company

Is it important for you to work with a firm that has been around for a number of years, or would you consider working with a younger company? Certainly, older companies have a proven track record, enabling you to check on their successes and failures. But newer companies may be hungrier for sales and more willing to take a chance on someone new. Therefore, the age of the company may be worthy of your consideration.

The Size of the Company

It is important to check out the size of any publishing house you may be considering. A quick and easy way to do this, without going into a company's finances, is to find out how many titles the firm turns out each year. The fewer books produced, the smaller the company;

the more titles, the larger the company. Will you be satisfied working with a small publisher, or is the status of a large well-known company what you really want? The answer is different for every author. Just keep in mind that, as you learned in Chapter 3, there are advantages and disadvantages to each size house.

The Quality of the Company's Work

Some publishers invest only a minimal amount of money in production costs—a fact that is more than clear when you see the cheap paper, unimaginative typefaces, and uninspiring artwork characteristic of their books. Others invest quite a bit of money and time in their books, producing beautiful hardbacks with quality paper and a variety of typefaces, as well as original high-quality interior art.

If you have strong feelings about this aspect of the process, take time to examine the existing products of any prospective publisher. The quickest way to do this is to visit a bookstore or a library, where you can feel the paper stock and glance through the pages. As a general rule, the thinner the paper, the cheaper it is. If you can see the type and art on the back of any given page by looking through the front of the page, the paper is inexpensive. If the typeface is one you've seen every day, the art director wasn't being particularly creative. As for artwork, despite the fact that we writers don't like to hear it, the phrase "a picture's worth a thousand words" couldn't be more true when it comes to children's books. Most publishers know this, but some rely on simple ink drawings that make even my adult eyes glaze over. If you don't have time to perform a hands-on inspection of a publisher's books, be sure to request the company's catalogue or visit its website, as this will give you a good idea of the quality of the work it produces.

While a catalogue can tell you a lot about a company, you'll have to make a hands-on inspection of the publisher's books if you want to determine their quality. Visit your local bookstore or library, and examine the books' binding, paper, printing, and artwork. It shouldn't take long to determine if that company's work meets your standards.

The Company's Marketing and Sales

Getting your book out there—whether "there" is a bookstore, library, classroom, or website—is an important consideration when looking at publishing houses. That's why when you research each potential publisher, it's so important to get answers to certain questions. What kind of marketing and sales program does the company have? Does it have an in-house sales force to market its books, or does it employ the services of outside salespeople? In addition to promoting its books through catalogues, how else does the company sell its titles? Does it have a distributor? What marketplaces does it reach? Are the publisher's books available through Internet bookstores and other online sites? How much money and effort does the firm spend on advertising? How many bestsellers does it have within a marketplace?

To get answers to these important questions, you might begin by questioning the manager of your local bookstore. Your own powers of observation—a search of library and bookstore shelves, for instance—may offer some answers as well. You might also want to look through back copies of *Publishers Weekly*, which regularly runs articles about the book campaigns of various publishers. And if all else fails, don't hesitate to call the marketing and sales department of the publisher to get some basic information about the company's operation.

The Company's Publicity Department

From *Through the Looking Glass* by Lewis Carroll

Illustration by John Tenniel

Closely related to marketing is publicity, which is the dissemination of information about books, authors, and the publishing company itself via magazines, newspapers, radio, and television outlets, as well as other media. Each publisher has its own methods of promoting its titles. During your research, it's important to ask questions concerning this facet of each company's operation. Does the company have a designated publicity department, or does it hire freelance publicists to work on a project-by-project basis? Is it run by one person or by a group? Does it have well-established connections with the media? Does it promote its books through media tours, book signings, or guest spots on radio or television programs? Are books reviewed in appropriate publications? How heavily does the company rely on its authors to generate their own publicity?

Again, you can start your search for information at your local bookstore, where the manager should be able to tell you which publishers routinely arrange book signings. Also read your local paper and check trade publications such as *Publishers Weekly* and *School Library Journal* to see if the company's books are regularly reviewed. And, of course, you should feel free to call the publicity department of the publisher for answers to any remaining questions. In all cases, writers today have to be willing to publicize their own books. But if the company puts a good deal of effort into publicity, it will certainly lighten your load and enable your book to get sufficient media exposure.

The Company's Offer

What type of advance or royalty payment do you expect to receive for your book? Not all publishing companies, particularly smaller ones, offer their authors advances. Since the money offered in an advance will be deducted from future royalties, this may not be an important issue for you as you search for a publisher. On the other hand, if you need the immediate income an advance provides, you should consider only those publishers that make such offerings. For more detailed information about the different types of offers that publishing companies make, see Chapter 7, "The Deal."

The Location of the Company

Does the geographical location of a publisher matter to you? If your book has specific relevance to your region, perhaps a local publisher could best handle all aspects of publishing and promotion. In that case, I suggest that you first check out the publishers within the area related to your work. If, however, you simply want to work with a publisher in your city and state, consider that in this age of e-mail, faxes, and overnight delivery, every publisher—even a company on the other side of the continent—is as close as your keyboard. That's why in most cases, location should not be a factor in the selection of a publisher.

Don't be put off by the fact that a publisher is located on the other side of the country. These days, e-mail, faxes, and overnight delivery make it easy to work with any publisher anywhere.

These criteria should be helpful as you search for potential publishers for your work. Add your personal requirements, and you will find yourself on the right path. Please don't skip this important step. Once you know what you want from a publisher, both personally and professionally, you will be ready for the next step—creating that initial list.

STEP TWO—CREATE THE LIST OF PUBLISHERS

You've already figured out why you want to be published and what

The Importance of Writer's Guidelines

If editors could give writers just one piece of advice, it would be this: Find out what the publisher wants before submitting your proposal so that you don't waste everybody's time by sending the wrong materials to the wrong company. Fortunately, most publishers make this a fairly simple task. In their writer's guidelines, publishers tell you exactly what genres and categories they will and won't accept, as well as how they want to be contacted and what they want to receive. And these companies mean what they say. In fact, some writer's guidelines bluntly state that the publisher will return any proposal—unread—if it does not conform with the company's guidelines.

Writer's guidelines are not difficult to understand. They are generally clear and to the point, and although the occasional publisher offers several pages of do's and don'ts, the average company offers only a page or two of instructions. The guidelines provided by a nonfiction book publisher, for instance, might look something like this:

Author Specifications and Guidelines

Our company is looking for nonfiction picture books for children ages 2 to 6 that feature a new approach to sports, adventure, science, biography, and history. Please note that books about other topics for other age groups will be returned.

XYZ Publishers will consider unsolicited manuscripts. However, manuscript submissions should be no longer than 1,500 words. They should be typed doubled-spaced and accompanied by a cover letter that includes a brief biography of the author, including your publishing history and qualifications for writing about the topic. The letter should also state if the manuscript is a simultaneous or an exclusive submission. All submissions must include a self-addressed envelope with adequate return postage or they will be discarded. Please send complete manuscripts rather than queries.

Reporting time is within three months. Questions regarding the status of a submission after that time should be made in writing to the address below. Please do not call. We regret that due to the

you expect from a publisher, so now the time has come to roll up your sleeves, grab a notebook and pencil, and lay some important groundwork. First, you are going to create a rough list of possible publishers to produce and market your work. Next, you will be narrowing that list to include only those publishers that meet your personal criteria and are most likely to respond positively to your proposal. This step requires a good amount of effort, but your work will be rewarded in the long run.

You will start by compiling an initial rough list, which, depending on your category, subject, and genre, can range anywhere from a few dozen to a few hundred names. This first list should include the names of publishers only—nothing else. Once this list has been cre-

large quantity of submissions, we can't guarantee a personal response.

Please send submissions to: XYZ Publishers, 222 Main Street, USA, Attention: Nonfiction Submission. We don't accept e-mail submissions.

Is that straightforward enough for you? This information is relatively easy to come by, too. The standard practice, used for years, is for you to obtain the company's name and mailing address from the resources listed elsewhere in this chapter. You then send the infamous SASE (self-addressed, stamped envelope) along with a note requesting the publisher's writer's guidelines. Within a few weeks, you should receive the requested information.

With the creation of the Internet, alternative means of acquiring the guidelines have become available, of course. By performing an Internet search for the publisher of your choice, you should be able to find the company's website. Once there, click on the writer's guidelines—and save yourself an SASE, as well as several weeks' waiting time. Another option is to use the handy searchable database of more than 1,500 writer's guidelines found at www.writers-digest.com. To use this database, however, you have to pay a small yearly fee to subscribe to WritersMarket.com.

Finally, although publishers certainly don't encourage phone calls, you can always try giving the company a call to request the guidelines. Usually, the person who answers the phone will jot down your address or other contact information and either mail, fax, or e-mail the guidelines to you. Be aware, though, that some publishers will not respond to requests made over the phone.

Remember that it's up to you, the author, to obtain and follow each publisher's guidelines to the letter. If you think that someone's requirements are too restrictive or difficult to follow, just cross that publisher off your list. But when the time comes to mail out your proposals, you'll know that you have all the information necessary to send out the best submission packages possible to the most appropriate publishers for your work.

ated, you will take a closer look at the companies to see if they fit your personal criteria. Those that don't will be deleted from the list. Those that do will be placed on a new list along with some basic contact information, including street, e-mail, and website addresses; phone and fax numbers; contact name for submission proposals; and other pertinent information you come across during your search.

Finding Those Publishers

Where should you begin your quest for the best publishers for your work? Inexperienced authors may simply visit their local bookstore or library, jot down the names of the companies that produced the most bestsellers, and send their book proposals directly to them. Good idea? Let's just say that there are much more effective ways for prospective authors to find publishers. It has been my experience that when looking for children's book publishers that meet certain criteria, the most valuable references are *Children's Writer's & Illustrator's Market, Literary Market Place,* and *The International Directory of Little Magazines & Small Presses.*

Children's Writer's & Illustrator's Market

Children's Writer's & Illustrator's Market should be your first stop in the search for a publisher. As its name implies, this resource focuses on the children's book market. In fact, it lists several hundred publishers in the United States and other English-speaking countries.

I believe that the best place to start your research is the *Children's Writer's & Illustrator's Market.* This reference lists hundreds of publishers, including United States companies and—in a separate section—publishers in English-speaking countries, including Canada, Australia, and the United Kingdom. Also included are articles and interviews featuring children's book writers and illustrators, as well as information on literary agents, organizations, workshops, clubs, conferences, awards, and grants.

Children's Writer's & Illustrator's Market is updated annually. While it's available in the reference section of your library, the relatively small price tag of the softcover edition makes it a wise purchase for any children's book author—especially since you'll want to dog-ear the pages and highlight entries as you research various publishing houses.

This book contains a number of indexes, including a *Poetry Index* for poetry writers, and a *Photography Index* for freelancers who wish to submit photo submissions to publishers. But the indexes that make the book so useful for a writer of children's books are its *Age-Level Index, Subject Index,* and *General Index.*

The *Age-Level Index* is very helpful when you're trying to figure out which houses publish the category of books into which your work falls. The categories used in the *Children's Writer's & Illustrator's Market* include Picture Books, Young Readers, Middle Readers, and Young Adult/Teen.

The *Subject Index* provides an alphabetical listing of several dozen subject categories, which are divided into two general groupings: Fiction and Nonfiction. Under each subject heading is a listing of the publishing houses that produce books in that area. Two small samplings of subject categories are provided on the next page.

Fiction	Nonfiction
Adventure	Activity Books
Animal	Biography
Concept	Careers
Fantasy	Concept
Hi-Lo	How-To
History	Music/Dance
Problem Novels	Religious
Special Needs	Sports

Finally, the *General Index* lists all of the children's publishers included in the other indexes.

Each entry in *Children's Writer's & Illustrator's Market* first provides standard contact information—mailing addresses, phone and fax numbers, e-mail addresses, and websites, for instance. In addition, the entry includes the name of the editor who manages acquisitions, as well as the number of books published each year in each of the publisher's categories. In most cases, you'll learn the percentage of titles that comes from first-time authors, and the percentage that comes from agented writers. Following this, the entry lists the types of books published by that company, along with titles of books recently published in each category. The publisher generally includes its requirements for manuscript submission and, in some cases, its policies on advances and royalty percentages. Finally, many publishers offer a useful "Tips" section that clearly states the kind of book the publisher is looking for, as well as books that the company will *not* consider producing.

The *Children's Writer's & Illustrator's Market* makes research easier by providing the names of those editors who manage acquisitions. Other important bits of information offered include the percentage of titles written by first-time authors, the types of books published, and requirements for manuscript submission.

Using the Children's Writer's & Illustrator's Market to Create a Rough List

Now you know what the *Children's Writer's & Illustrator's Market* has to offer. But how do you use this reference to begin making your list? The best way to explain the process is by using an example. So here's a scenario—you have written a book for children ages one to three about a little girl who is afraid of the wind. In Chapter 2, you learned to identify this book's category along with the three classification levels. It's broken down in the following way:

Category

Toddler Book

Level One

Fiction

Level Two

Prose / Nature

Level Three

Three-year-old Lois is reassured by her mother that the wind isn't as mean as it sounds. Through photographic images, toddlers will learn, along with Lois, about all the things the wind helps us do.

With a free afternoon ahead, you open your copy of *Children's Writer's & Illustrator's Market*, and turn to the Fiction section of the *Subject Index*. Thumbing through the categories, you come across Nature/Environment, which is followed by a list of fifty-six publishers that produce works of fiction on this topic. Your first job is to write down the names of the publishers or—better yet—to photocopy the page.

Next, because your book is in the toddler category, you turn to the *Age-Level Index* and look under the Picture Books category. In Chapter 2, you learned that picture books are broken into four different age levels: baby, toddler, early picture books, and picture books for older readers. But this reference book groups them together, which is fine, as in most cases, publishers of picture books handle all relevant age groups. You can specify the particular age group for which you're writing when you compose your query letter.

For now, under the Picture Books category, you find well over a hundred children's book publishers listed. You know, however, that not all of these publishers produce fiction, and not all create books for your age group. Moreover, not all of the publishers that make up your rough list of fifty-six names produce picture books. Your next step, then, is to compare your list of fifty-six publishers of fiction books that have a nature theme with the publishers of picture books, and you find that only forty-four of the publishers on your rough list are also found on the list of picture books publishers. (The remaining twelve publishers produce novels for older kids.)

So now you are left with the names of forty-four publishers who produce fiction picture books with a nature theme. But at this point, that's all you have—names. You don't know anything about the companies themselves. Your next step is to get more information on the companies to see if they might be the right publishers to represent your work. For this, you turn to the A-to-Z directory of *Book Publishers*. Begin to move through your list systematically. One of the great things about the *Children's Writer's & Illustrator's Market* is that it clearly states the types of books that each publisher produces, as well as the number of books the company publishes each year (an indicator of the size of the house). In many cases, too, it provides tips from the publisher, as well as the publisher's mission statement. This can be a big help in determining if a company's publishing philosophy matches your own. As you read through the listings, you can remove the names of those firms that are not appropriate, and obtain contact information and other pertinent data for the companies that are.

Begin a new list for those companies you believe may be right for your book—the ones you might choose to receive your book proposals. This list should include as much of the following information as possible:

☐ The company's name.

☐ The company's address.

☐ The company's phone number, fax number, and e-mail address.

☐ The company's website.

☐ The materials that should be submitted.

☐ The individual who should be contacted.

☐ The company's payment policy.

☐ The company's response time.

Be sure to do your homework. Taking the time to research those publishers who seem best suited to represent your work will yield benefits as you pursue your dream.

The last two items on the above list aren't necessary for contacting a publisher, but you'll want to have this information handy. The first is important because we all want to have an idea of how much money we could earn. The last, because you'll want an idea of when you can expect to hear from the publisher after sending in your proposal.

Ideally this refined list should include twenty or more publishers. You'll be referring to this list later on when you begin sending out your submission packages, as explained in Chapters 5 and 6. For now, while it's important to get as much company information as possible, don't worry if the listing doesn't include an acquisitions editor, for instance. You can fill that information in later, as detailed in Chapter 6.

Let's get back to you and your rough list of forty-four publishers. When checking the companies out in the *Children's Writer's & Illustrator's Market*, you'll find that the information you need is usually fairly easy to locate and understand. In the next few pages, you'll find three sample entries—fictional versions of the types of listings you can expect to find for small, moderate-sized, and large publishers. Let's look at them one by one to see how you can use this reference book to assess each company's suitability.

By looking at the "Fiction" section of the For Kids Publishing entry (see page 107), you can see that this press produces picture books in the area of nature/environment, so it's a good match for your work. With an annual publication of twenty to thirty books, this is most likely a small house, which is another good sign, as small publishers are often willing to take a chance on new writers. Moreover, 80 percent of the company's books are by first-time authors! This doesn't guarantee that the company will take on your project— but it might. So unless your personal goals demand a big-name firm, For Kids Publishing is a "keeper" and belongs on your list.

As you research different publishers, be open-minded about smaller companies that may be new to you. Usually, these are the houses that are most willing to take a chance on new writers.

A simple glance at the Northwest Publishers entry (see page 108) and you can quickly eliminate the company from your rough list. Although this publisher does produce picture books that deal with nature, its focus is on regional themes, while the focus of your picture book is much more general. Moreover, the entry makes it clear that this publisher is interested only in authors from the Northwest—and you live in Boston. Sending this company a submission package would be a waste of time, effort, and money.

FOR KIDS PUBLISHING, 6280 Berkshire Drive, Suite D, Los Angeles, CA 95118. (408) 555-2010. Fax: (408) 555-2014. E-mail: forkids@tac.net. Website: www.forkids.com. Estab. 1998. Specializes in fiction, educational material, multicultural material, nonfiction. Book publisher. **Manuscript Acquisitions:** Jessica Surman, senior editor. **Art Acquisitions Editor:** Ellen Passeretti, art director. Publishes 20–30 picture books/year. 80% of books by first-time authors.

Fiction: Picture books, young readers: activity books, animal, biography, concept, history, multicultural, nature/environment, poetry, special needs, mystery. Average word length: picture books—450 words. Recently published *The Mystery of the Missing Tabby,* by Barbara Toland (young reader); *The Flight of the Daffodil,* by Eileen Connor (picture book).

Nonfiction: Picture books, young readers: activity books, animal, biography, concept, history, nature/environment, religion, special needs, textbooks. Average word length: picture books—450 words. Recently published *Birds, Beas, and Butterflies* by Muriel Freeney; *My First Origami Book* by Joanne McDougall.

How to Contact/Writers: Fiction: Submit complete ms. Nonfiction: Submit complete ms for picture books; outline synopsis and 2 sample chapters for young readers. Responds to mss in more than 2 months. Publishes a book 1–3 years after acceptance. Manuscript returned with SASE.

Illustration: Works with 20–30 illustrators/year. Uses both color and b&w artwork. Reviews ms/illustration packages from artists. Submit ms with dummy or ms with 2–3 pieces of final art. Contact: Jessica Surman, senior editor. Illustrations only: Arrange personal portfolio review or send résumé, portfolio and client list. Contact: Ellen Passeretti, art director.

Photography: Works on assignment only. Contact: Jessica Surman, senior editor. Model/property releases required. Uses 35mm transparencies. Submit portfolio, résumé, client list.

Terms: Pays author royalty of 5% based on retail price. Offers advances (Average amount: $2,000). Pays illustrators by the project (range: $2,500 minimum) or royalty of 2–5% based on wholesale price. Send galleys to authors; dummies to illustrators. Originals returned to artist at job's completion. All imprints included in a single catalogue. Writer's, artist's and photographer's guidelines available for SASE.

Tips: "Write from the heart. Submit only one manuscript per envelope. Only one per month please."

CHILDREN'S WRITER'S & ILLUSTRATOR'S MARKET **SAMPLE ENTRY SMALL PUBLISHING COMPANY**

Dynasty Press is a large company that publishes over 400 books a year. A quick glance at the sample entry on page 109 shows that Dynasty produces children's books of all types, so it might very well consider one like yours. However, you also note that only 3 percent

CHILDREN'S WRITER'S
& ILLUSTRATOR'S
MARKET
SAMPLE ENTRY
MODERATE-SIZED
PUBLISHING
COMPANY

NORTHWEST PUBLISHERS. 2040 W. 12th Ave., Eugene, OR 11732. (503) 555-2939. Fax: (503) 555-3723. E-mail: northwest@optagon.com. Website: www.northwestbooks.com. Book publisher. Estab. 1945. "We publish primarily regional fiction, and are particularly interested in works that are set in the Pacific Northwest." **Manuscript Acquisitions:** Elizabeth Thomas. Publishes 60 picture books/year; 75 young readers/year; 70 middle readers/year. 20% of books by first-time authors.

• Northwest only accepts work from writers who reside in the Northwest United States.

Fiction: Picture books, young readers, middle readers: animal, folktales, multicultural, nature/environment, poetry. Multicultural needs include themes reflecting cultural heritage of the Pacific Northwest, i.e., first nations, Asian, East Indian, etc. Does *not* want to see generic books with no sense of place. Recently published *Hawk in Trouble,* by Catherine Littlefoot; *Mountain Man,* by Tom Hemmings.

Nonfiction: Picture books: concept, reference. Young readers: reference, nature/environment, multicultural issues. Middle readers: reference, multicultural issues. Recently published *Trees of the Northwest,* by Michael Bell.

How to Contact/Writers: Fiction: Query. Nonfiction: Submit outline/synopsis and sample chapters. "Submission must be accompanied by SASE for response." E-mailed or faxed proposals are not accepted. Responds to queries in 1 month; mss in 6–8 months. Publishes a book 1 year after acceptance. Will consider simultaneous submissions.

Illustration: Works with 10 illustrators/year. Reviews ms/illustration packages from artists. Query first; 3 chapters of ms with 1 piece of final art, remainder roughs. Illustrations only: Submit tearsheets or slides plus résumé. Responds in 3–10 weeks.

Terms: Pays authors in royalties of 10–14% based on wholesale price or buys ms outright for $2,000 minimum. Pays illustrators by the project based on retail price. Sends galleys to authors; dummies to illustrators. Book catalog, ms/artist's guidelines for 9 x 12 SASE.

of the company's books are written by first-time authors. You realize that it's difficult to get a book proposal accepted by a large publishing house, but you've always admired Dynasty's publications. You therefore decide to keep Dynasty on your list, along with all of its contact information.

By the time you've completed your work with the *Children's Writer's & Illustrator's Market,* you may still have nearly forty-four publishers to contact, or you may have whittled your list down to half that number. Meanwhile, realize that as valuable a tool as this book is, it's important to check other resources as well. The *Literary*

> **DYNASTY PRESS.** Children's Trade Books, 335 Barkley Street, Boston MA 02116-3942. (617) 555-3927. Fax: (617)555-1014. E-mail: childrensbooks@ dp.com. Website: www.dynastypress.com. Book publisher. **Manuscript Acquisitions:** Caleb Claiborne, submissions coordinator. Kim Couric, managing editor; Phaedra Ridley, Neil Crosby, senior editors; Elaine Caufield, editor; Kate Joyce, books editor; Maureen Erin, editor. **Art Acquisitions:** Victoria Smallwood, creative director. Publishes more than 400 titles/year. 95% of books published through agents; 3% by first-time authors.
>
> **Fiction:** All levels: all categories except religion. Recently published *The Happy Bunny Moves to the Country*, by Joseph Corvin (ages 4–8), picture book.
>
> **Nonfiction:** All levels: all categories except religion. Recently published *Understanding Rocks*, by Hilda Hazor (ages 12 and up).
>
> **How to Contact/Writers:** Fiction: Submit complete ms. Nonfiction: Submit outline/synopsis and sample chapters. Always include SASE. Responds within 4 months.
>
> **Illustration:** Works with 70 illustrators/year. Reviews ms/illustration packages from artists. Manuscript/illustration package or illustrations only: Query with samples (colored photocopies are fine); provide tearsheets. Responds in 4 months. Samples returned with SASE; samples filed if interested.
>
> **Terms:** Pays standard royalty based on retail price. Offers advances. Illustrators paid by the project and royalty. Manuscript and artist's guidelines available for SASE.

CHILDREN'S WRITER'S & ILLUSTRATOR'S MARKET SAMPLE ENTRY LARGE PUBLISHING COMPANY

Market Place and *The International Directory of Little Magazines & Small Presses*, which are discussed below, are excellent choices.

Literary Market Place

While I suggest the *Literary Market Place*—or *LMP*, as it's commonly called—as your second stop for information on children's book publishers, this reference book is generally considered to be the bible of the publishing industry. A directory of United States and Canadian publishers of both children's and adult literature, the *LMP* lists about 3,500 publishers, both large and small. True, the scope and setup of the book makes it a somewhat unwieldy tool for our purposes. Moreover, a lot of the helpful information found in *Children's Writer's & Illustrator's Market*—the name of the person in charge of manuscript acquisition, for instance—is not included in the *LMP*. However, the *LMP* does list many children's book publishers not found in *Children's Market*. In addition, the *LMP* is a great means of exploring the

Considered the bible of the publishing industry, the *Literary Market Place* lists thousands of publishers. Because the *LMP*, as it's called, is designed for use within the industry, you may not find it as author-friendly as other books of its type. But don't skip this resource, as it's likely to inform you of companies not listed anywhere else.

business side of publishing companies. For instance, it will tell you whether the company in question has its own sales force, and it will show you whether the company sells foreign-language rights.

The *LMP* is available in the reference section of your library. The cost of buying a copy is quite high, as is the cost of using the online version available at www.literarymarketplace.com. Fortunately, your local library's copy should be perfectly adequate for your needs. Further, if you make friends with your reference librarian—as any professional writer should—she may be happy to give you last year's volumes when the current books become available in the library. At the very least, she may let you borrow them indefinitely.

Updated yearly, the *LMP* is published in two volumes, and it is Volume 1 that you—an author in search of a publisher—will find most helpful. Volume 1 is divided into subsections. For your needs, you will be focusing on the first section, which lists book publishers. This section begins with an A-to-Z directory of book publishers that are located in the United States. Each entry provides standard contact information—mailing addresses, phone and fax numbers, e-mail addresses, and websites—as well as the types of books published by the firm. In addition, most but not all listings include the names of key personnel and information such as the year in which the company was founded, the number of books it publishes annually, and its total number of titles in print.

Wherever applicable, an entry includes the publishing house's divisions, subsidiaries, and/or imprints, which are also cross-referenced and listed individually. Excluded from the *LMP* are "author-subsidized" publishers, also known as vanity presses, which characteristically charge authors significant fees to get their books into print. (For more information about vanity presses, see Chapter 8.)

After the *LMP's* A-to-Z directory come the *Geographic, Type-of-Publication*, and *Subject Indexes*, which include listings of publishers by name only. As you might have guessed, in the *Geographic Index*, companies are listed alphabetically by state, which is useful if you are interested in working with publishers in a specific region. In the *Type-of-Publication Index*, companies are listed according to the type of books they print. This is the easiest way to find names of children's book publishers, as you can look under headings such as Children's Books, Juvenile & Young Adult Books, Textbooks—Elementary, and Textbooks—Secondary.

Finally, the *Subject Index* provides an alphabetical listing of over 100 subject categories. Under each subject heading, there is a listing of the houses that produce books in this area. Although these listings include children's book publishers, note that they are not identified as such. Below is a small sampling of subject categories.

African-American Studies	Mysteries
Americana, Regional	Religion
Animals, Pets	Science Fiction, Fantasy
Art	Romance
Biography	Self-help
Crafts, Games, Hobbies	Sports
History	Western Fiction

Using the LMP

Because you already have a preliminary list of publishers from your work with the *Children's Writer's & Illustrator's Market*, you will be using the *LMP* to expand and refine this list.

As a first step, I suggest seeking out more information about those publishing houses already on your list—especially those companies about which you have some doubts. As already mentioned, the *LMP* is a great means of learning about various business-related aspects of a company. Does it sell its books in foreign markets? Does it have foreign offices? Does it use outside distributors? In most cases, the *LMP* will answer these questions, and will also tell you the year in which the company was founded, which is one way to judge whether this is a solid firm with well-established channels of distribution. Any new information provided by the *LMP* may help you decide which publishers might best serve you and your book.

Once you've filled in any information gaps about the companies already on your list, you'll want to locate those publishers that are listed in the *LMP* but are not listed in the *Children's Writer's & Illustrator's Market*. You'll find that a surprising number of companies are included in one source, but not the other.

Because the *LMP* does not focus specifically on children's books, you'll have to put more work into your search than you did when using *Children's Market*. Again, let's use the example of a work of fiction for children ages one to three about a little girl who's afraid of

Because the *LMP* provides a good deal of information about business-related aspects of publishing companies, you'll want to use this resource to learn more about the companies already on your list. And, of course, the *LMP* is sure to guide you to a few publishing houses not found in other reference works.

the wind. First, use the *Type-of-Publication Index* to find the listing of children's book publishers. There, you'll find the names of well over three hundred companies. Write the names down or, even better, make a photocopy of the relevant pages. Now, to weed out those publishers that don't produce fiction, turn to the *Subject Index*, and check your list of children's book publishers against the company names that appear under Fiction. This should enable you to cross out a good many names.

Once you've created a rough list of publishers' names, turn to the directory of *U.S. Book Publishers* and read through the information provided. Just as you did when you gathered information from the *Children's Writer's & Illustrator's Market*, you can remove the names of those firms that are not appropriate, and obtain contact information and other pertinent data for the companies that are.

As the *LMP* is primarily a directory for use within the publishing industry, rather than a resource designed for writers, it offers only basic statistical data and few details. However, by understanding how to analyze the entries, as shown in the fictitious sample entries that begin below, you will be able to determine company

LMP SAMPLE ENTRY
SMALL PUBLISHING COMPANY

COMPANY NAME.	**Phoenix Kids Press**
THIS IS IMPORTANT CONTACT INFORMATION TO INCLUDE IN YOUR LIST.	3214 Hudson Dr., Phoenix, AZ 85014 *Tel:* 602-555-9900 *Toll Free Tel:* 800-555-5990 *Fax:* 602-555-9909
THE ONLY EDITOR IN THIS ENTRY IS MEGGIE ABRAMS. ADD HER NAME TO YOUR LIST. LATER ON, YOU WILL BE VERIFYING THAT SHE IS THE PROPER CONTACT.	*Key Personnel* Pres: Allan McConnach Ed: Meggie Abrams
AGE OF COMPANY.	Founded: 1975
SUBJECTS PUBLISHED.	Children's illustrated picture books, nature & science, nonfiction, multicultural, concept & fiction, board books, supplemental educational materials K–8.
ASSIGNED INTERNATIONAL STANDARD BOOK NUMBER(S).	ISBN Prefix (es): 0-914846; 1-885590
ANNUAL NUMBER OF TITLES SHOWS THE SIZE OF THE COMPANY. FIFTEEN TITLES MEANS THAT THIS IS LIKELY A SMALL FIRM.	Number of titles published annually: 15 Print Total titles: 100 Print

LMP SAMPLE ENTRY
MODERATE-SIZED PUBLISHING COMPANY

COMPANY NAME.	**Snapdragon Publishing**
THIS SHOWS THAT THE COMPANY IS A DIVISION OF A LARGER COMPANY.	Division of Snapdragon Communications Inc
THIS IS IMPORTANT CONTACT INFORMATION TO INCLUDE IN YOUR LIST.	35 Frederick St, Fairfield, CT 06430 Mailing Address: 35 Frederick St, Fairfield, CT 06430 *Tel:* 203-555-3200 *Toll Free Tel:* 800-555-9868 *Fax:* 203-555-3220 *E-mail:* info@snapdragon.com *Web Site:* www.snapdragon.com
THESE ARE NAMES OF COMPANY EXECUTIVES FOR YOUR LIST. YOU WILL WANT THE NAME OF THE ACQUISITIONS EDITOR, BUT NONE IS GIVEN. SELECT THE NEXT LIKELY PERSON. IN THIS CASE, IT WOULD BE THE EDITORIAL ADMINISTRATOR— JESS CARA. LATER ON, YOU WILL BE VERIFYING THAT SHE IS THE PROPER CONTACT.	*Key Personnel* Pres: James F. Ciara Exec VP & Prodn Mgr: Deb Wilson Publisher and CEO: Gabriella Abrams Busn Mgr: Stephen Love Edit Administrator: Jess Cara Publicity: Elle D'Amico Intl & Subs Rts: Jason James
AGE OF COMPANY.	Founded: 1983
SUBJECTS PUBLISHED.	Radio communication hobby books; general nonfiction; children's books.
ASSIGNED INTERNATIONAL STANDARD BOOK NUMBER(S).	ISBN Prefix(es): 0-945257; 0-866224
ANNUAL NUMBER OF TITLES SHOWS THE SIZE OF THE COMPANY. FIFTY TITLES MEANS THAT THIS IS LIKELY A MODERATE-SIZED FIRM.	Number of titles published annually: 50 Print Total Titles: 400 Print
HAS ITS OWN SALES OPERATION AND OUTSIDE DISTRIBUTORS.	*Sales Office(s):* 35 Frederick St, Fairfield, CT 06430 *Distributed by:* The Chrysler Group
SELLS ENGLISH-LANGUAGE BOOKS IN FOREIGN MARKETS.	*Foreign Rep(s): Merrimac Int'l*
SELLS FOREIGN-LANGUAGE RIGHTS.	*Foreign Rights:* Fred Claus Agency
THIS INFORMATION IS NOT NECESSARY FOR YOUR INITIAL LIST.	*Advertising Agency:* Snapdragon Marketing Services, 35 Frederick St, Fairfield, CT 06430, ChaunceyMasters, Tel:203-555-3500 Fax: 203-555-3520 E-mail: mmasters@aol.com *Billing Address:* 35 Frederick St, Fairfield, CT 06430 *Shipping Address:* Merrimac Dist Ctr, 400 Avery Dr, Edison, NJ 08837 *Warehouse:* Merrimac Dist Ctr, 400 Avery Dr, Edison, NJ 08837 *Distribution Center:* Merrimac Dist Ctr, 400 Avery Dr, Edison, NJ 08837

LMP SAMPLE ENTRY
LARGE PUBLISHING COMPANY

COMPANY NAME.	**Douglas International Publishing Group**
THIS IS IMPORTANT CONTACT INFORMATION TO INCLUDE IN YOUR LIST.	2500 Third Ave, Suite 1500, New York, NY 10017 *Tel:* 212-555-2300 *Toll Free Tel:* 800-555-2704 *Fax:* 212-555-2333 *E-mail:* douglasint@tac.net *Web Site:* www.douglasint.com
PLACE BOTH THE VP/SENIOR EDITOR, DARLA STUART, AND THE MANAGING EDITOR, INGRID JUDD, ON YOUR LIST, ALONG WITH THEIR TITLES. YOU WILL BE VERIFYING THE PROPER CONTACT LATER ON.	*Key Personnel* Pres & Pub: Albert Will Douglas, Jr. Exec VP & Assoc Publisher: Tuesday Cirrus Exec VP & Gen Mgr Rts & Perms: Erica Rubin VP & Sr Ed: Darla Stuart Man Ed: Ingrid Judd Prod Coord: Roslyn Carl Dir Electronic Publishing: Michael Thomas Mktg Asst: Joshua Shan Wilson Premium Sales Dir: Elaine Shriver Art Dir: Gary Berg
AGE OF COMPANY.	Founded: 1980
SUBJECTS PUBLISHED.	Adult trade paperbacks & hardcovers, mass market, reprints & originals. Children's hardcover picture books, fiction & nonfiction, trade paperbacks, picture book paperbacks, novelty books, daily calendars.
ASSIGNED INTERNATIONAL STANDARD BOOK NUMBER(S).	ISBN Prefix (es): 0-4372; 0-7760
ANNUAL NUMBER OF TITLES SHOWS THE SIZE OF THE COMPANY. WITH 885 TITLES, THIS FIRM IS A LARGE ONE.	Number of titles published annually: 885 Print Total Titles: 21,000 Print
INDICATES THAT COMPANY DISTRIBUTES BOOKS FOR OTHER PUBLISHERS.	*Distributor for:* Christiana Press; Green Gables Ltd., Old World News Group; Rhodes Books; Cable Publishing
COMPANY SELLS BOOKS IN FOREIGN MARKETS.	*Foreign Rep (s):* Ashland Southampton (UK); Brightwaters Associates (Europe); Canadian Winston Group (Canada, UK); General Books (Europe, UK); Taylor & Taylor (Asia, South America, UK); Unity Press (Japan, Korea)
THIS INFORMATION IS NOT NECESSARY FOR YOUR INITIAL LIST	*Advertising Agency:* Williams Roth Advertising *Shipping Address:* Douglas International Publishing Group, 77 Kingston Rd, Providence, RI 02904

size, editorial interests, and a variety of other relevant facts. Because the *LMP* doesn't always provide detailed information on the types of books published by a company, in many cases, you will want to do further research on any firms that seem promising. If, for instance, you're not sure whether a certain company produces young children's concept books or middle readers, you'll be able to obtain more information by visiting the company's website, sending for its catalogue, or perusing the shelves of your local library or bookstore.

When using the *LMP*, it's very easy to be seduced by the large companies, whose listings are long and impressive. And, unfortunately, it's easy to miss the shorter listings characteristic of smaller companies. Always remember, though, that it is the small or medium-sized publisher who is most likely to be open to first-time authors and unsolicited manuscripts.

When using the LMP, the long, impressive listings of big-name publishing companies are certain to attract your attention. Be sure to give equal consideration to mid-sized and small publishers.

The International Directory of Little Magazines & Small Presses

A good means of locating small publishers, *The International Directory of Little Magazines & Small Presses* includes over 5,000 small presses and journals. The entries are quite brief, but each of them presents enough basic information about the publisher to let you know if the company is worth looking into. Subject and regional indexes are included to help you target appropriate presses.

Many of the publishers listed in this book are so small that they can be found in no other reference work. True, some of these presses produce only a couple of titles a year, and many are very niche-oriented. But if your book fits into that niche, you may have found a home for your work.

Using the International Directory of Little Magazines & Small Presses

In your search for small publishers that might be a good match for your toddler book, the first place you should turn to in this directory is the *Subject Index*. There, you find three categories that might be appropriate for your book: Children, Youth; Juvenile Fiction; and Environment. As you did when using the other reference books, you determine the publishers that are common to all three lists, and write

LITTLE FEET PRESS. Mike Mansel, Senior Editor, PO Box 2445, Los Angeles, CA 90056, 213-555-6776; fax: 213-555-6777. 1983. Fiction, art, photos, nonfiction. "For board and picture books: submit entire manuscript and photocopies of 3 sample illustrations. Fiction/nonfiction: submit 3 sample chapters, outline/synopsis." Avg press run 3–5M. Pub'd 4 titles 1999, expects 4 titles 2005, 5 titles 2006. 21 titles listed in the *Small Press Record of Books in Print* (28th ed, 2003–04). Avg. price, paper: $15. Discounts: for resale: 20–40% off; distributor discounts negotiable. 250pp; 6x9. Reporting time: due to increased volume, we cannot reply unless interested. Publishes less than 1% of manuscripts submitted. Payment: 9% of net. Copyrights for authors. Memberships: Publishers Marketing Association (PMA).

down their names only. You will probably end up with only a small handful of companies.

Next, flip to the A-to-Z publishers listing and read about those companies you have selected from the *Subject Index.* Although the information in the entries may vary, for the most part, each provides the following: the name of the acquisitions editor, company address, year the company was founded, subject areas published, average print run, number of titles published in the previous year and number expected this coming year, average copy price, discount schedules, average number of pages per book, average page size, printing method, reporting time on manuscripts, payment or royalty arrangements, rights purchases and/or copyright arrangements, number of titles listed in the current edition of the *Small Press Record of Books in Print,* and membership in publishing organizations. A sample entry is provided above.

When your research is complete, you will probably have only a couple of new companies to add to your final list of prospective publishers. Because the entries in *The International Directory of Little Magazines & Small Presses* are rather brief, and sometimes provide scant information on a company's interests, you may want to visit each company's website or request a catalogue before sending off your proposal.

Other Methods of Finding Publishers

While the *Children's Writers & Illustrators Market, LMP,* and *Little Magazines & Small Presses* are excellent resources for writers, they are not the only means of finding publishers that might be interested in your book. Depending on your goals, on the nature of your project, and on the time and money you are willing to commit to getting your book into print, a number of other resources should be considered.

International Resources

With the exception of the *Children's Writer's & Illustrator's Market*—which in 2004, began listing publishers in several English-speaking countries around the world—most of the resources discussed earlier in the chapter offer information only about firms located in the United States and Canada. If you're interested in further exploring publishing houses in other English-speaking countries, the *Writers' and Artists' Yearbook* is a good place to look. This resource includes listings of publishers in the United States, the United Kingdom, Ireland, Australia, and New Zealand.

If you're looking for a comprehensive listing of worldwide publishers in both English- and non-English-speaking countries, refer to *Publishers' International ISBN Directory*. This resource lists well over 600,000 publishers in over 200 countries, regions, and territories, along with up-to-date contact information.

The *Writers' and Artists' Yearbook* is affordably priced, so you may decide to add it to your home library. *Publishers' International ISBN Directory* is quite expensive, though, so you'll want to look for it in the reference section of a large public library.

If you're interested in exploring publishing houses in other countries, refer to the Writers' and Artists' Yearbook *to learn about publishers in other English-speaking countries, and to* Publishers' International ISBN Directory *to find publishers in both English- and non-English-speaking countries.*

Online Resources

The Internet provides a wide variety of means to learn about new publishers, or to research publishers you may already have in mind. For starters, you may want to check out online bookstores such as Amazon.com or Barnesandnoble.com and browse subject areas of interest. Very likely, you will be able to get a listing of books in your category, along with their publishers.

A great online resource is provided by the Children's Book Council (CBC), a nonprofit trade association whose membership consists of U.S. publishers and packagers of trade books for children and young adults, and producers of related literacy material. Authors and illustrators of children's books can locate potential publishers through the CBC Members List, which includes each member's address, main phone number, representatives, publishing program description, and general manuscript submissions guidelines (when provided). The list, which is updated every month, is available online free of charge, both as a read-only document and as alphabetical links to the members' websites. Single print copies may be purchased for a nominal fee.

Yet another directory of publishers is offered by Yahoo. (See page 261 of the Resource List.) Click on the "Children's" category, and you'll find an alphabetical listing of links to publishers' websites.

Finally, don't forget that these days, most publishers have websites that include online catalogues, as well as guidelines for writers and information on their distributors. Don't hesitate to visit these websites as a means of judging if your manuscript would be a good fit for the company—and if the company would be a good fit for you.

Trade Shows

Trade shows—events designed to enable publishers, booksellers, writers, and other people in the industry to network, sell rights, and conduct business—provide another excellent means of gathering information about publishing houses. If possible, try to visit BookExpo America (BEA), which is the annual trade show for the publishing industry. Just about everyone associated with the book industry is in attendance, giving you the opportunity to meet representatives of many different children's publishing houses, and get a good sense of the types of books their companies produce.

Many editors and marketing representatives attend the BEA, and you might be able to steal a few moments of their time and discuss your project with them. Keep in mind that while your first instinct may be to approach a company's editors at one of these shows, you might be better able to gauge a firm's interest by speaking with someone from the marketing department. In many companies, an editor can't acquire a book unless the project has the support of marketing.

WORDS FROM A PRO

Dandi Daley Mackall

Author of *101 Ways to Talk to God* (Sourcebooks, Inc.)

Dandi Daley Mackall has found that as a writer, you sometimes have to go the extra mile to get your work published. She once wrote a baby book designed as a shower gift item. She then found an appropriate conference to attend and searched for a pregnant editor. When she showed the manuscript to the editor, the woman immediately presented it to her publishing house and pushed it through to publication.

(Remember that in the last chapter, you learned that the number-one question most publishing houses ask before acquiring a book is, "Will it sell enough copies to make money for the company?") And if the people whom you contact don't feel that your project fits into their publishing program, they will often steer you toward a more appropriate house.

Another important trade show is BookExpo Canada, which is Canada's largest book industry event. A showcase of books in all formats and of all types—including children's books—this convention is attended by thousands of industry professionals, and usually enjoys a good turnout of small publishers.

If you are interested in writing books for the Christian market, consider attending the annual convention held by the Christian Booksellers Association, or CBA. This event attracts thousands of bookstore owners and buyers, literary agents, and media. Moreover, part of its expressed purpose is to enable publishers to meet new authors and artists.

Every year, Volume 1 of the *Literary Market Place* provides a comprehensive listing of worldwide industry-related conventions, conferences, and trade shows. *Publishers Weekly,* the book industry's trade magazine, also announces upcoming shows. You can also check out the Trade Show News Network (www.tsnn.com)—an Internet site that provides a listing of shows for a number of different industries, including book publishing. Finally, if you are interested in attending the BEA, you can visit www.bookexpoamerica.com for full information.

If you plan to attend a show, be aware that there will be an admission fee, which varies from show to show. Don't hesitate to call ahead and inquire about the cost.

MOVING ON

At this point, you have created a customized list of potential publishers for your work. Not only should these companies be the ones best suited to handle your book's category, they should also meet your personal criteria. If you've taken the time to develop this list carefully, it will increase your odds of getting published.

But you'll have to put that list aside for a short time. Your next step will be to prepare that all-important submission package, which you will be sending to the publishers on your list.

Every April, the world's leading children's publishing event is held in Bologna, Italy. The Bologna Children's Book Fair brings together several thousand publishers, authors, illustrators, literary agents, and other members of the children's publishing community from seventy different countries. Participants buy and sell copyrights, establish new contacts, learn about the industry's latest trends and developments—and discover new authors and illustrators.

CHAPTER 5

PREPARING THE PACKAGE

First impressions do count in the world of business and beyond. This is certainly true in the case of your submission package. This package will be your representative in the world of publishing, and the only means by which an editor can initially judge you and your book, and decide if he wants to consider your proposal. That's why the components of your package must be treated with the same care you'd give to your appearance before a job interview.

This chapter was designed to guide you through the writing of a winning submission package—a package that will invite the editor's attention, give the editor the best possible impression of both you and your book, and provide the editor with all the information he needs to make an initial decision about your project. You'll learn exactly what should be included and, just as important, you'll discover what should never be included. Assembling a winning package is probably easier than you think. As I explained in Chapter 4, editors know exactly what they want to see, and make that information available to you through their writer's guidelines. The problem has always been that most authors don't take the time to find out exactly what that is. This chapter will let you in on industry secrets, and help you put together a proposal that will get the best possible results.

THE GOAL OF THE SUBMISSION PACKAGE

Before you begin work on your submission package, it's important to understand the goal of the material you'll be writing. This goal is really threefold.

First, a winning package is designed to get *read*. That may sound ridiculously obvious, but many submissions are so poorly written, so confusing, or so overwhelming in size that they are destined to be "killed"—rejected, in other words—before the editor even finishes reading the first paragraph. Above all, a winning package is so brief and otherwise so inviting that it maximizes the odds that the editor will actually read enough of it to learn the merits of the project.

Second, a winning package shows the editor that this is a viable project—a project with potential. It does this by demonstrating that the book addresses a specific segment of the children's audience, and that it provides these readers with a product in which they are interested. An important point to remember is that you're not only selling the idea of the book, but are also selling yourself as the author. Reading your package, the editor will have a chance to assess your writing ability. A good package can convince him that you are credible, and that you have what it takes to produce a good book.

Finally, the winning package evokes a *positive response* from the editor. If he is interested, the editor will probably send a form letter, asking for further material. If he is sufficiently excited, he might take the time to write a personal letter, send an e-mail, or even make a phone call to discuss the project.

> Always remember that the goal of a submission package is not only to sell the idea of your book, but also to sell you as the author. An effective package will convince the editor that you have what it takes to produce a good children's book.

THE COMPONENTS OF THE SUBMISSION PACKAGE

I've said it before and I'll say it again: You must obtain the writer's guidelines for every publisher on your list, and then send in only what the guidelines request—no more, no less. If you already have the writer's guidelines from several companies in hand, or if you've simply read some of the "How to Contact/Writers" sections in *Children's Writer's & Illustrator's Market*, you know that these instructions can vary quite a bit from publisher to publisher. While some companies request a "query with outline/synopsis," others want "cover letter, table of contents, 1–2 sample chapters."

If this seems confusing, relax. The remainder of this chapter will tell you how to craft each of these components. Throughout, you'll find samples that will keep you on track. By paying careful attention to each detail of your submission package—and sending it to the appropriate editor—you will maximize the chance that your package will prompt a positive response.

The Cover or Query Letter

Is there a difference between a query letter and a cover letter? Technically, yes. A cover letter is the letter that accompanies your manuscript. A query letter is the letter you send to a publisher to ask—to query—if he's interested in seeing the manuscript. Cover letters are most often used for fiction, as fiction editors often want to receive a full manuscript, or at least several chapters. Query letters are usually used for nonfiction, as nonfiction editors more often want to receive just a proposal. There are many exceptions to this rule, though, which is why it's so important to read and follow each company's guidelines. In fact, increasingly, to cut down on the amount of mail they have to plow through, editors are requesting query letters rather than submission packages for fiction as well as nonfiction.

Although cover and query letters clearly have to be somewhat different, they have more in common than you might expect. In both cases, this letter is the first part of the package that the editor sees, so it serves as an introduction to you and your book. It is therefore the most crucial portion of your submission package. Unfortunately, most of these letters miss some or all of the elements needed to capture the editor's full interest and motivate him to read the remainder of the package. In other cases, the necessary information is there, but is presented so poorly that it casts serious doubts on the author's ability to write. Very few editors will pursue a project further when the letter is poorly written.

The Square One letter is designed to provide all of the information that the editor needs in four well-organized paragraphs, which are described on the next few pages. With a few minor changes, this letter can serve as either a cover or a query letter, as both of these letters must make the same major points about you and your book. As you read the following, keep in mind that the letter should range between one and two pages in length. You'll find a sample query letter on page 124, and sample cover letters on pages 127 and 128.

WORDS FROM A PRO

Hans Wilhelm

Author and Illustrator of *I'll Always Love You* (Dragonfly Books) Hans Wilhelm says, "There is no one *perfect* way to submit your material to a publisher." But Wilhelm points out that a strong cover letter and manuscript are key ingredients.

The Salutation and First Paragraph

Every letter, of course, should begin with a salutation, such as "Dear Mr. Smith." Although a letter, whether query or cover, can begin with

Sample Query Letter for a Nonfiction Book

44 Essex Road
Cleveland, OH 11747
Phone: (330) 555-1218
Fax: (330) 555-1837
E-mail: erigby@rivercenter.org

(Current Date)

Ms. Carol Smith, Editor
Kids Press
999 Lexington Street
San Francisco, CA 11937

Dear Ms. Smith:

I lost eight years of my adolescence and young adulthood to the eating disorder bulimia. But that does not have to be the case for other boys and girls. The goal of *Bulimia Nervosa: The Secret Cycle of Bingeing and Purging* is to reach young people before their body image and their relationship with food and weight become distorted, and to provide them with accurate information about bulimia, as well as proven tips for developing a positive self-image. The enclosed table of contents, overview, and sample chapters offer more details about the scope and contents of this young adult book, which I expect to be approximately 40,000 words in length.

An estimated 8 million people—children and adults—are affected by some type of eating disorder, with almost 90 percent reporting an onset of the illness before age twenty. This book is designed to address twelve- to fourteen-year-old boys and girls, who are just approaching the age at which this problem may develop. Although other books deal with this important issue, they either overwhelm the young reader with scientific data or tell only one person's story. *Bulimia Nervosa,* however, uses an easygoing, approachable style that clearly defines the problem without using technical lingo. Scattered throughout, young eating-disorder survivors share their stories in their own words. Both the book's format and style would allow it to fit in well with your superb "Talking About" series.

Due to my personal experience with bulimia, I have long been interested in helping others avoid this devastating disease. After receiving my master's and doctorate degrees in clinical psychology from Ohio University in 1989, I joined the staff of the Cleveland River Center Clinic, where I continue to work with young eating disorder patients. My related articles have appeared in *Newsday;* teen publications such as *Listen* and *Blue Jeans Magazine for Girls*; and consumer magazines like *Ladies' Home Journal, Better Homes & Gardens,* and *Parents.*

Thank you for taking the time to review my proposal for *Bulimia Nervosa: The Secret Cycle of Bingeing and Purging.* Please let me know if you would like to receive any additional materials. You can reach me by phone at (330) 555–1218 or by e-mail at erigby@rivercenter.org. A self-addressed, stamped envelope has also been enclosed for your convenience. Note that this is a simultaneous submission.

Sincerely yours,

Ellen Rigby

Ellen Rigby

"Dear Editor," I recommend that you use the appropriate editor's name when possible. By placing the name at the top of the letter and, more importantly, on the outside of the package, you not only will make sure that the package gets to the right person, but will also demonstrate that you have done your homework. (More about getting the appropriate editor's name in Chapter 6.) If the editor's name makes his gender unclear—if the name is Robin Smith, for instance—use both the first and last names in the salutation: "Dear Robin Smith." And *never* refer to the editor by his first name. Assuming familiarity isn't going to win you any points.

Below the salutation comes the first paragraph, which is the introductory paragraph. This portion of the letter has to capture the editor's attention and at the same time introduce your book. How can you get the editor's attention? This can be done in a number of ways.

Because it serves as an introduction to you and your book, your cover or query letter is the most crucial portion of the submission package. Make sure you've crafted a strong letter before moving onto the next component of your package.

For instance, if a well-known author or critic has suggested that you send your manuscript to the editor, be sure to mention that. But don't wax poetic about how much that person loved your work. Editors like to make up their own minds, and that kind of sales pressure can turn into a strike against you. Certainly if through attendance at writer's conferences or through research you've discovered that the editor has a new imprint or was recently promoted, you could refer to that: "Congratulations for being named senior editor of XYZ Books." Perhaps you've read a quote by him or learned that five of the books for which he served as editor recently won awards. It's a smart move to show that you follow the industry. But be genuine in all you write, not gimmicky, and be sure to get your information correct! What if you know nothing about the editor, and no well-known person has endorsed your project? In that case, do your best to make your lead sentence a strong and intriguing statement about your book or its subject. (See the first sentence of the query letter on page 124.)

The next part of the first paragraph should include a one- to four-sentence summary that explains what the book is about. In Chapter 2, you wrote a brief description of your book. Use this information within the first paragraph, describing your book in an enticing manner and using a spare amount of words, like the copy found on book jackets and in catalogues. In fact, if written well, this copy will be used by the publisher in all promotional materials. Many writers find that these words follow them throughout the life of their book!

At the end of the paragraph, tell the editor what you have enclosed—perhaps a table of contents and an overview of the book, or perhaps the entire manuscript, for instance. In this line, you'll also want to indicate the approximate length of the book either in double-spaced pages or an approximate word count.

The Second Paragraph

This paragraph is designed to show the editor that you, as a writer, have a reasonably clear idea of the book's audience—the age range and, perhaps, the gender of your readers. As explained in Chapter 2, an author who demonstrates that he understands his book's category and audience is viewed as an asset by the editor—as a partner in the publishing process. Unfortunately, all too many authors show their ignorance of the book world by misidentifying their audience

Sample Cover Letter for Picture Book

25 Preston Street
Brooklyn, NY 10013

(Current Date)

Harold Nimrod, Executive Editor
Patriots Press
1535 Patriots Street
Boston, MA 02102

Dear Mr. Nimrod,

"A is for Apple, B is for Barn" might appeal to a child living on a farm, but the urban preschooler lives in a very different world. *A is for A-Train* introduces children to letters and sounds through the exciting world of the city. Enclosed is my 300-word manuscript for this concept picture book.

The alphabet is one of the first things that children learn, and as you—the editor of the Alphabet Soup series—know, alphabet books are ideal tools to introduce children to this important concept. With our population growing increasingly metropolitan, and millions of children now living in urban areas, it's vital that these tools address not only the rural and suburban child, but also the city dweller. Designed for the preschooler, *A is for A-Train* is an early picture book that will not just teach city children the alphabet, but also alert them to the many unique sights and opportunities that surround them, from the A-train (A) to museums (M) to planetariums (P) to zoos (Z).

I have lived in the city all my life, and have taught in Bedford-Stuyvesant elementary schools in New York for twenty years. Thus, I have learned that many children's books seem to ignore kids whose experience includes trains and bodegas—not farms and fields. But when children are shown a book about *their* world, their faces light up and their minds eagerly open to new concepts!

I very much appreciate your taking the time to review my manuscript. A self-addressed stamped envelope has been enclosed for your convenience. Please be aware that this is a multiple submission.

Sincerely,

Rachel Kline

Rachel Kline
(555) 555-1234

Sample Cover Letter for Fiction

Noel Lucas
43 Roy Street
Big Rock, NC 28714
Phone: (704) 555–9779
E-mail: noell@bakerhigh.com

(Current Date)

Ms. Finola Finn, Senior Editor
Teen Machine Press
116 Adolescent Address
San Francisco, CA 11937

Dear Ms. Finn:

Congratulations on your promotion to the new department of Teen Troubles. I understand that you have begun a new line of problem novels aimed at the adolescent reader. To that end, I have enclosed a proposal for my problem novel for fourteen- to eighteen-year-olds. *The Perfect Girl* tells the story of seventeen-year-old Callie, who is struggling to hold her life together and to hide the family secret—her mother's alcoholism. This package includes an annotated table of contents, synopsis, and two sample chapters of the book, which is approximately 50,000 words in length.

The *American Journal of Public Health* states that approximately one in four United States children under the age of eighteen is exposed at some time to familial alcohol dependence (alcoholism), alcohol abuse, or both. At the core of my book are the family dynamics that situation can create for teens, told through the voice of Callie, a character to whom adolescents can relate. Through her experiences, I hope that readers will be able to understand not only how their lives may be affected by alcohol abuse, but also how they can seek and find help for this all-too-common problem.

I have been a young adult librarian for fifteen years, working at the Baker Memorial High School in Big Rock, North Carolina. In that capacity, I am often asked by adolescents to help them do more than find a book. They want to know how to cope with the difficult issues they face, and they ask for available resources to help them through troubling times. Family alcoholism issues seem to be near the top of their list of concerns.

Thank you for taking the time to review my proposal for *The Perfect Girl*. Please let me know if you would like to receive any additional materials. You can reach me at (704) 555–9779 or noell@bakerhigh.com. I have also enclosed a self-addressed, stamped envelope for your convenience. Please note this is a simultaneous submission. I look forward to receiving your response.

Sincerely yours,

Noel Lucas

Noel Lucas

or showing no recognition of it at all. Again, you might want to refer to the work you did in Chapter 2, where the category of your book defined your readers.

In this second paragraph, you should, if possible, support the assertion that your book has an audience by giving some idea of the size of your potential readership. If your book, whether fiction or nonfiction, focuses on a specific topic—eating disorders, for instance—you might be able to provide statistics: "Studies show that 6 to 10 percent of all children and adolescents in this country suffer from some type of eating disorder." If your book does not focus on a topic but fits into a certain genre or popular category, you can provide information about that: "The popularity of middle grade fantasy novels is skyrocketing, accounting for 40 percent of all books sales in the middle grade category in 2005."

If you've found that your book would be perfect for that publishing house because it fits beautifully into a specific line of books or imprint, this would be a good place to mention it. Such a statement will not only show that you've done your homework, but will also help the editor better identify the book's audience. Another effective strategy is to mention the titles of books that are similar to yours, and then explain how your book is different from or better than its competitors. For instance, while other books on eating disorders may be frightening to the young reader, or may overwhelm him with scientific information, yours may use an easygoing, approachable style that informs the reader without scaring him off.

Should you actually state your *marketplace*—traditional and children's bookstores, for instance—in your cover letter? If you have done your homework and carefully selected appropriate publishers as explained in Chapter 4, the companies on your list should both know all of the outlets through which your book may be sold and have established means of reaching them. For this reason, in most cases, it is not necessary to identify your book's marketplaces in your letter. However, if you have a difficult-to-reach audience and have found an unusual and effective way of accessing it, it would be wise to highlight this fact. Similarly, if you know that an upcoming event would make your book particularly timely—if, for instance, the publication of your book on American railroads would coincide with the bicentennial of a major railway—this would be the place to let the editor know about it.

The Third Paragraph

As important as it is to establish your credibility as an author by mentioning relevant accomplishments, it's equally important to avoid citing irrelevant achievements. Your success as a stamp collector, for instance, won't help to convince an editor that you're suited to write a book about horses.

The goal of this paragraph is to establish your credibility as the author of your book. Here, you can mention a variety of credits, from your educational background to work experience to hobbies. The key is to mention only relevant experience. For instance, if you've written a book on pet care and you have a veterinary degree, you should definitely state the college you attended and the degree you received there. Similarly, if you're an elementary school teacher and you've written an easy reader, that, too, would be relevant.

It is equally important to avoid citing irrelevant accomplishments, however meaningful they may be to you. For instance, the writer of the pet care book should not mention that he's the commodore of a local yacht club. On the other hand, if he were writing a book on sailing for young boaters, his experience in boating *would* be pertinent.

Of course, the best credential of all is having had something published, be it a book, a magazine article, or even an article in a local newspaper. If any of your writings have been in print, certainly mention this within the third paragraph, as it will show that your work has already been approved by another editor and that you are capable of completing a project. However, keep in mind that while it is a plus to be published, it is not a prerequisite to having a winning submission package, as editors also like to discover "new talent."

Editors are always impressed by authors who already have something in print, whether it is a book or a magazine article. If you want to build your credentials as an author, consider writing for children's magazines. (See page 233.)

The Fourth Paragraph and Closing

The purpose of this concluding paragraph is to wrap up the letter. First, express your appreciation for the editor's consideration and, if appropriate, offer to send any additional materials. Also indicate that you've enclosed a SASE or self-addressed, stamped envelope, and, if you desire, specifically mention other ways in which you can be reached. (For more on this, see "Contact Information," below.) If you plan to send out multiple submissions, this is the section of the letter to indicate that you'll be doing so, without providing any other details. (Again, you'll find more on this in the inset on page 132.) Finally, add your complimentary close—"Yours truly," "Sincerely yours," or "Sincerely" are all appropriate—and type your name, placing your handwritten signature above it.

Contact Information

Although it may be hard to believe, many authors fail to provide the information the editor needs to contact them by mail, phone, fax, or e-mail. If the submission package is truly outstanding, the editor may try to track down the missing information—but don't count on it! The very fact that this information was omitted is a red flag to the editor, who may then have serious doubts about the writer's commonsense and organizational abilities.

Years ago, an author simply typed his address at the top of the letter. But now that so many methods of contact are available, a number of options are considered acceptable. I strongly suggest that you invest in business stationery that shows your name, address, phone number, and fax number and e-mail address, if any. If you do not choose to make this investment, but you own a decent printer, con-

Multiple Submissions

Multiple submissions—the practice of submitting a proposal to several publishers at the same time—used to be frowned upon in the children's book industry. But these days, most editors recognize that it can take months to get back to a writer about his proposal, making it unfair to expect a writer to wait indefinitely for a response—only to have to go through the same process again and again, in most cases. At that rate, it could take years for the average writer to learn the fate of his proposal!

Some publishers still do demand exclusive submissions, and that's a consideration you'll have to keep in mind if a company's guidelines include a statement such as, "Will not consider simultaneous submissions." But even though most companies don't like the idea of multiple submissions because of the possibility that more than one house may end up competing for the same contract, they do understand that most authors send their proposal to more than one publisher.

Although multiple submissions are now acceptable, it's important to inform each editor that you are sending your submission out to other companies. It is *not* good etiquette to imply through omission that the editor is the only one receiving the proposal. If and when you have the good fortune to be offered a deal by two pub-

lishers, and you have to reject one in order to accept the other, you won't be making any friends at that second publishing house. This may not seem important to you now, as the idea of being offered a book contract is so exciting. But remember that people in publishing tend to move from company to company, so the rejected editor may become part of your life down the road. And editors do talk to other editors from other houses. It will be to your advantage to keep all of your business relationships positive and on the up-and-up.

As discussed on page 131, the best course of action is to include a sentence at the end of your cover or query letter, stating that you are sending out multiple submissions. In addition to keeping your business dealings honest, this statement will show you're savvy about the submissions process. Just as important, it will add a sense of urgency by giving the impression that another editor at another house may snap up your manuscript at any moment. So by including this one simple statement, you will do quite a bit to increase the impact of your letter.

A final caveat: Don't send simultaneous submissions to several editors in the same house. If they find out about this ploy, they will *all* reject your proposal.

sider creating your own letterhead. If neither of these options seem right, simply place your contact information at the top of the letter; place it beneath your typed name at the end of the letter; or work it into the last paragraph of the letter.

Even though I print my queries on business letterhead, I always repeat the contact information in the final paragraph of each letter. This makes it all the easier for the editor to reach me.

The Annotated Table of Contents or Outline

Many publishers request a table of contents or an outline. In either of these cases, an annotated table of contents will fit the bill.

As the samples on pages 134 to 136 demonstrate, unlike the standard table of contents (TOC), which lists only chapter titles, the annotated TOC provides descriptive information about each chapter. In a work of fiction, each annotation should briefly state what occurs to the major characters within that chapter. In a work of nonfiction, the annotation should provide a clear yet concise explanation of that chapter's coverage. Be aware that although all parts of the book—including prematter and postmatter sections like the preface and glossary—should be listed in the annotated TOC, you do not have to annotate sections of the prematter and postmatter.

No matter what you're writing, it can be tricky to summarize each chapter's coverage or plot. The rule of thumb is to pull out the most important components of your story or nonfiction material. To avoid taxing the editor's patience with pages and pages of copy, try to write no more than two to three sentences for each chapter. For most children's books, the entire table of contents should run no more than three pages. Your annotations should be informative but concise.

Note that although all works of nonfiction have chapter titles, and that the same is true for works of fiction designed for the younger reader, many young adult fiction books have chapter numbers only. If you are writing fiction for the older child, you are certainly not required to write chapter titles for your work. If, however, your chapters do have names, do your best to come up with clever ones, as this will make your proposal all the more appealing.

If you have not yet written a table of contents for your book—which is likely only if your book is still in the planning stages—doing so will give you an opportunity to assess the organization of your material. In fact, I've found that preparing an annotated TOC before I even begin writing a book is a wonderful exercise that helps me with organization, regardless of whether I'm working on fiction or nonfiction. Seeing my whole book laid out on the page often helps me determine what will work best in terms of pacing. Then when it comes time to send out the proposal, my TOC is complete and ready to go.

If the chapters of your book have titles, try to make them as intriguing as possible. This will make your proposal all the more appealing.

Sample Table of Contents for Fiction Book

The Perfect Girl
Contents

Chapter One

Callie Brown performs her nightly ritual of getting her drunk mother to bed and dealing
with her withdrawn father. She oversleeps in the morning and is once again late for school.
Chronic tardiness—coupled with the school's zero-tolerance policy—is jeopardizing
Callie's honor roll status, while problems at home are making her lose touch with friends.

Chapter Two

Callie is offered the chance to work on a special series for the school newspaper. She's teamed
with Andy Simon, who later asks her out. She declines the invitation, but doesn't explain
that her refusal is due to her home situation—not to feelings about him.

Chapter Three

Another volatile evening at home acts as a catalyst, prompting Callie to reach out to Andy
and other friends. As she begins her new series, one of her jobs is to work with Ms. Manos,
the school psychologist—someone whom Callie has always done her best to avoid.

Chapter Four

That night, when Callie attempts to get her mother to bed, her mother struggles and injures
Callie. On a date with Callie, Andy notices her bruises. Although she first pretends that nothing
is wrong, when Andy shares a family secret of his own, Callie finds herself opening up about
her situation for the first time.

Chapter Five

When Callie and Andy become a steady couple, Callie spends more time away from home,
which greatly affects her family life. Callie argues with her parents at Thanksgiving dinner,
and leaves to visit Andy's family, where she learns more about their secret—that Mr. Simon
was arrested for driving while drunk years before.

Chapter Six

When school opens after the holiday, Callie meets with her guidance counselor, Jessica Porter, to discuss college choices. Ms. Porter encourages Callie to apply to the top journalism schools, which would mean her going away to school. When Callie tells her parents, they forbid her to apply.

Chapter Seven

Callie decides to apply to the colleges despite her parents' objections, and during the Christmas vacation, Callie and her mother have a huge fight. Callie realizes that her problems at home are too big to handle on her own, and she calls Ms. Manos, the school psychologist.

Chapter Eight

Although Callie feels guilty to be "airing her family secrets to a stranger," as her mother would say, she finds that her visits with Ms. Manos are helping her. But she and Andy have a fight and break up when she discovers that he's been sneaking beers at the florist where he works.

Chapter Nine

Callie is offered early acceptance to the college of her choice, as well as a partial scholarship. She tells her parents that she's going regardless of what they think, and her father surprises her by lending his support. That night, she finds her mother lying unconscious on the bathroom floor, and she calls an ambulance.

Chapter Ten

Andy surprises Callie by meeting her in the emergency room of the hospital. They talk, and Andy volunteers that he's going to visit Ms. Manos the next day. When Callie's father calls her into her mother's hospital room, she and her parents have their first honest conversation about her mother's alcoholism.

Chapter Eleven

The newspaper project on which Callie has been working earns her community-wide recognition. The story that wins the most attention is that about being the child of an alcoholic. And it's Callie's mother—now, in a rehab program—who offers her the highest praise of all.

Sample Table of Contents for Nonfiction Book

Bulimia Nervosa: The Secret Cycle of Bingeing and Purging
Contents

Preface
Introduction: The Hidden Disease

Chapter One: What Is Bulimia?
Bulimia is a major social concern that has a devastating effect on millions of girls, boys, women, and men. This chapter explores the warning signs, explains how bulimia is different from other eating disorders, and identifies who is at risk.

Chapter Two: Why Do People Develop Bulimia?
Young people and adults can develop an eating disorder for many reasons, including media influences, family issues, depression, drug abuse, and physical and sexual abuse. Each of these potential causes is explored in Chapter Two.

Chapter Three: How Bulimia Affects the Body and Mind
This chapter details the physical, psychological, and emotional consequences experienced by a person who has bulimia. Some of the potential effects discussed are the female athlete triad (disordered eating, amenorrhea, and loss of bone mass), vitamin and mineral deficiencies, stomach and organ damage, and emotional problems.

Chapter Four: Recovering From Bulimia
This chapter first informs the reader that people can recover from bulimia, and then explores the many resources that can help sufferers battle the disorder. Possibilities include help from a loved one, individual therapy, hospitalization, family therapy, group therapy, and support groups.

Chapter Five: Developing a Positive Body Image
How can you prevent an eating disorder in the first place? This chapter takes a positive approach to helping young people develop a healthy self-image.

Glossary
Where to Go for Help
For Further Reading
Index

The Book Synopsis or Overview

As already discussed, many publishers ask for a synopsis—a concise summary of the plot. Why, then, does this section also cover overviews? As you know, not all books have plots. Our hypothetical book on bulimia nervosa—see the sample query letter on page 124 and the sample TOC on page 136—does not present a story, but is a methodical examination of its subject. What I have found best, then, is to provide the publisher with a synopsis for fiction books, as well as for nonfiction books that have a story line—a biography, for instance; and to provide an overview for nonfiction books that do not have a story line. Let's look at each of these submission package components in turn.

The book synopsis summarizes your story. It discusses the setting, the major characters, the plots, and the subplots. Be aware that it should not give a blow-by-blow account of your story, but should explain it briefly, while making it as interesting and tempting as possible. Think about the copy you might find on a book jacket or in a book catalogue. You want the reader to know what the book is about, but you don't want him to know everything that happens. Most of all, you want him to be intrigued enough to read more. For inspiration, try reading book jackets for stories that are similar to yours. Also see the sample synopsis on page 138.

An overview is designed to explain clearly and in reasonable detail just what your book is about, and to show why readers would be interested in the title. It demonstrates the scope and thrust of the book, and clarifies your point of view. It may help you to understand that the overview is very often used as a basis for the book's introduction. Thus, the overview can be viewed as a sort of "hook" that heightens the editor's interest in the book so that he wants to read more. It should be upbeat and enthusiastic, without sounding like an advertising piece. For more ideas, read the introductions of children's books on related topics, and see the sample overview on page 139.

Although you don't want your synopsis to recount every event of your story, you also don't want to tease the editor by stating that if he wants to find out what happens, he'll have to read your manuscript. Editors don't like guessing games, nor do they like surprises. Be sure to clearly indicate where the plot is going, but paint the picture using broad strokes—not minute detail.

WORDS FROM A PRO

Kathleen Duey

Author of *The Mountains of the Moon*
(Aladdin Paperbacks)

Kathleen Duey says that synopsis writing is a necessary skill for all writers. Your synopsis, she notes, is a demonstration of your book. By introducing the characters, evoking the setting, stating or implying the theme, and summarizing the story, you want to intrigue the editor so much that he asks to see the book. All of this takes time, of course, and Duey believes that the people who fail are usually those who give up too soon.

Sample Synopsis

The Perfect Girl

Seventeen-year-old Callie Brown is having a hard time holding it all together. Her nights are disrupted by her parents' frequent arguments about the family secret—her mother's alcoholism. As a result, Callie's grades are slipping, and her history teacher Mr. Harmon seems determined to humiliate her in front of the class. Yet she keeps her troubles to herself, fearing that a cry for help would expose her family to embarrassment. Not knowing how to spend time with her friends without airing family problems, Callie withdraws. It takes a special school project—and a unique relationship—to help Callie see that in trying to be a perfect girl, she is only hurting herself.

As Callie struggles between the desire to care for her parents and an enjoyment of her new-found social life, she has to come to grips with the fact that her parents are unwilling to take responsibility for themselves. Still, she understands that she must pursue her dreams. Her relationship with Andy Simon, who has family secrets of his own, is also tested when Callie is able to face her reality, but is unable to help Andy confront his own demons.

Through a series of painful experiences, Callie learns that in order to find herself, she has to first be willing to give herself permission to be imperfect.

Remember that like everything else in your submission package, your synopsis or overview is a sample of your writing style and ability. If you are including a portion of the book in your package, you want this piece to inspire the editor to pick up the chapters and read further. If you are not including sample chapters, you want to pique the editor's interest, as well as to convince the editor that you are capable of writing a high-quality book.

Whether you're writing a synopsis or an overview, aim for brevity. You don't want to tax the editor's patience or bore him with countless details. Although it may take time to pare the piece down without omitting important information or robbing it of its flavor, it's critical that you do so. Most books require a synopsis or overview that is only a page or two in length. If you've written a novel for older readers, a slightly longer piece may be acceptable. Ideally, though, this component of your package should be short and punchy.

Sample Overview

Bulimia Nervosa: The Secret Cycle of Bingeing and Purging

Nearly 8 million girls, boys, women, and men in the United States have an eating disorder. It is not known how many of them have bulimia. Why? Because this disorder is so often a closely guarded secret. People with bulimia binge on enormous quantities of food, and then—when no one is around—purge their bodies of the food to avoid gaining weight. Unlike those with anorexia, who have noticeable weight loss, sufferers of bulimia often have normal weight or are slightly overweight. That's why even those closest to them are often unaware that their loved one is struggling with a disease that can profoundly affect both body and mind.

This book begins by providing basic information about bulimia. Readers learn what bulimia is and how it differs from other eating disorders. They also learn the warning signs and identify who is at risk. Following this, each chapter explores a different aspect of the bulimia puzzle. In Chapter 2, readers discover the many possible reasons that young people and adults develop bulimia, including media influences, family issues, depression, and more. Chapter 3 examines the physical, psychological, and emotional consequences of bulimia. Chapter 4 explains that despite bulimia's devastating physical, psychological, and emotional consequences, people can and do recover from the disease, and then goes on to explore the resources available to the bulimia sufferer. Finally, Chapter 5 helps the reader cultivate a positive self-image that can prevent the development of an eating disorder, and promote a lifetime of health and happiness. Throughout the book, young people who have battled with bulimia—and won—tell their stories in their own words.

Bulimia destroys thousands of lives every year. Although it affects girls more often than boys, it can attack anyone, male or female, young or old. But it can be stopped. It is my hope that *Bulimia Nervosa* will reach children before they are affected by this disease, and—through clear information and practical guidance—help them develop healthy attitudes about food, their world, and themselves.

The Sample Chapters

Although many publishers prefer to receive only a query letter and, perhaps, a table of contents and overview, others request sample chapters or—when picture books are concerned—the entire manuscript. Be aware that even when publishers desire samples, their requirements vary greatly. While some want a single chapter, others

Sample First Manuscript Page for Picture Book

Rachel Kline   300 words
24 Preston Street
Brooklyn, NY 10013
(555) 555-1234
E-mail: rkline@bedstuyel.net

A Is for A-Train

by

Rachel Kline

A is for A-Train which speeds through a tunnel.

B is for Broadway where people act, dance, and sing.

C is for the Carousel with painted horses and carts.

D is for the Docks where we watch ships pull in.

E is for the Escalator that rises high above the ground.

F is for the Frankfurter you buy from a cart.

Sample First Manuscript Page for Book With Chapters

Noel Lucas   50,000 words
43 Roy Street
Big Rock, NC 28714
(704) 555-9779
E-mail: noell@bakerhigh.com

The Perfect Girl

by

Noel Lucas

Sample Second Manuscript Page for Book With Chapters

Lucas, The Perfect Girl   2

Chapter One

Callie Brown was late again. But she leaped out of bed, pulled on jeans and a sweater,

stuffed her feet into loafers, and quickly glanced in the mirror. She grimaced at her

reflection. The skin under her large, green eyes was smudged with dark circles.

Impatiently, she combed her fingers through her long, dark brown hair.

Glancing at her watch with anxiety, she raced to her parents' room. "Mom, Mom,"

she called, gently nudging her mother's shoulder. "You have to get up or you'll be late

for work."

Carol brushed her hand away. "Leave me alone," she mumbled.

Callie felt her chest constrict. She took a deep breath and then dashed down the

Sample Full Text Page for Picture Book or Book With Chapters

Lucas, The Perfect Girl   3

stairs and out into the October sunlight, trying to remember her history class lectures so she would have some chance of passing that morning's test.

The test was already in progress when Callie slipped into the classroom. Her teacher was writing something on the blackboard, so she stealthily approached the pile of test papers on his desk. As she reached for the paper, a hand clamped down on hers.

"Miss Brown, is there some reason why you feel that my class starts later for you than for everyone else?" Mr. Harmon asked in his clipped voice. "I can't remember when you last saw fit to arrive with the crowd. Are you perhaps better than the rest, Miss Brown?"

Callie stood before her classmates. They were more interested in her confrontation with Horrible Harmon than the Battle of Gettysburg. A few of them giggled. With her shoulders squared and her face blazing, she looked into her teacher's eyes and said, "I'm very sorry, sir. I was studying for the test, and I lost track of the time. It won't happen again."

When sending sample
chapters, be sure to follow
each publisher's writer's
guidelines to the letter
and submit only what's
been requested.

want three chapters, and still others request five. Some want the first
two chapters, but others want to see a middle and last chapter. As
always, my advice to you is to read the writer's guidelines and follow them carefully, sending no more and no less than what the publisher requests. If the guidelines ask for three chapters, don't send the
whole manuscript even if it's complete and ready to go. Most editors
are already overwhelmed by piles of paper, and won't appreciate
your adding unnecessary materials to the pile. Moreover, in the case
of nonfiction, it is very likely that the editor will want to shape your
manuscript and make alterations to your table of contents. In a case
such as this, a completed manuscript can actually cool the editor's
interest in your proposal.

At this point, it should go without saying that your sample chapters should be flawless in terms of spelling and grammar, and should
showcase your abilities as a writer. Don't fool yourself into thinking
that your concept is so unique that an editor will jump at the chance
to buy your work even if the text doesn't read as well as it might.
While this could be true, it's more likely that the editor will use the
sample chapters as a means of judging your ability, and will turn the
project down if your skills as an author are not up to snuff.

Finally, while the editor probably won't toss out your proposal if
the format of your manuscript pages is not perfect, it is important to
provide certain basic information on the first page of your manuscript, and on each page that follows, as well. To make your sample
chapters look as neat and professional as possible, you'll want to follow the guidelines provided below. Also look at the sample manuscript pages found on pages 140 to 143.

❏ When setting up *any* kind of book, make sure to create 1-inch margins around every sample manuscript page. In the upper left-
hand corner of your title page, type your name, address, phone
number, and e-mail address if you have one. This copy should be
single-spaced. In the upper right-hand corner of the page, type
the approximate word count. Halfway down the page, type the
title, centered. Double-space, and type the word "by," centered.
Double-space again, and type your name or pseudonym, centered. Do *not* place a page number on the title page.

❏ If your book is a picture book—a book without chapters—the
actual text will start on the title page. Simply double-space twice

after your name, and begin typing your text. Do *not* indicate page breaks. Instead, let the text flow on, indenting each new paragraph, and start a new page only when you've run out of room on the old page.

❑ If your book has chapters, begin each chapter on a new page. Place your last name, followed by a comma and the title of the book, in the upper left-hand corner of the page. Place the page number in the upper right-hand corner of the page. Type the chapter title—or simply Chapter One, Chapter Two, etc., if appropriate—a third of the way down the page, centered. Double-space twice, and begin the actual text of the chapter.

❑ Whether writing a picture book or chapter book, on all subsequent pages, type your last name, followed by the title of the book, in the upper left-hand corner of the page, and the page number in the upper right-hand corner of the page. Double-space twice, and start typing your text.

The Self-Addressed Envelope

As a courtesy to the editor, it's important to always include a self-addressed stamped envelope (SASE) in your submission package. If you don't, a number of things will happen. First, you will show a lack of understanding of standard submission procedures. Second, you will imply that you don't want the materials back, which is a bad message to send. Third, you will decrease the chance of receiving a response.

I always leave my submission package open when I take it to the post office so that the postal worker can weigh the package. I then place the proper postage on my SASE—a 9-x-11-inch envelope—fold it and tuck it inside the envelope before sealing and mailing the package.

You won't always get all of your contents back. In fact, I've had editors use my large-sized envelope, complete with extra postage, just to send back a one-page rejection letter. But most of the time, you will receive everything but your cover letter.

Instead of enclosing an SASE, some writers like to enclose a response postcard. If you opt to use this, the editor will be able to simply check the appropriate response and drop the card in the outgoing mail bin, rather than running off a standard letter. And, of course, you will save a few cents on postage.

By including a self-addressed stamped envelope (SASE) in your package, you will help ensure that you receive a response to your proposal. Just as important, you will show that you are a savvy writer who is aware of standard submission procedures.

The response postcard can read something like the following:

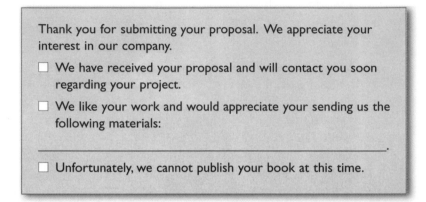

Thank you for submitting your proposal. We appreciate your interest in our company.

☐ We have received your proposal and will contact you soon regarding your project.

☐ We like your work and would appreciate your sending us the following materials:

_____.

☐ Unfortunately, we cannot publish your book at this time.

Naturally, the card should be self-addressed and stamped, just like the envelope it's meant to replace. Be aware, though, that not all editors are impressed by the response postcard. Some, it's true, are happy to check the appropriate box and place the card in the mail. But other editors have told me that checking the box is just one more thing for them to do, and that they would rather follow routine procedures. Certainly, if the writer's guidelines specifically request an SASE, that's exactly what you should send.

POLISHING THE PACKAGE

All along, I've emphasized how all the details of the submission package are worthy of your attention. Since this package is your calling card—your one chance to make an editor sit up and take notice—it's important to take a little extra time and make sure that your package is the best it can be. This involves two steps: checking your material for spelling, grammar, clarity, and flow; and making the materials attractive and professional in appearance. Let's look at each of these in turn.

Perfecting the Language

As a magazine editor, I'm always amazed by the many poorly written query letters I receive on a day-to-day basis. In addition to typos, a good number of these letters contain rambling paragraphs and poor grammar. Almost always I determine that I don't have time to work with someone who can't present the core of what they do in a professional, polished manner.

Are book editors likely to be more forgiving than magazine editors? Probably not. That's why it's so important to perfect the language, spelling, and grammar in every component of your submission package. Just keep in mind that even if the language is reasonably perfect, editors are likely to make changes. Editors have to follow their in-house style guidelines. Moreover, because they have the benefit of objectivity, they can sometimes see how to better phrase a sentence. Nevertheless, it is vital to demonstrate that you can produce copy that is well organized and clear. You also want to show that you are a careful and conscientious writer, who can and will do any work that is necessary to bring the book to completion.

After you've drafted your letter and the other components of your package, read through the materials carefully. Don't forget to do the same for your manuscript or sample chapters, if these are to be included. Check for spelling, grammar, and organization. Even if everything seems fine to you, run a spell-check on your computer. Then carefully check any changes you made per your computer's advice. Sometimes computers *don't* know best, and will replace a correct word with an incorrect homonym, substituting "they're" for "their," for instance. While the spell-check is a good tool, like all tools, it must be used with care.

Be aware that the more familiar you become with your work by reading it over and over, the more likely you are to become blind to it. So once you've perfected your package as much as possible, put it aside for a day or two. This will place a little distance between you and your work so that the next time you review the material, you will have a fresh perspective and a bit more objectivity. Correct any further errors that you find.

Finally, consider asking someone else to read through your package and provide an appraisal of your work. I'm fortunate to be married to a high school English teacher who regularly reviews my work when asked. If you can find someone in the publishing industry or another writer to read your proposal, that's best. If not, a teacher, librarian, or someone else who is well read and has a good ear for language will fit the bill. But make sure this person isn't going to just

Consider asking a friend to read through your submission package. Someone in the publishing industry, a teacher, or a children's librarian would be a good choice.

tell you the nice things you want to hear. He has to be willing and able to provide an honest response.

When you hand the material to your "reader," explain that you want him to read the material through for clarity, organization, spelling, and grammar. Point out that the package is *supposed* to be brief and easy to read; it is not intended to be lengthy or technical. Also mention what the package is supposed to contain. Then walk away. You don't want to stand over the person's shoulder, figuratively or literally, and you don't want to even inadvertently give him your "take" on the material. Then, when he's finished, make sure you're willing to listen with an open mind to any comments or criticism. Did he tell you that your package is clear, logical, well written, and interesting? Did he find anything misleading or offensive? Keep in mind that you don't have to change everything the reader mentions, but chances are that if something you've written jars one person, it could easily bother an editor. Thank your reader politely and make those suggested changes that you can live with and that are in line with your objectives.

Getting the Mechanics Right

Once you feel that you have perfected the wording of your submission package, you'll want to make the package as attractive and professional in appearance as possible. This serves two purposes. It makes the copy easy to read, and it shows the editor that you understand what a publishing company expects from a prospective author.

Let me warn you that some of this will sound very basic. But because many people don't know about these basics, they bear repeating.

First, choose $8\frac{1}{2}$-x-11-inch white paper. Standard photocopying paper will do fine, although a nice white bond is even better. Use 1-inch margins and type—don't handwrite—all of the submission package materials. The only handwritten element in your package should be your signature on the letter. Everything else should be printed on a computer or typed on a typewriter, even if you have to borrow your friend's computer or use the typewriter at your local library.

If you have letterhead, you can, of course, use that for the query or cover letter only. But please don't use any cutesy images or type-

Protecting Your Work

When you send out copies of your submission package, you may wonder if any of the editors you're contacting might be so unscrupulous as to steal your idea. Or perhaps this notion won't occur to you until an editor requests sample chapters and you worry if your painstakingly worded text might end up in someone else's book!

If you start to get a little overprotective, you're not alone. The fear that someone, somewhere, will steal or modify your work is a common concern for the writer who is just starting to submit queries and manuscripts to publishing houses. Keep in mind that this rarely if ever happens, simply because an editor is most interested in finding a writer who can produce a marketable book—not just an idea that might someday be developed into a book. But if the possibility of theft remains a concern for you, you'll be glad to know that there are at least three ways of protecting your work.

Register a Copyright

You may have noticed that every commercially printed book contains a copyright notice on the back of the title page. What you might not realize is that unpublished works can also be copyrighted.

What does a copyright mean? When a copyright is issued in your name by the United States Copyright Office, you will have the legal right to exclusive publication, production, sale, or distribution of your work. In other words, once it is registered, no one else will be able to legally print your work unless you formally grant him or her the right to do so. If anyone does violate your copyright by publishing part or all of your work, the formal copyright registration will speed up any legal battle and avoid complications. And if the work is registered with the copyright office within three months of its appearance in print or before any violation of your rights occurred, you will be awarded the money to pay for any attorney expenses, as well as compensation for the wrongs committed against you.

It is simple to register your copyright with the United States Copyright Office in Washington, DC. And you can register the work at any time—even years after your manuscript is written. First, you will have to fill out an application form, which can be downloaded from the Internet or obtained through the mail. (See page 259 of the Resource List for further information.) You will then send the completed application, the manuscript, and a check covering the copyright fee. The office will mail you a certificate of registration once your application has been reviewed and accepted. Be aware that neither the fee nor the manuscript will be returned to you.

One last point should be made. When a copyright is issued in your name, only your actual *words*—not your concept—are protected. It is impossible to copyright a concept, be it the central idea of a book or a unique format or method of presentation.

Obtain a Notary Public's Stamp

A notary public is a person who has been officially authorized to certify or witness the placing of a signature on a document, and to confirm that the paper was signed on a given date. Every notary has an exclusive ink stamp that contains his or her identification number. Therefore, when you have your work notarized and then, at a later date, someone prints your work, the notary seal will prove that this work was in your possession on the recorded date.

It's easy to have your work notarized and thus establish visual proof of possession. If you don't already know a notary public, you will be able to find one at a bank, a financial office, or a professional office. Bring with you the manuscript itself, as well as two forms of identification, one of which must include a photo. In the presence of the notary, place your signature on the first page of each chapter—it is unnecessary to notarize more than this. Then, for a small fee, the notary will stamp, sign, and date each signed page. Keep the notarized documents in a safe place.

Mail Yourself a Copy of the Work

If copyrighting or notarizing your work sounds like too much fuss or too time-consuming, another option is available. First, sign and date the manuscript, and seal it securely in an envelope. Then buy small paper adhesive-backed seals—small blank address labels will do—and place one on each and every seam of the mailing envelope. Take the package to the post office and ask the person at the desk to hand-stamp each paper seal with an official *dated* post office stamp. Finally, mail the package to yourself. When the package finds its way back to you, it will not only bear the regular postmark, which shows the date it was sent out and the location at which it was mailed, but will also show the stamped unbroken seals on the seams, which will prove that you did not tamper with the package after receiving it in the mail.

The rationale behind this practice, of course, is that the sealed, postmarked document will serve as visual evidence that the piece of writing was complete and in your possession prior to the postal stamp date. Then, if anyone plagiarizes your work, you will be able to present the package—which, of course, must still be closed with all seals intact—in a court of law.

Secure a Trademark

In recent years, many children's books have generated other products, from dolls and stuffed animals to games, videos, and TV shows. If you create a great character or concept that you think will be saleable, you might want to consider having it trademarked. This will protect it more completely than a copyright. You can secure the trademark on your own through the U.S. Patent and Trademark Office, or you can hire a trademark attorney to complete the filing for you. Your best bet is to start by doing some research at your library or online. (See page 259 of the Resource List for contact information.)

A Final Caution

Any of the methods described above should allow you to protect your work as you send it out to one or several editors. But do keep one important point in mind: The material you submit should not actually bear a copyright notice, notary seal, or trademark symbol. Why? Simply put, such practices are insulting to the editor, as they give the impression that you don't trust his integrity. Perhaps just as important, such practices demonstrate that you lack experience and professionalism. Keep the copyright certificate and the notarized pages in your home records, and send the editor an unmarked copy of your material. That way, you'll both protect your work and project a professional image.

faces. If you ordinarily have little rainbows or kittens on your letter-head, skip the letterhead and use the plain white paper on which you're printing the rest of the submission materials. Editors are pro-fessionals, and writers should be, too.

Your ink should be basic black, even if you have a color printer. Black is clear, legible, and professional. Similarly, if you have a choice of typefaces, you'll want to choose a basic, readable font such as Times Roman or Courier, and use 12-point type. Avoid fancy or exot-ic typefaces, as editors generally don't appreciate hard-to-read copy. And make sure that your ink cartridge is working well so that your printout doesn't have feathery, blotchy, or fading type.

Start each new part of the package—the letter, table of contents, etc.—on a new sheet of paper. If you're sending several sample chap-ters, also start each of these on a new sheet. Single-space the cover letter, but double-space all the other materials.

One last caution is in order regarding the appearance of your package. Many editors tell me that some of the proposals they receive have been stained by food or coffee. As you may imagine, this is not an attractive sight. If there's one time to keep the coffee mug or buttered roll off the table, it's when you're preparing your submis-sion package! Professionalism always wins points.

> To maximize the readability of your submission package and ensure a professional appearance, you'll want to choose 8$\frac{1}{2}$-x-11-inch white bond paper, select a basic no-frills typeface, and use a printer that produces letter-quality type.

SHOULD YOU INCLUDE ILLUSTRATIONS IN YOUR SUBMISSION PACKAGE?

As you'll learn when you read the inset on pages 152 to 153, many first-time children's book authors feel compelled to include illustra-tions with their manuscript. Perhaps you're one of them. Is this a good idea? To a large extent, the answer depends upon your abilities as an artist.

If You're a Writer, But Not an Artist

In Chapter 2, I mentioned that children's book editors don't want or expect to receive illustrations with a manuscript proposal. Most edi-tors have a list of established illustrators whom they use regularly, and are experienced in matching each manuscript with the best illus-trator. Generally, to help ensure sales, they will pair a new author with an artist who has some name recognition. Further—as you may

Ten Common Submission Package Errors

Throughout this chapter, I've mentioned several submissions package "don'ts," but as long as authors keep making the same mistakes, these warnings bear repeating. Of all the errors shared with me by book editors, the following ones are the most common. Avoid them, and at the very least, you will avoid raising a red flag.

1 **The author includes a headshot in his submission package.** You may be a very attractive person, but your appearance isn't going to make or break the deal. If you get a contract and the publicity department needs your headshot for press releases or the design department wants to add it to your book cover, they'll let you know. Until then, keep the photographs in your home file.

2 **The proposal is submitted as an e-mail attachment.** Editors say that they have no time to print out an attachment, and even if they did have the time, they wouldn't print it out because of the paper and ink expense to the company. Unless the writer's guidelines say that e-mailed queries are okay, make the editor's job easy and send in a hard copy.

3 **The submission package includes Pringles, Beanie Babies, Sour Patch Kids, or other treats.** As one editor said, "I just need the manuscript, thanks." Don't try to bribe the editor; it won't work.

4 **Feeling that a picture book isn't complete without pictures, the author—who can't draw—submits art along with his manuscript.** Unless your art is of professional quality, do not include it in your submission package. At best, it will not be used. At worst, it will call your professionalism into question and result in the rejection of your proposal. (For more information about submitting art, see pages 151 to 156.)

5 **The author states that his children, his grandchildren, or his neighbor's**

already know by perusing published books and scanning book catalogues—most houses favor a specific style of art. For that reason, if your art is not of professional quality, you should not send your illustrations along with your manuscript. The same is true of illustrations created by your best friend or brother.

Keep in mind that if and when you secure a publishing contract, you can always suggest an illustrator. But if you submit your proposal along with illustrations that you feel must accompany your words, and the illustrations are not up to par, the editor will not look favorably upon your submission. In fact, with many editors, this will pretty much guarantee rejection. Rest assured that if your proposal is well written and your story is compelling, the editor's imagination

children just loved his story. Editors prefer to make up their own minds about submitted material, and are unlikely to be impressed by your grandchildren's opinions. Such words even call the editor's judgment into question. It's as if you're saying, "If you don't like it, you're wrong." If you're a good writer who knows his audience, that will come through in your work. There's no need to spell it out.

6 **The author stops by the editor's office on a whim.** It's the manuscript they want to see, not you. Chances are you won't get past reception anyway, so don't waste your time.

7 **The manuscript proposal is filled with spelling errors, grammatical errors, and awkward sentences.** Don't send a rough draft hoping that the editor will edit it, and don't believe that your concept is so outstanding that the editor will be willing to overlook sloppy writing. If you've read the section "Perfecting the Language" on pages 146 to 148, you already know what to do. Take the time you need to make the package as good as possible.

8 **The submission package includes a resumé.** You're not applying for a job. If you have been published, by all means, mention it in your letter. (See page 131 for details.) But don't send a resumé.

9 **The submission package is sent to the wrong type of publishing houses.** Authors have been known to submit their picture book manuscripts to companies that publish only young adult books, and to send nonfiction nature books to houses that specialize in fantasy novels. To avoid wasting both your time and theirs, do your homework, and send your submission package to the appropriate editor at the appropriate publishing house.

10 **The package doesn't follow the rules presented in the company's writer's guidelines.** I've said it before and I'll say it again: You must read the writer's guidelines and send in only what the company wants. If you submit the appropriate materials and address them to the correct editor, you will greatly increase your chance of seeing your book in print.

will be captured, and he will become excited about your book—even without illustrations.

If You're a Writer and an Artist

If you are a professionally trained illustrator, and would like to produce the art for your book, you should still submit the required materials—cover letter, sample chapters, etc. In addition, though, you'll want to send a *dummy*—a mock-up of the final book that, ideally, is the same size as the finished volume, and has the text glued onto separate pages. Insert black-and-white sketches where you plan to have illustrations, including only two or three finished color pieces. Do

Creating a "Dummy" Picture Book

If you've never created a dummy book before, it may seem to be a daunting task. It's really quite simple, though, if you follow these steps:

1. Determine the number of pages you'll need for the book, including prematter and post-matter pages.

2. Divide the number by four.

3. Cut white paper into a size that is *double* the width of the desired book page, but the exact length of the desired page, creating the number of sheets determined in Step 2. For instance, if the size of the finished page is 10 inches in length and 9 inches in width, and the book will be 48 pages long, you'll want to cut 12 pages ($48 \div 4 = 12$), each of which is 10 inches high and 18 inches across.

4. Place the paper in a stack, and fold the stack in half, folding the left side over the right side so that it forms a book. Then place staples down the center, where the binding would be, to hold the sheets together.

5. Generate the text on a computer or type-writer, and paste each block of text on the appropriate page.

6. Create your black-and-white sketches and two or three pieces of completed art, paste them on the appropriate pages, and you're done!

not go to the trouble of completing all of the art for the project, as this will be quite time-consuming and will not improve your chances of having the book accepted. Then make color copies of the mock-up and send the copies—not the original mock-up. Be sure to mention the enclosed dummy in your cover letter. (For step-by-step instructions on creating a dummy picture book, see the inset above.)

Although it is ideal to submit the dummy described above, it is also permissible to omit the mock-up and simply send color copies or printed samples of illustrations that you have created for other projects. (Do not send slides!) Again, you'll want to mention in the cover letter that you would like to create the illustrations for your own book.

If You're an Artist or Photographer, But Not a Writer

Just as editors are always looking for that new writer, both editors and art directors are always open to acquiring new illustrators. They're also interested in photographers for their nonfiction books, as well as for those fiction books that they feel would best be complemented by photos rather than other types of illustrations.

If you're predominantly an illustrator and wish to have your work considered by a children's publishing house, start by researching the various companies—just as if you were a writer looking for a home for his book. Look at catalogues, and page through children's books at libraries and bookstores. You'll find that some houses use black-and-white art, while some use only color illustrations—that some use photos, and some don't. And while some use photos of only nature, for instance, the needs of other publishers vary from book to book. It should go without saying that you'll want to contact only those publishers who are a good match for the type of art you produce.

Just as a writer should always secure writer's guidelines, an illustrator should always obtain illustrator's guidelines for every company of interest. You'll soon discover that illustrators should submit materials to the company's art director, rather than an editor. The guidelines will also tell you exactly what the company wants to receive. Many prefer *tearsheets*—printed color samples of published work, torn out of a magazine or other source. Other companies, however, prefer to receive different materials, such as slides. You'll want to submit exactly what the publisher requests, accompanying the material with a cover letter and—when requested—a resumé that shows your work experience. You'll also want to include an SASE if you wish to have the materials returned to you.

When you send in your samples, never, never, never (got that?) send in originals. Originals can easily get lost or damaged. Moreover, you'll want to make a number of copies so that you can send your work out to several companies at the same time. Remember that you hope to have your work put on file for future projects. It's unlikely that any company will be able to give you a job right away.

If you happen to live near any publishing houses, consider dropping off your portfolio at the front desk—as long as the company's guidelines permit this approach. Be sure to include a note saying when you'll be picking the portfolio up.

Here are some other tips for illustrators:

❏ Unless company guidelines request only images of wildlife, for instance, make sure that your samples include images of children!

If you're interested in illustrating children's books, be sure to obtain the illustrator's guidelines from each publishing company of interest. The guidelines will tell you exactly what the company wants to receive and exactly who should receive it.

Recently, while attending a conference, I was approached by an illustrator who months before had sent original artwork to an editor in hopes of landing a job. How, she asked, might she go about getting the art returned to her? I didn't have the heart to tell her that she would probably never see those illustrations again. The lesson is clear, though: Never send originals!

❏ Don't make the mistake of presenting your artwork in elaborate packages. Let your art speak for itself.

❏ Obtain critiques of your work at writer's and illustrator's conferences, and make good use of what you're told. If an editor or art director returns your work with suggestions for improvement, take his words to heart, redo the art, and send it back with a follow-up letter.

Finally, if you are truly committed to getting your illustrations into print, consider working with an art representative—especially if you want to work for a large publishing house. Just as the larger firms are generally most receptive to manuscripts presented by literary agents, most will give greater priority to artwork presented by a rep.

CONCLUSION

If you have prepared each component of your submission package with thought and have carefully selected the publishing houses to which you will submit your work, you have greatly increased the chances that your proposal will elicit a positive response. In the next chapter, I present a proven system for sending your package to the publishers you've chosen. This system will help you keep your costs down and capitalize on any feedback you receive, all the while maximizing your chance of success.

CHAPTER 6

*U*SING THE SQUARE ONE SYSTEM

When I finish preparing a submission package, I'm sometimes so excited that I want to send it to all of the publishers on my list at once. At other times—when I have a specific publisher in mind—I'm tempted to mail out a single package in hopes that the chosen house will snap it up. But over the years, I have learned that neither of these strategies is a good option.

For starters, the first choice—mailing the proposal to everyone on the list—would be quite expensive. Moreover, as you'll learn later in the chapter, the job of gathering the data you need to complete the mailing can be daunting if you decide to research every company at once. Finally, it's important to keep in mind that although most publishers are likely to respond to your package with form letters, some may offer valuable feedback. If your letters are sent out all at once, you will receive this feedback only after the publishers on your list have been contacted, and will therefore not have the opportunity to fine-tune your package during the submission process.

What about the alternative of sending your proposal out to only your "dream" publisher? While this may seem cost-effective, it's certainly not time-effective. It can take six weeks or more to receive an answer from a publisher. If that publisher does *not* opt to give you a contract, do you really want to wait that long before sending out additional submissions? At that rate, over a year may pass before you receive any positive word about your proposal!

The Square One System for proposal submission is a carefully planned program that guides you in sending out your proposal in groups, with the first group going to those publishers who best meet the criteria you established in earlier chapters. Therefore, this program can save you time and money by having you first contact those companies that you favor most highly. (If the publisher you really want to work with accepts your proposal, there may be no need to contact the editors at the bottom of your list.) This system also breaks the submission process into small steps, each of which can easily be managed, and enables you to benefit from any feedback you receive along the way. But most important, the Square One System maximizes your chance not only of getting your manuscript into publication, but of getting it into publication with a company that will work with you to produce a book of which you can be proud. This chapter will show you how it's done—step by step.

STEP ONE:
PRIORITIZE THE PUBLISHERS ON YOUR LIST

In Chapter 4, you formulated your criteria for choosing appropriate publishers for your submission, and composed a list of likely candidates. You now hopefully have a list of at least two dozen publishing houses. But chances are that all of these publishers are not equally appealing. Depending on your criteria, you may, for instance, favor only the smaller publishing houses, the best-known publishing houses, or the houses found in your particular area of the country. Whatever these preferred companies may be, you probably feel a certain thrill at the idea of seeing one of their logos on the title page of your children's book.

Now it's time to prioritize the publishers on your list. Start by selecting the five companies that you feel best meet your criteria, and write the names of these A List companies at the top of a piece of paper. Look at your long list again, and choose the *next* ten companies that appeal to you. Write the names of these B List companies below the A List. Finally, write the names of the remaining companies—the C List—at the bottom of the page. Your prioritized list should, of course, contain all of the companies that appeared on your original list, but should name them in order of preference, with the most promising and desirable ones appearing at the top. In Step Two, you'll work with the first five publishers on your list, verifying the information needed to send out your first submission packages.

STEP TWO:
DETERMINE THE CORRECT ADDRESSES & EDITORS

In Chapter 5, I mentioned how important it is to direct your package to a specific editor rather than to the company as a whole or, for instance, to "The Picture Book Division." Publishing companies are busy places, and everyone from the receptionist to the publisher usually has more work than she can comfortably handle. For that reason, you cannot assume that the person who opens your package will take the time to forward your proposal to the appropriate editor. To prevent your manuscript from remaining in the so-called slush pile for days, weeks, or months, it is necessary to find the name and title of the appropriate editor and to send the package directly to her. And, of course, to make sure that package reaches that editor, you'll have to find the correct address—the address of the building that actually houses the editorial department and not, for instance, the company's corporate headquarters or warehouse.

When you composed the list of publishers in Chapter 4, you jotted down the appropriate contact information for each publisher, including the address, phone number, and—to the best of your ability—the name of the editor who should receive your submission package. Even if you feel that your research provided you with exactly the information you need, you must double-check it through a phone call. As I've mentioned in earlier chapters, the world of books is a fluid one in which editors come and go and companies merge and sell off divisions, all at a dizzying speed. So the person who edited middle grade fiction when the book you used as your resource went to press may not be the editor of that category of books by the time you send out your submission packages. Just as important, like any company, a publishing house can change its address. So to get the up-to-the-minute information you need, you'll have to place a phone call. And, of course, if your source books were unable to provide you with the name of a likely contact person, a phone call to the editorial department is your best bet.

If you're intimidated by the idea of calling an editor, relax. You do not want to speak to the editor at this time, as most won't discuss a project with an unknown author until they have a submission package in hand. You simply want to ask the person who answers the phone—probably an editorial assistant—if your proposal for, say,

Even if you managed to find complete contact information in your resource books, you'll want to double-check it through a phone call. The world of publishing is one of rapid change, and the acquisitions editor of yesterday may not be the acquisitions editor of today.

**From *Beating the Bounds*
by Thomas Hughes**

Illustration by Kate Greenaway

a nonfiction easy reader should be sent to the address and editor you have noted. If you're in luck, the person you contact will politely provide you with the information you're seeking. You should then confirm the spelling of that editor's name, her title, the name of the publisher (in case it has changed since you composed your list), and the mailing address. However, don't be surprised if the staff member refuses to give you the name of the appropriate editor. Many publishing houses are very protective of their editors and try to screen them from unwanted phone calls and unsolicited manuscripts. But don't cross a publishing house off your list simply because the person who picked up the phone is not especially cooperative. Simply verify the address, and direct that particular package to the editor of the appropriate division—the Early Picture Book Editor, for instance—so that when it arrives, those who route the mail will deliver it to the correct person.

Occasionally, even though your initial research indicated otherwise, the editorial assistant may tell you that the company is no longer accepting unsolicited manuscripts. This is most likely to happen after a company or division has been inundated with submissions. In this situation, just remove that company from your A list and place it on the B list. In a couple of months, contact the publishing house again to see if it has reversed its policy. If not, move it to your C list. Eventually, that publisher may have to come off your lists altogether, but for now, don't rule it out.

Every once in a while, you may actually get an editor on the phone. While this may be unnerving, try to make the best of this wonderful opportunity. No, this isn't the time to launch into a five-minute speech about your book proposal. But you could quickly indicate, in ten words or less, the type of book you're sending, and confirm that she's the person to whom you should address the proposal. If so, be sure to modify your cover letter so that it leads with the words, "As we discussed in our phone conversation of April 5. . . ." Sometimes an editor will tell you that your proposal sounds interesting. At other times, she might reject it outright, possibly saying that she's just signed on a book with a similar theme. If she is even remotely encouraging, ask her if you can send her your next proposal. Then be sure to keep her name and number on file.

At the end of each phone call, be sure to request a company catalogue. Why? A catalogue can tell you a great deal about the company that produced it, and therefore may be useful later, when you may have to choose which of several companies you want to publish your book. If the person on the phone gives you a choice, ask for the specialty catalogue—in other words, a catalogue that contains only those titles in your area of interest. If a specialty catalogue is not available, ask for a full catalogue and a frontlist catalogue. (For more information on this, see the inset "Reading a Catalogue Like a Book" on pages 162 to 163.)

STEP THREE: FILL OUT YOUR TRACKING CHART

You now have all the information you need to send your submission package to the first five companies on your list. But instead of rushing out those first packages, take the time to fill in the information on your Tracking Chart. (See pages 164 to 165.) At this point, of course, you'll be able to fill out only the first two columns: the publishing company's name, address, phone number, and other contact information, including the name and title of the appropriate editor; and the date that you requested the catalogue. As you actually mail out packages and, later, receive the responses from the publishing houses, though, you can fill in the Date Catalogue Received, Date Package Sent, Date Response Received, Outcome, and Feedback columns.

If you choose to recreate the Tracking Chart on paper and to write in the information by hand, be sure to leave space between the different entries so that you'll have room to fill in the information as you receive responses and review catalogues. Another option is to create a table in your computer and fill it in as appropriate during the submissions process.

You may wonder why it's desirable to keep track of your mailings and responses. Although you may be one of the lucky authors who immediately receives a positive response from the publisher at the top of your list, chances are that it will take some time to actually go to contract on your book. In the meantime, you'll probably be sending out a lot of letters and receiving a lot of letters and catalogues in return. A conscientiously filled-out Tracking Chart will allow you to quickly check when you sent the submission package out to a particular publisher, when—and if!—you received a catalogue, and when you received a response to your proposal. The data on your sheet may also provide clues about the publishing company

If possible, create your Tracking Chart on your computer. This will enable you to easily add information as you receive responses to your proposal.

Reading a Catalogue Like a Book

Before writing your book, you may have received book catalogues in the mail from time to time. Perhaps you leafed through them to see if they contained anything of interest. What you probably did not realize is that a publishing company's catalogue provides the reader with far more than a listing of its books. As an extension of the company's marketing department, it is a clear reflection of how that company packages and markets its products—not only through its catalogues, but through all its marketing tools.

Depending on the company, it may offer only one catalogue at any given time, or it may produce several, each of which serves a different purpose. Some companies—especially small companies—may produce only a *full catalogue*. This catalogue includes both frontlist titles, which are new releases brought out for the current selling season, and backlist titles, which were published prior to the current season. Most companies offer both a full catalogue and a *frontlist catalogue*—a catalogue that presents only new books. Some companies also offer *specialty catalogues,* which include only the books in a specific area of interest. For instance, a company may produce a catalogue of education-related books for schools and libraries.

When you receive one or more catalogues from a publishing house, first look at the covers. Are they attractive and enticing, or are they dull and unappealing? Are they printed in full color, or are they black and white? Some companies invest a great deal of time, money, and care in their catalogue covers so that their catalogues will be noticed and read. Others, unfortunately, farm the cover design out and use whatever is given to them—even if the result is unattractive. As a

writer, you want your book featured in a catalogue that invites the reader to pick it up and look inside.

Now, open the catalogue and examine its listings. Note whether the interior is printed in black and white or in color, whether the covers of the books are displayed, and whether the format invites you to look further or lulls you to sleep with its ho-hum layout.

Pay special attention to the titles of that company's books. Some publishers work hard to choose book titles that are both appropriate and catchy—that both tell the reader what the book is about and engage her interest. Don't underestimate the power of a title. When your book is displayed on the shelf of a bookstore, it is often the title that determines whether the consumer takes the book off the shelf or leaves it there to gather dust. A title can make or break a book.

Now read the book descriptions. The quality and length of these descriptions can vary widely from catalogue to catalogue and from company to company. In the catalogue you're examining, are the descriptions full or skimpy, lively or boring? Do they give you a clear idea of what each book is about, or do they fail to provide any useful information? In other words, do they make you want to order the books, or do they make you want to toss the catalogue into your recycling pile?

Finally, compare the company's presentation of its frontlist books with that of its backlist books. While most companies devote a little more space to a frontlist title than to a backlist book, some nevertheless feature both frontlist and backlist titles in full-color pages, display the book covers of all their titles, and provide well-crafted and intriguing descriptions for every single book. Other companies, unfortunately, give their backlist titles little attention. They may, for instance, merely list their older books in a lackluster black-and-white section, and omit both a photo of the book cover and a description of the book. Why is it so important to analyze the company's treatment of backlist and frontlist titles? Think about all those wonderful children's books—from older classics like *Little Women* to modern classics like *Goodnight Moon*—that generate sales year after year, decade after decade, as new readers discover them. That's what you want to happen to your book. If you work with a company that will give your book only one chance to be a frontlist success, and then relegate it to an unappealing backlist, chances are that this won't happen. But as many small publishing companies have shown, continual promotion of an older title can lead to a long life—and a profitable one.

When you have finished reviewing a catalogue, don't forget to note your impressions in your Tracking Chart and to put the catalogues away for safe keeping. You have learned how to "read" a catalogue, and this skill will serve you well as you review the responses to your submission packages and—if you're lucky!—pick and choose among the positive responses, selecting the company that will provide you with the most rewarding working relationship.

itself. For instance, if the catalogue you requested fails to arrive or arrives only after you've made several follow-up phone calls, you will have learned something about the operation of that company. This, like the catalogue itself, will help you select the company with which you ultimately choose to work.

STEP FOUR:
MAIL OUT THE FIRST FIVE SUBMISSION PACKAGES

And now the moment you've been waiting for—the release of your creations into the hands of the five editors at the top of your list! First, finalize the five letters by adding the date; the name and address of the publishing company; and the editor's name and title. (See the sample letters on pages 124 to 125, and 127 to 129.) Remember that unless you know the editor, this is no time for informality. The salutation should read "Dear Ms. Jones" or "Dear Mr. Jones," for instance—not "Dear Susan" or "Dear Bob." Do not use the titles "Mrs." or "Miss" unless you know that this is how the editor prefers to be addressed.

Experience has taught me that if you're using a computer template to generate your cover letters, you have to take special care to

TRACKING CHART

Publisher/Editor/ Contact Information	Date Catalogue Requested	Date Catalogue Received
Kids Press Carol Smith, Editor 999 Lexington Street San Francisco, CA 11937 Phone: 310-555-1222, ext. 342 Fax: 310-555-1122 E-mail: Kids@bks.bks	November 13	November 26 Black and white; boring.
Teen Machine Press Finola Finn, Senior Editor 116 Adolescent Street San Francisco, CA 11937 Phone: 310-555-9721 Fax: 310-555-2943 E-mail: TeenMach@bks.bks	November 14	December 1 Full color; well written.

make all the changes necessary in each individual letter. That means that if your first letter is to Mr. John Smith and your second is to Ms. Ellen Randolph, you must remember to change the name not only in the address field but also in the salutation, and you have to make sure that any references to the editor or publishing house that appear within the body of the letter—as well as references to the materials being enclosed—are changed as well. Never send anything to an editor until you've read it over several times and you're certain of perfection.

Take the time and care to spell both the name of the editor and the name of the publishing company correctly. Remember that spelling counts in every element of a submission package. And while a busy editor may not notice your misspelling of the word "transcendental"—although I wouldn't count on it!—she will certainly notice a misspelling of her own name. I can't tell you how many letters I have received addressed to "Lisa Burby" or "Liza Berby." While I didn't toss the packages into the kill pile, these errors certainly did not assure me that the author was a careful and conscientious writer.

Date Package Sent	Date Response Received	Outcome (yes/no/maybe)	Feedback
November 20	December 20	No	None
November 20	January 2	Maybe	Liked concept. Asked for remainder of ms.

Make a copy of each cover letter, and place it in a file. Then type out the envelopes using the correct editor's name, title, and address. Again, be careful. This is no time to make a careless error. (For more guidelines regarding this final step in sending out submission packages, see "Your Submission Package Checklist" on page 166.) If your package is only a few pages in length, a standard white #10 envelope—one that is $4\frac{1}{8}$-x-$9\frac{1}{2}$ inches—is just fine. The editor will find it easy to handle, and it will look businesslike. Of course, you will have to fold the letter, table of contents, and other materials in thirds, and the self-addressed stamped envelope in half so that everything will fit in your envelope. If your sample chapters, if any, run more than a few pages in length, though, you'll want to use a 9-x-12-inch envelope. Although this will increase your mailing costs by a few cents per package, it will accommodate the bulkier enclosures and will enable everything to lie flat. In my opinion, it also looks neater when it arrives in the editor's hands, which is why I use this size envelope for all my submissions. Rightly or wrongly, I also feel that it is less likely to get lost in the slush pile. Is bigger better? I don't know, but at least it's neater. And if your submission package is sizeable, it's really the only way to go.

I highly recommend that you use regular mail to send out your submission packages. Registered or overnight mail may get the envelope there sooner, but it's not going to get your submission read any faster. And avoid faxing anything to an editor unless you're specifically asked to do so. Faxed materials can easily be lost, and even if they aren't, they are never as attractive and readable as originals and photocopies. You want to put your best foot forward, so do all you can to ensure that your package is as neat and attractive as it can be.

Your Submission Package Checklist

Throughout this chapter and Chapter 5, I present some important submission package do's and don'ts. As you begin mailing your packages out to publishing houses, keep in mind that all of this information is intended to help your package earn a positive response. The following checklist will ensure that the all-important details will not be forgotten. As you prepare to mail out your packages, be sure that you:

☐ Include a cover or query letter, as well as any other materials requested in the company's writer's guidelines, such as an annotated table of contents, a book overview, and sample chapters. Be sure to enclose a self-addressed, stamped envelope (SASE) in every package.

☐ Type, rather than handwrite, all the elements of your package, including the mailing label.

☐ Place the elements of your package in order, with the cover or query letter on top; followed by the contents, the overview or synopsis, and the sample chapters, per the writer's guidelines requests; and, finally, the SASE.

☐ Address both the cover letter and envelope to a specific editor by name, or at least to the editor of the appropriate division. Make sure to spell the names of both the editor and the publishing company correctly.

☐ Make a copy of each cover or query letter for your files and fill in your Tracking Chart with all the appropriate information.

☐ Place your materials in a plain envelope—either a #10 business-size envelope or a 9-by-12-inch envelope, as the bulk of your mailing requires.

☐ Avoid "protecting" your envelope by enclosing it in plastic wrap or sealing it with packing tape. The envelope should be neat in appearance and easy to open.

☐ Make sure to use the proper amount of postage on both the outgoing envelope and the SASE. You don't want your package to arrive on the editor's desk marked "postage due," and you don't want to delay your receipt of the editor's response by having the SASE returned to the editor for insufficient postage.

Finally, fill in the Date Package Sent column of your Tracking Chart. You can sit back and relax now, or better yet, you can get to work on your next book!

STEP FIVE: BE PATIENT!

Now that your first five submission packages have been sent out, you may be tempted to start checking your mailbox every day, looking for a response. But, as mentioned earlier, it may take days or weeks for some of the editors to even open your package. So try to cultivate patience during this time. The responses will arrive; they just won't arrive as quickly as you might want them to.

Some authors call each editor a few days after they have sent out their submission packages. They hope that if the editor has already looked at the package, she will discuss it with them, and that if the editor has *not* yet opened the package, the call will inspire her to do so. I strongly suggest that you avoid making these phone calls. The editor will get to your package as her workload allows, and will probably not appreciate your efforts to hurry her. And if she has already reviewed the package, there is a very good chance that she won't remember your proposal simply because she sees so many of them. All editors tell me that while they sympathize with a writer's anxiety, they don't want phone calls. Therefore, it is highly unlikely that your call will result in a satisfying and helpful response. And if the editor feels she's being pestered, your follow-up call will work against you.

Once your first group of submission packages is in the mail, avoid the temptation to make follow-up phone calls. This tactic is unlikely to increase your chance of getting a contract, and may actually work against you.

During this waiting period, can you do anything that will increase your chance of getting your book published? You can, of course, begin performing the research needed to send out the second group of proposals. And you can review any catalogues that arrive so that you can start learning more about the publishing companies on your list. (Don't forget to record everything you receive on your Tracking Chart.) If you have not already examined books published by these companies, this would be a good time to visit your local bookstore or library. Pay particular attention to those books that are in the same category as yours, and examine them as critically as possible. Are the covers attractive? Do the books seem to have been well edited? (In other words, do they read well?) Is the typeset page pleasing to the eye? Are the illustrations of good quality? Does the publishing company ever highlight its books by arranging for special displays in bookstores? The answers to these questions will tell you a great deal about each of the publishing houses.

I suggest that, hard though it may be, you wait six weeks before sending out the second wave of submission packages. That's the time that most editors say it takes to get to the proposals on their desks. Hopefully, during that time, you will receive responses to some or all of the initial five packages. Perhaps one of the editors you contacted will even request further material! If so, consider yourself fortunate, and respond in as timely a manner as possible. In this situation, I usually call the editor and ask if I can fax the new material to her or send it overnight. Then I write "Requested Materials" on the fax cover page or envelope, as the case may be, to indicate that I'm responding to a specific request. Just don't stop sending out submission packages! I cannot overemphasize the fact that a letter expressing interest in your project is not the same as a signed contract. Many writers, including me, have received these requests only to find a rejection letter in the mailbox a few weeks later. Sometimes, after seeing the additional material, the editor may decide that the project is not right for her company. And, of course, after learning more about the publishing company, you may decide that you'd be happier working with another house.

If you do not receive a positive response from this first group of editors, don't be discouraged. Keep in mind that most writers have to contact quite a few publishing companies before they elicit any interest on the part of an editor.

When an editor decides that she is not interested in a project, she usually responds to the author via a form letter. However, occasionally—and I do mean only occasionally—an editor does provide the author with some feedback on the proposal. For instance, the editor may say that the topic of the book is great, but that the focus is too limited and should be expanded. Or she may want the book to be written for a different age group. If you are lucky enough to receive feedback such as this, try to consider the editor's recommendations with an open mind. You may decide that they are just what your book needs to make it more marketable—or you may find the suggested changes very unappealing. Whatever your response, I do suggest that you call the editor and thank her for her comments. During your conversation, remind her of the letter she sent and ask if she

---

If you do not receive a positive response from the first group of editors to whom you send your proposal, don't be discouraged. Keep in mind that most writers have to contact quite a few publishing companies before they elicit any interest on the part of an editor.

would be interested in the book if you made the recommended alterations. If she answers in the negative, ask if she knows of another publishing company that might be interested in your book. Though this may strike you as a rude question, it can actually be quite fruitful, as editors get to know other editors in the course of their work.

Sometimes an editor will reject a book because she has already signed on a similar project. Try to see the silver lining in this cloud. It means that you've hit upon a desirable topic, and that your book might be of interest to another publisher. If you receive a rejection for this reason, again, give the editor a call, thank her for her letter, and ask if she might be interested in considering your book a year from now. If she says yes, and if you don't get any other bites in the meantime, you can always resubmit the package, along with a reminder of your earlier conversation. While you're speaking to the editor, also ask her if there are any other topics in which she might be interested. If she suggests a subject that holds appeal for you, get to work, but only after determining that she will consider it when you have it in proposal form. When you send in the proposal, be sure to write "Requested Material" on the envelope and to remind the editor of your earlier conversation, mentioning the date of your talk in the first paragraph of your cover letter. Also be sure to get the package out quickly, before the idea ceases to have appeal for the editor.

Finally, if an editor's comments make sense to you, make any necessary changes in your package before mailing out the next round of submissions. Perhaps the modifications will lead to a more encouraging response from the remaining companies on your list.

If an editor is not interested in your current book, but suggests another project that appeals to you, be sure to submit a new proposal as soon as possible, before the editor loses interest in the concept.

STEP SIX:
MAIL OUT THE NEXT TEN SUBMISSION PACKAGES

About six weeks after sending out the first wave of proposals, prepare and send out submission packages to the next ten companies—the B List. Be sure to follow Steps Two, Three, and Four carefully, researching names and addresses, filling out your Tracking Chart, and finalizing each package by adding the appropriate information.

As discussed earlier in the chapter, if you received feedback from any of the editors on the first mailing list, you may want to amend one or more portions of your submission package. If you decide to do so, be sure to take the same care you took when preparing the

E-Mail Submissions

As we all become more computer savvy, it can be tempting to save yourself the time and expense of mailing your proposal the old-fashioned way by opting for an e-mail submission. After all, your proposal elements—the cover or query letter, annotated table of contents, etc.—can easily be sent as attachments. And they'll get there so much faster than they would by snail mail! In addition, wouldn't an e-mail lend some measure of urgency to your proposal?

Well, it all sounds good in theory, but there's no guarantee that an e-mail submission will receive prompt attention from an editor. Why? Because when I asked editors if they accept e-mail submissions, they all sighed and said, "Do you know how many e-mails I get a day? I can go out of the office for an hour and come back to 400 messages!" In fact, editors complain that e-mail has only made their job harder because now in addition to submissions sent by regular mail, they have all those e-mails to worry about. As a result, many editors admit to ignoring a good number of their e-mails. Think about how you feel when your message in-box is filled with e-mails from people you don't know. Your first impulse is to treat them like junk mail and delete them unread.

Also realize that if an editor were to open your attachments, she would still need to print them out so that she could review a hard copy. That takes time as well as money in the form of paper and ink. Editors are also understandably concerned about opening attachments, which could carry viruses. So, you see, as lovely as the idea may be, there are many reasons why your proposal won't get the red carpet treatment if it arrives by e-mail.

I suggest e-mailing your proposal under only two conditions—if the writer's guidelines specifically say that it's okay to do so, or if you've made contact with an editor who has given you permission to send an electronic submission. In either case, be sure to send your proposal components as attachments. Otherwise, the documents can lose attributes ranging from paragraph breaks to italics, and arrive as a jumble of hard-to-read words. If the editor has asked you to send a proposal by e-mail, make sure your subject field says something like, "Requested proposal materials for *The Perfect Girl*." This will prevent the editor from deleting it as an unsolicited message.

Finally, because you can't always tell if your e-mail has actually arrived in the editor's in-box or is floating in cyberspace, call the editor to let her know that you have sent an e-mail, and request that she inform you of its safe arrival. After reviewing the proposal, she may e-mail you her response or she may call you. But chances are that you'll have to wait just as long as you would have waited if the submission had been mailed from a post office.

original package. Read through the new letter, table of contents, and other package components, checking for spelling, grammar, punctuation, flow, organization, and style. It should go without saying that any change made in one portion of the package should be reflected, as necessary, in all the other portions. For example, if an editor suggests that the book be reworked for middle grade students rather than the young adult readers you initially targeted, you want this to be reflected not only in your sample chapters but also in your cover letter.

If you feel that you benefited from the comments and suggestions of the friend who read your original submission package, by all means ask that person to review any subsequent revisions. And as the catalogues and letters arrive in response to your phone calls and submissions, be sure to keep your Tracking Chart up-to-date.

STEP SEVEN:
MAIL OUT THE REMAINING SUBMISSION PACKAGES

After you mail out the second group of packages, wait a month to six weeks. Then repeat all of the steps necessary to send out the remaining proposals.

If you've already received several requests for additional material as a result of your earlier mailings, and they came from publishers who are high on your list, there's no requirement that you continue the submission process. You may want to channel your energy into perfecting the material requested by the editors, like sample chapters. If these companies continue to respond in a positive manner, you may never have to send out another submission package for your book. And, of course, if the editors decide that your book isn't for them, you can always continue the submissions process where you left off.

If you receive a number of requests for additional material, don't feel that you have to continue the submission process. It may be best to focus your energy on perfecting the material requested by the editors.

STEP EIGHT: REVIEW YOUR RESULTS
AND ASSESS YOUR OPTIONS

At this point, you've sent out proposals to every publisher on your list. Now is the time to assess the results of your efforts.

Maybe you've received positive responses from one or more companies who are prepared to offer you a contract. If so, congratulations! You should now turn to Chapter 7, "The Deal," to learn about publishing contracts. You'll want to understand all you can to make the most of this important document. And if two or more companies

From *Through the Looking Glass* by Lewis Carroll

Illustration by John Tenniel

are vying for the opportunity to publish your book, by comparing the contracts, you may be better able to decide which working relationship would benefit you the most.

Possibly some editors had requested additional materials, but after reviewing the complete manuscript, they rejected your project. I know how disappointing this can be. But don't take it personally, as there may be absolutely nothing wrong with your book. As I said back in Chapter 2, there are many factors beyond your control that can affect an editor's decision, from personal bias against a topic to poor timing. Sometimes writers are simply in the wrong place at the wrong time. Maybe the editor has been inundated of late with easy readers with a grandparents theme so that no matter how unique your book is, she can't get beyond the topic to give it a chance. Or perhaps the sales department determined that the book wouldn't earn the company enough money. Whatever the reason, at this point, it's fine to give the editor a call. Once an editor has become sufficiently interested to request further materials, she may be willing and able to provide you with feedback. If what she says makes sense, you'll be able to use it as a guide for reworking your book into a more marketable project.

Sometimes It Pays to Listen . . .

Earlier in the chapter, I mentioned that editors are sometimes interested enough in a manuscript to suggest changes. Of course, it may not be in your best interests—or, for that matter, the book's best interests—to make the suggested revisions. But at one time or another, a number of now-famous children's authors did follow an editor's advice, and enjoyed truly remarkable results. Here are just a few examples:

☐ Virginia Lee Burton's *Mike Mulligan and His Steam Shovel*—a 1939 Caldecott Medal winner—was originally a story about a traveling dust bunny! Fortunately for generations of children, the editor suggested that the author rewrite her book with a slightly different focus.

☐ Initially, *The Carrot Seed* by Ruth Krauss was a manuscript of 10,000 words. Then an editor sug-

gested that the author pare it down. The version published in 1945 had only 109 words—and decades later, the book is still in print.

☐ Ever heard of *A Week With Willie Worm*? That's because an editor told author Eric Carle that the story was silly and should be reworked. The result was the best-selling *The Very Hungry Caterpillar*, first published in 1969.

If you didn't receive any positive responses to your proposals, you need to analyze the reason for this result. While the Square One System is designed to increase your odds of eliciting a positive response from editors, when there's a problem with the package itself, the system isn't likely to work. To help determine if the package may be the problem, turn to Chapter 8, "When It Doesn't Happen." This chapter is designed not only to guide you in pinpointing any flaws, but also to help you rectify them so you can enjoy more positive results with later submissions. In addition, it looks at a number of proven alternatives, including self-publishing.

Perhaps you feel strongly that your package isn't the problem. Or maybe you have already revised it and believe that it's ready to meet the needs of the publishers in which you're interested. What are your options now? First, consider waiting about six months from the time you began the submissions process, and resubmitting the package to the publishers on your original list. Why would someone who rejected your proposal be interested several months from now? For one thing, if you've changed the focus or scope of your book or otherwise altered your package, these modifications may make the book more marketable. But another important element—one alluded to earlier in the chapter—is timing. To a great degree, acquisitions editors look for books that are in line with their company's publishing program—a program that guides editors to certain types of books in certain areas of interest. These programs change periodically according to consumer demand. And as they change, editors begin looking for books in areas that they may have previously ignored. For example, until *Harry Potter* came on the scene, children's fantasy had a loyal following, but didn't have the same widespread appeal it does today. As the public's demand for this genre grew, more and more juvenile fantasy books appeared on the market. Similarly, after the events of September 11, 2001, nonfiction topics that had previously been ignored or mentioned only as parts of other books—subjects like Islam—became popular, and acquisitions editors become anxious to fill the need.

But editors are affected by far more than just their company's publishing program. Every editor is an individual who is influenced by many factors, from the people she knows to the television shows she watches to the books and magazines she reads. Many times, an editor will simply become excited about a subject because of a story

Any number of factors— from a change in a company's publishing program to an editor's new awareness of an issue— can cause an editor to be interested in a project that she rejected only a few months earlier. That's why it sometimes pays to wait six months after the time you began the submission process, and resubmit your package to the companies on your original list.

or a bit of information that she heard or read somewhere along the line. Then, when a proposal for a book on this topic lands on her desk, she can't move quickly enough to contact the author and request further material. While you may find this a bit maddening—do you have to pray that an editor develops an interest in the plight of endangered tigers the day before she receives your submission package?—it does mean that a door that was once closed to you may suddenly open. And the result may be that your book, once rejected out of hand, may now be in great demand.

Is any other option open to you at this point? Consider creating an entirely new list of publishing houses and sending your submission package to them. Literally thousands of publishing companies dot the United States, with new ones cropping up all the time, so it's highly unlikely that your initial list of companies included every house that might be interested in your book. Perhaps when you were compiling your first list, you did not seriously consider the many small companies that are more likely to accept the works of first-time authors. If so, now is the time to look into these smaller houses. Or perhaps you did not sufficiently home in on the publishers that focus on books in your particular area of interest. By creating a new list of publishers and following the system outlined in this chapter, you will greatly increase your odds of finding the right company for your project.

Finally, don't give up! Stay positive and keeping working towards your goal. Many authors receive scores of rejection letters before landing a contract. As you have already gathered, this doesn't mean that you should indiscriminately send out proposals to every publisher large and small, regardless of the company's areas of interest and the quality of its books. (If this book has taught you anything, I hope it's taught you the importance of zeroing in on the publishers that are right for you and your project!) It does, however, mean that it may take longer than you expected to find an editor who appreciates the special merits of your manuscript and has faith in you as an author. By following the Square One System with care, consistency, and perseverance, you will greatly improve your chances of ultimately making contact with the editor who will champion your project and work with you toward the realization of your dream.

CHAPTER 7

THE DEAL

The day you receive your first publishing contract may seem like a dream come true. You've worked long and hard to get to this point and deserve congratulations. It may appear that your work is over—that all you have to do is sit back and wait for your sales to take off. But as you pull the contract out of the envelope and start to scan it, your heart sinks. Printed in small densely packed type, the multi-page document coldly refers to your treasured book as "the said work." Terms like "indemnities" and "force majeure" send a chill up your spine. What does all this legal gobbledygook mean?

Most people are intimidated by contracts, and even if you have dealt with contracts in the past when buying a house or leasing a car, a book contract is a very different animal. But there's no need to panic. The majority of publishing agreements are relatively standard. Although they may vary in length, in the wording used, and in the order in which the topics are covered, all of them cover pretty much the same subjects and offer similar terms. This chapter was designed to explain the standard publishing contract, and to make you aware of the types of terms you are likely to encounter. By the time you finish this chapter, you will have a greater grasp of the rights and responsibilities conferred on you by the agreement, and you will know the warning signs that can alert you to a publisher who may be less than scrupulous in his dealings.

Please be aware that this chapter is *not* intended to provide you with legal advice. If you feel that legal advice is necessary, you should definitely contact a lawyer. In fact, this is one of the first topics I'll cover. But with the help of this chapter, you will be in a better position to figure out the terms of your agreement, and—either alone or with the help of a professional—to ask appropriate questions so that you can make an informed decision regarding the details of your publishing contract.

SHOULD YOU HIRE A LAWYER OR A LITERARY AGENT?

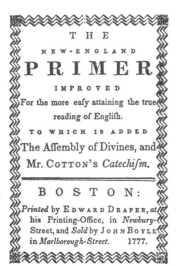

Title Page of *The New England Primer*

Upon receiving their publishing contract, many authors' first question is, "Should I hire a lawyer to review this?" The decision to hire a professional to represent you in negotiations with a publisher is one that is largely based on personal preference. Some authors prefer to manage any negotiations themselves rather than giving a piece of the pie to a lawyer or agent. Others feel that only a lawyer or agent can get them the best possible terms.

If you're not sure whether you want to finalize your contract on your own or with professional help, there are a few facts you should consider. First, while a smart and aggressive attorney can, to some extent, negotiate profitable changes in the agreement, unless he's an *intellectual property lawyer*—one who specializes in literary works and their inherent rights—he can wind up doing you more harm than good. As I mentioned before, publishing contracts are different from those of other industries. A lawyer who is unfamiliar with publishing contract terms could make unreasonable demands on a publisher or focus on the wrong issues. This could result in your starting off your relationship with a publisher on the wrong foot.

Second, although an experienced literary agent may be capable of getting a larger advance, limiting a publisher's rights, and even assisting you later in the publishing process if, for instance, you need someone to interpret a baffling royalty statement, you must pay a high price for this service. While a lawyer may be compensated with a one-time fee, an agent usually works on commission, garnering 10 to 15 percent of both your advance and your royalties. And these payments are expected for the life of the agreement.

When deciding whether to seek representation, it's important to think back to Chapter 2, where you spent some time considering the market for your book. If you feel that your potential audience is large—and that, therefore, your return should also be large—it may make sense to share the profits with someone who can help you get the best possible deal. If, however, your potential audience and expected return are relatively small, you may rightfully question the wisdom of sharing this smaller pie with someone else.

If you *do* decide to hire someone to represent you in negotiations, keep in mind that in addition to being experienced, your representative should be someone with whom you feel comfortable working. This is particularly important if you use a literary agent, as this person may continue to represent you for years to come. Also remember that you should never remove yourself from the bargaining process, leaving the fate of your contract in someone else's hands. Instead, read your contract carefully, and discuss your "wish list" with your representative before negotiations begin. Let him know exactly what is important to you. You may well care about issues that were of little concern to the authors he worked with previously. Only by developing contract literacy through the reading of this chapter and by staying involved in negotiations will you ensure that the terms of your publishing agreement are consistent with your wishes.

Before you hire a lawyer or literary agent to represent you in contract negotiations, consider if the royalties you anticipate receiving justify the cost of hiring a professional.

RULE # 7

Never sign a publishing agreement without understanding all the terms

Most of us have been told since childhood that we should always read something before signing it. But when faced with a long-winded document, many of us barely glance at the words before penning in our names. Trust me when I say that you must take the time to plow through the contract that you have received. Remember that your contract defines every aspect of your agreement with your publisher. When is your manuscript due? How long must the manuscript be? What might cause your book to be taken out of print? Are you expected to take part in a promotional tour? Are you expected to pay for any part of the production process? Your contract spells all of this out. So even if you have hired someone to represent you in negotiations, it is crucial that you read and understand each and every term of the publishing agreement. Whether or not you take the time to read the terms, you will be expected to live by them.

THE CONTRACT

You will be expected to live by the terms of your publishing agreement. For that reason, it is vital that you read and understand each and every term of your contract.

Usually referred to as the "Author/Publisher Agreement," your contract may be five pages or twenty-five pages in length. It may be couched in impenetrable legalese, or it may be worded in relatively plain English. But chances are that much of your contract is "boilerplate"; that is, it follows a formula used throughout the publishing industry, covering the same conditions treated in most publishing agreements. This certainly has been true of the many contracts that I've received. The remainder of this chapter will lead you step by step through a standard publishing contract, explaining the terms and examining the issues to be negotiated.

As you read through the following material, please keep in mind that although most publishing contracts deal with the same subjects, these subjects are discussed under different headings in different contracts. Similarly, the order in which they appear can vary. For ease of understanding, I have tried as much as possible to discuss the various issues in the order in which they appear in *most* contracts, and to choose headings that define the issue being covered. When possible, I have also indicated the headings under which they may be discussed in your own publishing agreement.

Please note that it is virtually impossible to consider every element that may be included in your contract. Some publishing contracts go on for many pages, detailing every situation that may be encountered in the life of the agreement. My intention is to cover only those terms that are most common and/or most important. Should you encounter terms that you don't understand and that cause you concern, do not hesitate to request clarification from your editor or from legal counsel.

Identifying the Parties

Contracts usually start off with a slightly dizzying round of terms that define the parties involved through the use of words and phrases that will appear throughout the contract. The writer of the manuscript is referred to as "the Author." The publishing company is referred to as "the Publisher." If the project involves a ghostwriter—a person who performs the actual writing but isn't credited as the author—he may be referred to as "the Writer." This introduction also states the tentative title of your manuscript and identifies it as "the Work," or "the said Work." Unlike the clauses that follow it, this introductory paragraph doesn't usually appear under a formal heading.

Rights

According to the current Copyright Act, the author is the owner of all rights to the literary work, including the right to publish the work in book form. The author may grant one, several, or all of his rights to the publisher, but such a grant *must* be in writing. The various rights that pertain to the publisher's production of, direct use of, and direct sale of the book are generally covered in a section called "Rights," "Grant of Rights," or "Author's Grant." (For those rights not covered in this section, turn to "Subsidiary Rights" on page 189.)

One of the issues generally defined in this section is "the Territory"—the geographical location in which the publisher has the right to sell this book. This territory usually includes the United States and Canada, North America, or the world.

The contract also generally defines the form of the work to which the publisher's rights extend. For example, it may grant the publisher sole rights to produce the work in book form and/or electronic data form—tapes, disks, diskettes, databases, networks, CD-ROMs, etc. The contract may also specify that the rights include both this edition and future editions, and may state that they extend to hardcover, trade paperback, and/or mass market paperback form. Be aware that if the contract does not specify a form such as hardcover, but does grant rights to print, publish, distribute, and sell the work in any form throughout the world, it means that the grant extends to all possible book forms, from hardcover to CD-ROM.

Usually, the contract specifies the language or languages to which the publisher's rights extend. It could extend the rights to publication or reproduction of the English language only, or it could extend them to "all languages," meaning that the publisher has been granted all translation rights. Stay alert when reading this section of the contract, and make sure that you're not going to be charged a fee for the translation of your book into other languages. Some small houses now charge authors who are unable to translate their own works. While having your book published in Spanish, for instance, may increase your sales, you may not want to have the translation performed at your own expense. If this situation occurs, do your best to negotiate terms that you find acceptable.

Finally, the contract usually defines the time in which the grant is extended in terms of the copyright, which is in effect for the author's life and fifty years thereafter. For instance, the contract might state that the rights are granted "for the full term of all copyright and renewals of copyrights." Rarely does the grant extend for less than the term of the copyright.

Work for Hire

Some publishers in the nonfiction library and school market—and increasingly publishers of fiction books, as well—ask authors to sign a work-for-hire agreement. This agreement is one in which the author is given a lump sum for the manuscript, but receives no royalties. The publisher owns all rights to the book, including the copyright. The author is viewed by the publisher either as an employee of the company or as an independent contractor. Unless otherwise specified, the author's name is printed on the book as the creator of the work.

Usually, a work-for-hire contract is very brief, as many of the issues covered in a standard royalty-based contract are irrelevant in a work-for-hire situation. The author, for instance, need not worry about subsidiary rights, as *all rights* belong to the publisher. However, this type of contract does stipulate when the book must be turned in, the form in which it should be submitted, and the desired length of the work. The contract may also state that the author is responsible for revising the work as desired by the publisher, and it may grant a small number of author's copies and a discount on any further copies desired. In return, of course, the author receives a flat fee and nothing more—no matter how many copies of the book are eventually sold. Moreover, the publisher reserves the right to make any revisions desired without the consent of the author, and to publish it at any time and in any form he sees fit.

Virtually everyone wants royalties. But it's important to remember that many authors who have been granted royalties never receive any money beyond their advance. So if a publisher offers you a decent sum to write a book, and you want to establish yourself as a children's book author, consider accepting the work-for-hire arrangement. Once you get your foot in the door of the publishing world, further opportunities—and far better contracts—may arise.

The Manuscript

Whether called "the Manuscript" or "Delivery of Manuscript," this section of the contract spells out your obligations regarding the delivery of the completed manuscript to the publisher. The contract specifies the date by which the manuscript must be delivered, as well as its length in terms of words. For instance, the contract may say that the manuscript should be "approximately 3,000 words in length"—in other words, about twelve double-spaced manuscript pages. The contract generally also states how the manuscript should be delivered—usually on floppy disk in Word, in English, with a printed-out hard copy as well.

At one time, an author was required to submit only a typed manuscript to the publisher. Now, most writers are expected to include a floppy disk as well.

Keep in mind that even if you've already sent the completed manuscript to the publisher and have received a contract in return, the editor will probably want you to rework it. Therefore, in many circumstances, the due date specifies the date by which the *revised* manuscript must be delivered. In rare instances, however, the Publisher will already have the manuscript in the desired state, and the delivery date will be the date the contract is signed.

Either within this section or within a section called "Publishing Details," the contract may specify the party that will bear certain costs and complete certain tasks relevant to the completion of the manuscript. For instance, the author may be charged with the responsibility of obtaining written permission to reprint any quotations taken from outside sources, or to use any illustrations or photographs required by the publisher. Some contracts specify that any expenses for such permission will be paid by the publisher. Others state that these permissions will be obtained "at the Author's expense." In the latter case, it is expected that the author will pay for the permissions out of his royalty advance. If the author has to bear the cost of preparing an index, this, too, is specified in the contract. Moreover, as discussed earlier, if the work is to be simultaneously printed in another language, the author may be charged with either performing the translation himself or bearing the cost of the translation. All of these points may be negotiable.

All contracts state that the delivered manuscript must be "acceptable to the Publisher" in content and form. In some cases, they also specify that certain items be included, such as a title page, preface or foreword, or table of contents. If the manuscript is not considered satisfactory by the publisher, the contract may demand that the author rework the problem portion of the manuscript within "a reasonable time." Most publishers reserve the right to either prepare the manuscript at the author's expense or terminate the contract if the author does not provide the company with an acceptable manuscript. While this sounds alarming, chances are that with editorial guidance, you will be able to correct any problems before such extreme measures are taken.

Editing, Proofs, and Publication

The publisher's rights and obligations regarding the editing, typesetting, printing, binding, pricing, and marketing of the book, as well as the author's rights and obligations in this regard, may be addressed under a heading such as "Publishing Details," "Publication," "Editing and Proofs," or simply "Proofs."

The publisher normally reserves the right to copyedit the manuscript according to his house style of punctuation, spelling, capitalization, and usage. In some cases, the contract will state that the meaning of the text will not be altered during this copyediting. Often, the contract also states that after the manuscript is edited, the author will have a chance to review it and then make any revisions and corrections, but then must return it within a set period of time. Keep in mind that even if your contract does not state that the author will review the edited manuscript, this is standard practice.

The contract also usually details the author's rights and obligations regarding the *proofs*—the typeset version of the book that is produced after the manuscript has been edited. Generally, the author of a children's book is permitted to review and correct the words themselves, but is not permitted to make changes to the illustrations. Authors—especially first-time authors—are usually sent only a few sample sketches as a courtesy. For the most part, the ultimate decisions regarding art rest with the editor and the artist.

Sometimes the contract specifies the time frame in which the proofs must be returned. The contract may also state that any author's alterations other than corrections of errors made in typesetting will be made "only at the Publisher's discretion," and may be paid for by the author if they are in excess of 10 percent of the cost of typesetting. This last term is included to prevent the author from rewriting

Although children's book authors are permitted to review the typeset proofs and correct the text, they are usually allowed little or no input regarding the illustrations—especially if this is their first book. All decisions about art rest with the editor and the illustrator.

portions of the book after it has been typeset, a situation that would incur extra costs and possible printing and delivery delays.

Normally, the publisher reserves the right to determine what are referred to as the "details of publication"—the format and design of the book; the paper, printing, and binding; the title and price; and the advertising, promotion, and distribution of free copies. Sometimes the contract specifies the form of the book, whether hardcover or paperback. It also may specify time constraints—for instance, that the edition shall be produced "within 18 months from the date of the Publisher's acceptance of the manuscript." And it may specify the imprint under which the work will be published—provided, of course, that the publishing company is large enough to have imprints.

The Author's Copies

Either in a section entitled "Author's Copies" or in one called "Publication," the contract may specify the number of copies that will be given to the author free of charge upon the book's publication. Generally, the author is offered fifteen to twenty-five copies, although some authors receive as many as a hundred free books. I've been offered as few as five copies from smaller houses. If the book is to be published in both hardback and softcover editions, the contract may specify that the author will receive X number of hardback copies and X number of paperback copies.

The contract may also state the discount the author will receive if he chooses to purchase additional copies. Usually a standard trade discount of 40 to 45 percent is given, although an author who wishes to buy a large number of books may be granted a 50-percent discount. Some companies also allow authors to purchase other titles from the publisher's list at a discount of 40 percent.

Be aware that if a contract doesn't spell out what your discount will be, the publisher may choose to give you only a minimal discount, if any. As an author, make sure you know what the price will be if you choose to purchase copies of your own book.

Author's copies are given to the author free of charge upon the book's publication. Additional copies can usually be purchased from the publisher at a discount.

Royalty-Free Copies

Some contracts state that no royalty or other fee will be paid on "Royalty-Free Copies." This means that books sold at or below manufacturing cost; copies that are destroyed; copies that are furnished free; editorial review copies, which are sent to the media to gain publicity; and copies otherwise used to promote the work will not be counted toward your royalties. Usually, books licensed for printing in Braille, or produced as mechanical audio recordings or visual recordings for the blind or other physically handicapped people, are also considered royalty free.

Although this clause may bother you, it's usually impossible to get the publisher to change these terms. After all, you can't charge a book reviewer for the right to read and comment in writing on your book.

The Author's Promotional Responsibilities

In today's competitive market, an author must promote his book in any way he can. If your publisher requests that you participate in publicity tours, newspaper and television interviews, and the like, try to cooperate as fully as possible.

Another subject that may be covered in the contract is the author's responsibility regarding the promotion of the book. For instance, the contract may state that at the publisher's request, the author must participate in a promotional tour of a stated duration, such as two weeks. It may also state that any expenses incurred during such a tour will be paid for by the publisher. Publishers who make such stipulations often explain that the author's participation in publicity activities was a "material inducement" to the publisher to enter the agreement. Other publishers, however, don't specify such activities in writing, although they may verbally request—not demand—that the author involve himself in publicity tours, newspaper and television interviews, and more. Frankly, in today's competitive market, you really must promote your book in any way you can.

If your contract doesn't address the topic of promotion, and you request such a clause as a means of ensuring that your book will, in fact, be promoted, it's unlikely that the publisher will add this term to your agreement. However, this doesn't mean that you shouldn't ask for the clause. By all means, make your wishes known. Then, if your request is denied, ask the publisher for a letter that outlines the proposed marketing program for your title. This will allow you to review the company's promotional plans and to understand the program as it moves forward.

The Out-of-Print Provision

Under a heading such as "Publishing Details" or "Out of Print Provision," the contract should define the circumstances under which the book will be taken out of print—in other words, will no longer be published by that company. The contract will probably indicate that the book will be taken out of print if it "shall cease to be profitable," if sales fall below a certain number of copies per year, or if the publisher doesn't reprint the book within a specified time after the existing inventory has been sold. Once the book has been taken out of print, the publisher usually offers the remaining copies to the author at cost—that is, at the unit print cost for each book—or at a specific discount, plus shipping. If the author doesn't choose to purchase the remaining copies "within a reasonable period of time," the publisher reserves the right to destroy the copies or to *remainder* the book—to sell it for a price that is slightly above or below the manufacturing cost.

Generally, the contract specifies that the rights to the book will revert to the author when the book is declared out of print. If your contract doesn't include this statement, you should make sure that such a provision is added. Remember that if the contract doesn't specify when a book will be declared out of print, the publisher may retain the rights to the book in spite of the fact that he no longer stocks, markets, or sells it. This would be a major problem for you if you decided to market the book on your own.

Royalties

Since most writers are not independently wealthy, they are understandably interested in their *royalties*—the money that will be received based on the sales of their books. Because this subject is one of both great concern and some complexity, it makes sense to explore it in some detail.

Royalties can be calculated in two ways. First, they may be based on the *retail price* of the book. This price is easy to determine in the case of children's trade books, as the retail price is almost always printed on the back of the book or, in the case of hardback editions, on the inside front flap of the paper cover.

Because customers aren't always charged the retail price, royalties are sometimes based on the *net price* of the book, which is the price actually charged by the publisher to the customer. When the book is sold by the company directly to an individual consumer, the net price

The concept of paying an author part of a book's profits was devised by American publishers in the mid-1800s. English poet Elizabeth Barrett Browning was one of the first authors to be offered a royalty by an American publisher. Before that time, publishers simply gave the writer a fixed sum in exchange for all the rights to a book. It is no wonder that so many well-known writers of the past—authors such as James Fenimore Cooper—chose to publish their own works.

is usually the same as the retail price of the book. In other cases, however, books are usually discounted. For instance, when books are sold to bookstores, the discount may range from 20 to 40 percent of the retail price. (In other words, the bookstore pays 80 to 60 percent of the retail price.) When sold to distributors, the discount may range from 50 to 60 percent. (The distributor pays 50 to 40 percent of the retail price.)

When royalties are based on the retail price of the book, they generally range from 5 to 10 percent. (In other words, if the book's price is $10.00, the author makes $.50 to $1.00 per copy.) When royalties are based on the net price of the book, they generally range from 5 to 15 percent. (The author receives $.50 to $1.50 per book.) Usually, trade publishers base their sales on the retail price, while most school and library and educational publishers use the net price.

It's important to be aware that your contract may base your royalties on the retail price in some instances, but on the net price in other instances. For example, a trade publisher may base royalties on the retail price if the discount given to the customer is less than 50 percent, but switch to a percentage of the net price if the discount is equal to or greater than 50 percent, or if the book sells to an outlet other than a bookstore—to a wholesale club, for instance. In such cases, the contract must spell these terms out.

A number of other variations may be found in a single contract. For instance, the publisher may use a sliding scale so that royalties increase as sales increase. As an example, the publisher may pay 10 percent of the retail price for the first 5,000 copies sold; 12.5 percent of retail for the next 5,000 copies sold; and 15 percent of retail for any sales in excess of 10,000 copies. The sliding scale may work in two different ways. When computed on an annual basis, the sliding scale begins at zero each year. When computed on a cumulative basis, all books sold over the years are included in the calculations.

Depending on the publisher's plans for the book, the section on royalties may include a staggering number of possibilities. The contract may, for instance, list different royalty percentages for hardcover copies, trade paperbacks, mass market paperbacks (sometimes referred to as rack-size paperbacks), large-print hardcover copies, large-print paperback copies, audio recordings, and more. The royalty percentage may also vary according to the territory in which the book is sold. The royalty percentage may be 7 percent for books sold within the United States, for instance, but 10 percent for books sold outside the United States.

Some contracts include a section on "holdbacks." This requires some explanation. The publishing industry is unique in that bookstores can send their unsold copies back to the publisher, in which case, the money paid for the books is returned to the stores. Because these returns can be large, some publishers hold back between 20 to 60 percent of the royalty payment until a specified date, at which point the balance is sent to the author. Most trade publishers, as well as some school and library and educational publishers, include a section on holdbacks in their contract. Others simply state that royalties will be paid "on sales, less returns."

Everything gets a little more complicated if an author has a co-author with whom he shares the royalties. In this case, the contract specifies the royalty split. Again, different contracts handle this differently, usually depending on the degree to which each author contributed to the finished work. The royalties may be divided evenly among the authors, or one author may receive a greater share than that awarded to the other contributors.

Note that when picture books are concerned, the illustrator generally splits everything evenly with the author. However, the author's contract does not indicate this split, but simply states the amount received by the author—usually 5 percent of the book's price. The illustrator gets his own contract, separate from the writer's agreement.

If you have written a picture book, remember that the illustrator of your book is considered a collaborator, and will probably be given 50 percent of the royalties from the sale of the book.

The "Royalty" section of the contract also specifies when the publisher will calculate and pay the royalties to the author or authors. Trade book companies generally calculate and pay royalties every six months. Most school and library and educational publishers pay royalties every twelve months

Your publisher will very likely specify both when your royalties will be reported and when you'll receive your actual royalty check. Generally, such reports of payments are promised to arrive within ninety days after the end of each royalty period, although some publishers mail out royalty payments within only sixty days. It's important to note, however, that some publishing agreements specify only when the author will receive the report, not when the amount will be paid. The actual payment may arrive months after the end of the royalty period.

The Advance

Although the advance is usually specified in the "Royalty" section of the contract, it is of such importance to most writers that it merits its own section. Since we all hear about the huge advances that some authors are awarded, this figure might be of more importance to you than the royalties—particularly if you plan to live on the advance while you complete your manuscript. But the reality is that the advance is actually an *advance against royalties,* meaning that the advance isn't additional to your royalties, but is a prepaid portion of future money earned. So if you receive an advance of $1,000, for instance, this amount will be taken out of any future royalty payments.

Advances are usually paid in installments, with the payment schedule varying from publisher to publisher and according to the size of the advance. For instance, the first portion may be paid on the signing of the contract; the second portion, on the receipt of the first two chapters of the manuscript; and the final portion, on the receipt of the balance of the manuscript. Or half may be paid on receipt of the prematter and the first two chapters; and the other half on completion of the manuscript. Almost every contract I've received has given me half the advance on signing, and the remainder upon approval of the manuscript. Only one contract gave me the balance of my advance when the manuscript was ready to be printed. In the case of large advances, payment may be made in as many as ten installments.

Most contracts specify that any portion of the manuscript received must be in "satisfactory" form as judged by the publisher before the corresponding portion of the advance is paid. This doesn't mean that the manuscript won't be edited in-house at this point; it almost certainly will. It means only that you must produce an acceptable first draft.

What happens if a book is put out of print, and the royalties earned by book sales total less than the amount of the advance? Based upon the existing language in the contract, the publisher may have the right to request that the author return the portion of the advance not covered by the sales of the book. While this rarely occurs, *rarely* does not mean *never.* In order to avoid this problem completely, you can request that the advance be paid out on a "non-returnable basis."

A word is in order about advance amounts. While five- and six-figure book deals are often reported in the media, the reality is that most new authors—including those who work with large publishers—usually start with an advance of no more than $3,000. And many new authors earn much less. There are exceptions, of course, but the majority of well-known children's writers—Paula Danziger, Judy Blume, and Gordon Korman, to name just a few—report first-time advances of around $3,000. Naturally, if your first book sells well, you'll be able to negotiate for a significantly higher advance the next time around.

Typical advances for first-time authors range from $1,000 to $5,000, with the average being about $3,000. Small publishers sometimes offer no advance at all.

Subsidiary Rights

The "Subsidiary Rights" section of the contract grants to the publisher certain rights not referred to in the earlier "Rights" portion of the contract. Thus, depending on the "Rights" section, this may include periodical or newspaper publications, either prior to publication of the book (first serial rights) or after publication of the book (second serial rights); condensations and abridgements; book club publications; foreign-language publications; English-language publications not covered in the "Rights" section; reprint editions; motion picture, television, radio, and stage interpretations; audio recordings; electronic recordings; CD-ROMS; public reading rights; Braille, large-type, and other editions for the handicapped; and merchandising/commercial uses, in which a portion of the book or its characters are used to make non-book products such as posters, calendars, greeting cards, coloring books, and toys.

In the case of each of these rights, the contract specifies the allocation of the money received by the publisher from the granting of these rights to third parties. In the case of those forms of the work with which the publishing company doesn't involve itself, the proceeds are usually shared with the author in a fifty-fifty or sixty-forty split. However, in the case of those forms in which the company does involve itself—if, for instance, the publisher owns an audio books company that produces an audio recording of the work—the split is likely to be based upon the standard royalty in that business.

The "Subsidiary Rights" section of the contract may also detail the allocation of any money received by the publisher for premium sales. This occurs when a business or organization wants to purchase a large number of copies for the purpose of providing the book free of charge or at a discounted rate to its customers or members. For instance, an environmental organization might purchase a book about ways in which children can clean up the earth, have it customized so that every cover bears the name of the organization, and then present it to every person who donates to the organization. In some cases, the publisher would make a special low-cost run of the book, using inexpensive paper and customizing it as desired, and sell the book to the organization at a low price. In other cases, the premium would be taken out of existing inventory rather than a special run, but would still involve a bulk sale of the book at a large discount. In the case of premium sales, the author generally receives a royalty of 5 to 10 percent of the amount received by the publisher.

Revisions

Some books become out of date in whole or in part as time passes. This is more of an issue with nonfiction books, as the information in certain areas—technology, for instance—changes frequently. However, publishers sometimes also want to make revisions in a work of fiction, perhaps because a specific term had become politically incorrect. And in other instances, a publisher may want to make changes and/or additions for a special anniversary edition of the title. As a result, some contracts specify that the author must revise the work if the publisher considers it necessary and in the best interests of the work. If the author doesn't prepare a revision "within a reasonable time"—either because he refuses to do so or because he is deceased—the publisher can have the revision prepared by another party, charge the cost against the author's royalties, and add the name of the person who revised the work to the authorship.

Accounting

Either under the heading "Accounting" or one such as "Royalty Statements and Payments," all publishing contracts include certain details about the publisher's records on the contracted book. In general, the publisher agrees to keep records of payments due the author, and to send statements of such payments to the author at times specified in the agreement. The contract may further detail exactly what these statements must include—for instance, the number of copies sold, the list price, the royalty rate, and the amount of royalties.

Most contracts also state that the author or a representative of the author has the right to examine the publisher's records for the book during normal business hours at the author's expense. The contract may or may not specify how often such an audit may be performed. If an error of 5 percent or more is found in the publisher's favor respecting a royalty statement, the money must be promptly paid to the author, and the publisher must contribute to or cover the cost of the examination. It should be noted that if the author or the author's representative accuses the publisher of underpaying the author, the publishing company can take issue with the author's interpretation of the accounting records. Thus, accusations of underpayment don't necessarily result in additional royalties for the author.

Warranty and Indemnification

The publisher must rely upon the author to produce an original work that has never before been published. So in the "Warranties" or "Warranties and Indemnification" section of the contract, the author guarantees that he is the sole proprietor of the work—in other words, that the book is original throughout and hasn't been plagiarized from other sources, with the exception of quoted materials that are being reprinted with written permission of the copyright owner. (For more about this, see "The Manuscript" on page 181.) The author may further guarantee that he has the full power to enter into this agreement and grant those rights granted within the contract; that the work doesn't contain any scandalous, libelous, or otherwise unlawful matter, and that it doesn't invade privacy or otherwise violate any right of privacy; and that no formula or instruction presented in the work would injure either the reader or others.

Either in this section of the contract or in a separate "Indemnities" section, the author usually indemnifies the publisher—that is, protects him—from any loss, damage, or expense that may be incurred if the author is, in fact, accused of breaching any of his warranties. It's worth noting, though, that most publishers have an omissions and errors insurance policy that covers the company if it's sued

Most publishers have an insurance policy that covers the company if it is sued for libel, copyright infringement, or invasion of privacy. To make sure that you are protected, request the addition of a clause which states that if any action is brought against you, you will be covered by the publisher's insurance policy.

for libel, copyright infringement, or invasion of privacy. To make sure that you're properly protected, you should request the addition of a clause which formally states that if any action is brought against you, you will be covered by the publisher's insurance policy.

Reserved Rights

Many publishing contracts include a "Reserved Rights" paragraph, which simply states that any rights not granted to the publisher in the agreement are reserved by the author, but that the author will respect the rights granted to the publisher within the contract. While it may seem a little strange that this clause doesn't simply spell out the rights to which it's referring, the clause does actually serve a purpose.

As you learned earlier in the chapter, in a standard publishing contract, the author grants the publisher the specific rights in which a publisher is usually interested—the right to sell paperback and hardback editions of the book, for instance. But, according to this clause, should a new area of rights emerge, this new area will be controlled by the author. While I always read this section of my contracts and think, "What rights can possibly be left?" the truth is that we don't know what may develop in the future. It wasn't that long ago that no one had thought a child's book could be made into a CD-ROM. Further, this type of stipulation is better than one which indicates that the publisher owns the rights to "all technologies currently in existence and any that may be developed in the future"—a clause that often appears in the contracts of freelance magazine writers. If you ever see this clause in your contract, I strongly suggest that you negotiate its removal.

Competitive Material

Under the heading "Non-Competition" or "Competitive Material," authors must agree that as long as the publishing agreement remains in effect, they won't prepare or cause to be prepared any work that is on the same subject, directed at the same audience, and treated in the same manner, *if* the new work would conflict with or lessen the sales of the present work. This doesn't mean that the author can never write a book on the subject addressed by his current work. However, it does mean that he can't write a book about the same subject if it would compete with the work under contract. For instance, sometime ago, I wrote a book about bulimia nervosa. Aimed at middle school students, it was designed for the library market. A year later, while the first book was still being offered in catalogues, I wrote a book about eating disorder prevention for adolescents. Because of their different markets, the books weren't in direct competition with one another, even though the topic of bulimia nervosa was certainly included in the prevention book.

Copyright

Sometimes within the "Rights" section of the contract, and sometimes within a special "Copyright" section, the publisher is charged with the responsibility of registering the book for United States copyright. In most cases, the contract states that the copyright will be taken out in the name of the author, who is the owner of the work. In some cases, however—in work-for-hire situations, for instance—the copyright is registered in the name of the publisher. (See the inset on page 180 for information on work-for-hire agreements.) The contract may specify that the publisher will print a copyright notice in every copy of the book. Since doing so is standard practice, however, the omission of such a statement shouldn't be viewed as a problem.

Most contracts state that the publisher will print a copyright notice in every copy of the book. Don't worry, though, if your contract doesn't include such a statement, as the printing of this notice is standard practice.

Sometimes the publishing agreement also specifies that in the event of any infringement of the work, the publisher "may employ such remedies as it deems advisable." The contract may even specify whether the author, the publisher, or both the author and the publishing house will pay for any such litigation. In such cases, it will also state how any recovered funds will be divided among the various parties.

Option

Some contracts give the publisher an option to acquire the author's next book before it's offered to another publishing house. This is referred to as the *right of first refusal*—not an especially positive way to phrase it, to be sure. Usually the publisher is given a specified amount of time—thirty days, for instance—in which to examine the new manuscript and determine whether he wants to acquire it. If he doesn't offer to publish it within the period specified, the author may show it to other parties and sign a contract with the publisher of his choice. The author may also offer it to other parties if the publisher *does* wish to produce the book, but the author and publisher are unable to agree on financial terms within a stated period of time.

Sometimes this clause gives the first publisher the opportunity to match the terms offered by another publisher competing for the next book. If the first company does offer the same terms, that company is entitled to the publication rights.

Occasionally a contract will stipulate that the publisher has the option to publish not just the author's next book, but his next two books or all subsequent books. While this may not seem significant to an author signing his first contract, it's important to understand both the pros and the cons of the option clause. If your first book is doing well with the publisher and you enjoy your relationship with him, most likely, you'll want him to publish any subsequent books. But if you're not happy with that publisher—perhaps because you feel that your current book has not been marketed properly—you probably won't want him to handle your next book. For this reason, it's usually prudent to request that the option extend to your next project only.

Some contracts stipulate that the publisher has the option to produce all of the author's subsequent books. In case your relationship with the company ends up falling short of your expectations, it is usually wise to request that the option extend to your next project only.

Rights of Termination

Some contracts include separate sections that spell out the circumstances in which the author and publisher can terminate the publishing agreement. For instance, if the publisher doesn't publish the work within a specified time, or if the work is out of print and the author sends the publisher a written request for a reversion (return) of rights, the contract may state that the publisher must return all rights to the author.

On the other hand, the publisher may have the right to cancel the agreement—and therefore, not publish the work—if the author fails to deliver the manuscript by the specified date or if a requested revision isn't judged to be acceptable by the publisher. The contract may further state that under such circumstances, the publisher has the right to recover any advances already paid to the author under the agreement.

Proceedings

Under a heading such as "Proceedings," "Arbitration," or "Applicable Law," the contract may specify that any major problem or disagreement relating to the contract, or to a breech of contract, will be settled in a specific manner, through legal proceedings or arbitration, and in a specific location—usually in the city or state in which the publishing company is located. For instance, the contract may specify that any legal proceedings will be governed by the laws of a particular state and be venued—in other words, take place—in that state. Or it may specify that any controversy or claim shall be settled by arbitration in the specified state. In the latter case, the contract may also state who shall bear the costs of the arbitration.

Because the financial resources of a publisher are generally greater than those of an author, publishers prefer to resolve differences in a court of law if they can't resolve them through direct negotiation. For the same reason, in most cases, it's in the author's interest to seek a remedy through arbitration rather than legal proceedings.

Benefit

A publishing contract usually states that should the publishing company be sold or acquired, the terms of the agreement will continue to apply to the new company or its successor. It may further specify that if the author is deceased, the terms of the contract will apply to the author's executors, administrators, or assigns (anyone to whom the author legally transfers the rights to the book). If there is more than one author, the surviving author or authors will have the authority to revise the book at the publisher's request without the consent of the estate of the deceased author. Note that the surviving author or authors will *not* receive the royalties of the deceased author—only the power to revise the work.

If you have one or more coauthors, and you believe that your book will be available for a long time through successive revisions, you and your coauthors should work out an appropriate arrangement for handling your book in the future. By arranging things correctly now, you may save yourself or your heirs many problems. For instance, you might decide that upon the death of a coauthor, the publishing rights of the deceased author will revert to the remaining

If you have a coauthor or several coauthors, and you believe that your book will be available for a long time through successive revisions, you and your coauthors should work out an appropriate arrangement for handling your book in the future. By arranging things correctly now, you may save yourself or your heirs a great many problems.

authors. Or you might decide that authors who don't participate in the revision of a future edition will have their royalty percentages reduced at that time. If, on the other hand, there is little likelihood that your book will be endlessly revised or kept in print for the next fifty years, the standard terms should be more than adequate.

Bankruptcy

Never a pleasant word, "bankruptcy" is certainly not a term you want to see in your contract. After all, if you're thinking about signing a contract with a particular publisher, you want to at least be confident that he'll remain in business for the life of your book. But the bankruptcy clause is actually designed to make the author feel more secure by assuring him that in the event the company does declare bankruptcy, all rights to the book will revert to him.

Know the Warning Signs

Hopefully, you'll be satisfied with the terms of your contract, or you'll be able to negotiate better terms— at least regarding the issues that are most important to you. Remember, though, that any contract is only as good as the parties who sign it. How will you know whether the publisher you're dealing with will honor the terms of your contract and treat you honestly and fairly? While there is no sure-fire method of gauging the character of a company, there are certain warning signs that should alert you to a possible problem. You may want to contact a lawyer or resume your search for a reputable publishing company if:

☐ The contract is so full of legalese and so convoluted in wording that it's impossible to understand without the help of a lawyer.

☐ When you ask the publisher or acquisitions editor for clarification of some of the terms of the contract, he never gives you a straight answer.

☐ When you attempt to negotiate the terms of the contract, you find that there is no give and take on the part of the publisher.

☐ Other authors who have worked with this publishing company report that the publisher is late with royalty payments and that he rarely makes good on verbal promises regarding marketing or other aspects of the publishing process.

☐ The contract states that the author will pay the publisher for one or several aspects of the publishing process. This is a bad sign *unless* the payment is expected to come out of the royalty advance—a practice that is acceptable and used by many legitimate companies. Any company that expects the author to pay for editing, typesetting, printing, or warehousing may be a vanity press masquerading as a commercial publisher.

Unfortunately, all is not exactly as it appears. In truth, when a publisher declares bankruptcy, his contracts are viewed by the court as company assets. This means that the rights in these contracts can't be reverted to the authors no matter what the bankruptcy clause states. Usually, if a buyer can be found for the publisher, the rights to the books are transferred to the buyer. If the company goes under reorganization—if it remains a working company with all contracts in place—it's protected under the bankruptcy laws. For authors, this means that the bankruptcy clause is unenforceable.

If you want actual protection in the event that your publisher declares bankruptcy, you might consider another option. One clue that a company is having financial problems is its failure to send out royalty checks. By incorporating a clear statement under the "Royalty" clause or the "Rights of Termination" clause that provides for the reversion of rights if the publisher doesn't make timely royalty payments, you may be able to protect the rights of your book. However, if the publisher seeks relief from the bankruptcy court before the appropriate reversion procedure is concluded, even this may not work.

The good news is that this issue doesn't come up often. However, it does highlight the benefits of working with a publisher who has a proven track record.

Although the standard bankruptcy clause may make you *feel* more secure, be aware that it will provide little actual protection in the event that your publisher declares bankruptcy.

Force Majeure

Many publishing contracts include a section on a so-called *force majeure*—an unexpected event that can't be controlled. In such a section, the contract usually states that the failure of the publisher to publish or reissue the work will not be considered a breach of contract if it's caused by events that are beyond the publisher's control. These events may include restrictions imposed by governmental agencies, labor disputes, and an inability to obtain the materials necessary for the book's manufacture. In such a case, the publication of the work would simply be postponed until the events no longer posed a problem.

THE NEGOTIATIONS

Hopefully, you now understand most or all of the terms of your contract. If you have any questions about the meaning of any portion of the publishing agreement, do not hesitate to speak to the editor or publisher with whom you've been dealing. He should be able to explain any and all of the terms to your satisfaction. And, of course, if you are working with an agent or a lawyer, he will be able to interpret the contract for you.

You may, at this point, find the terms of your agreement satisfactory, or you may wish to change some of them. The following discussion explores the negotiations process. Be aware that it is beyond the scope of this book to look at every possible contract term and then discuss if and how it might be changed. Rather, I hope to provide you with some insights into the "dance" of negotiations, as well as a closer look at a few important terms that are of interest to many authors. For a more detailed discussion of publishing agreements, refer to Martin P. Levin's *Be Your Own Literary Agent,* which includes a term-by-term review of a standard book contract, or *Kirsch's Guide to the Book Contract* by Jonathan Kirsch, a detailed clause-by-clause guide to the publishing agreement.

What Terms Can Be Negotiated?

By now it's probably clear that the contract you're holding is heavily weighted in the publisher's favor. This should not be too surprising, as it's the publisher who created the contract in the first place. In addition, it's the publisher who will invest the money and time to edit, typeset, print, bind, warehouse, ship, and market the book. The publisher therefore feels that he deserves the lion's share of the profits.

How will you know which terms of your contract are negotiable and which are not? You can determine this only by discussing them with your publisher.

On the other hand, over the years, I've learned that virtually any term, from the territory in which the grants apply to the subsidiary rights, can be amended. Remember that just as you need the publisher, the publisher needs you, so it's to his advantage to make those changes that will satisfy you. Also keep in mind, though, that for every publisher, there are certain points that are not negotiable. Which terms are and are not open to change in your case? You will have to discover this yourself through discussions with your publisher.

Before beginning negotiations, take out a sheet of paper and go through the contract term by term, deciding which points are most important to you. Maybe you need a larger advance in order to put aside other work while completing your manuscript, or maybe you want more author's copies or greater control over subsidiary rights.

Once you decide the specific changes you'd like to make, you'll be better focused and more likely to get what you want—as long as the terms you want to amend are among those that the publisher is willing to change, and as long as your requests aren't unreasonable. In any case, don't be afraid to at least request those changes that are important to you. The worst your publisher can say is "no."

While your publisher does expect some give and take, be aware that negotiations don't always end the way you want them to. If you insist on changing a term that the publisher is determined to leave as written, that term could prove to be a deal breaker. And if the negotiations drag on too long, the contract may be withdrawn. On the other hand, if you and your publisher can't agree at this early stage, it may be best to find another home for your book.

Before beginning contract negotiations, determine which points are most important to you. This will help you maintain focus during the negotiations process.

Important Bargaining Points

In the many years I've been signing book contracts, I've found that those issues which are important to me are not always equally important to my author friends. However, nearly everyone is interested in certain terms—advances, royalties, and subsidiary rights. Let's look at each of these in turn.

Advances

As already discussed, while we're all aware of the enormous advances awarded to some authors, standard advances for first-time authors range between $1,000 to $5,000, with some authors getting no advance at all. The size of any advance is dictated by many factors, including the policies of the company, the company's strength of interest in the manuscript, the size of the book's market, the author's need for money in order to complete the project, and the amount spent that season on advances to other authors. If, for instance, your book is on the same seasonal list as that of a well-known writer, the amount of company money available for your advance will be significantly reduced. Unfair? Perhaps, but if your book sells well, you may ultimately earn as much or more than that famous writer.

If you are dissatisfied with the amount of your advance, by all means, discuss it with your publisher. But in addition to considering the factors mentioned above, keep in mind that while your advance

From *Alice's Adventures in Wonderland* by Lewis Carroll

Illustration by John Tenniel

Keep in mind that large
advances are the exception
rather than the rule, and
are usually given to
known authors.

may provide you with ready income, this income is not additional to royalties. Rather, it is a prepaid portion of the royalties that your book will eventually earn, and will be deducted from your royalties.

Royalties

Money again, but what can you do? As long as authors have to earn a living, royalties will remain an important issue.

As I explained earlier, standard royalty percentages range from 5 to 10 percent of the retail price, and from 5 to 15 percent of the net price. While this may appear satisfactory on the surface—especially if your contract specifies 10 percent of retail—you do want to watch out for a common pitfall of many contracts. Some contracts reduce the royalty amount when the discount given to the customer is equal to or greater than 50 percent. What these contracts don't state—and what the publisher who offers such a contract isn't likely to explain—is that most books aren't sold directly to the bookstore, but are sold through distributors *at discounts of 50 to 60 percent*. Therefore, most of the royalties you collect are likely to be based on the smaller percentage listed in such a contract, rather than the more generous percentage.

Fortunately, you can avoid this pitfall. Simply request that the percentage and the basis for the percentage (net or retail) remain the same based upon discounts of up to *60 percent*, not 50 percent. This is a point worth negotiating for, as it will have a marked effect on any earnings you enjoy from the sales of your book.

Subsidiary Rights

As discussed earlier in the chapter, subsidiary rights are those rights derived from the literary work other than the primary right to publish the work. These rights are a common point of negotiation. Many authors want to retain various subsidiary rights, from the right to publish their book in a foreign language to the right to movie adaptations of the work.

If you want to retain one or more subsidiary rights, consider if you're able to sell them on your own. Many publishers have personnel devoted only to selling subsidiary rights—people who may have numerous contacts. If these rights are granted to the publisher, he will be committed to presenting your work to interested parties. After all, by doing so, both you and the publisher stand to gain, as any resulting proceeds will be divided with you as detailed in your contract. If you retain these rights for yourself, your publisher won't have a vested interest in contacting such parties, leaving you to your own devices—unless, of course, you employ a literary agent to represent you in this regard.

It's also important to explore your publisher's ability to sell subsidiary rights. Let's say, for instance, that you want to retain the rights to foreign-language editions. Ask your publisher about his track record in selling foreign rights. Are his books internationally distributed? Are his books represented by agents in foreign countries? Does he attend the Frankfurt Book Fair and the London Book Fair—two shows at which publishers often make contacts with companies from other countries? Does he attend BookExpo America (BEA), another show at which foreign rights may be sold? By asking appropriate questions about your area of interest, you will be able to judge who can best represent you in the selling of subsidiary rights.

If you do agree to grant subsidiary rights to your publisher, be sure to ask that they revert to you in a specified period of time—three years, for instance—in the event that the publisher hasn't exercised them. If the publisher just sits on those rights, you'll want them freed up so that you can make better use of your book.

If you want to retain one or more subsidiary rights, realistically consider if you'll be able to sell them on your own, or if the publisher will be able to do a better job. If the publishing house has personnel devoted only to selling subsidiary rights, it may be in your best interests to let the company represent you.

Tips for Negotiation

At this point, you probably have a good idea of the contract terms you can live with, the terms that make you a bit uneasy, and the terms that you are determined to change. But what is the best way to go about persuading the publisher that these revisions should be made? Is any strategy particularly effective?

Regardless of the area of the contract you wish to negotiate, I've found that the best way to discuss any of these changes is to start with one or two points that are of *least* importance to you—say, the number of author's copies that will be coming your way. These are the terms that you can graciously accept if the publisher insists on the original contract wording. Then, by the time you start discussing the areas of the agreement that you really want to change, you will be seen as a reasonable person, and the publisher will be more likely to negotiate.

What if the publisher calls your bluff and immediately agrees to those extra author's copies? Take it as great news since you can always use extra books. Besides, I'm not suggesting that you ask for something you don't want, as that would be a waste of time and energy. Moreover, the editor's ready agreement may indicate that he would be amenable to the more important changes you have in mind.

Is This Publisher Right for You?

Throughout this book, I've emphasized the importance of searching for a publisher who will meet your personal criteria as established in Chapter 4, and also produce a high-quality book, market your book aggressively, and deal with you fairly and honestly. In reality, you may be offered a contract by only one company. But if you're lucky enough to elicit the interest of more than one publisher, the following steps may help you choose the one that will provide you with the most rewarding relationship.

☐ Request and review the publisher's catalogues to see how the company markets its books. (For tips on assessing catalogues, see page 162.)

☐ Examine the publisher's books—especially those books that are in the same category as your own. Be critical, and look for specific things. Are the covers of the books inviting? Are the titles catchy and clever? Is the typeset page appealing? Are the illustrations of good quality? Unless your goal is simply to get your book into publication, you want a company that will produce an attractive, high-quality edition. Any books already published by the company will give you a fairly good idea of how your work will be treated.

☐ Ask the publisher who distributes his books in the relevant market. Also ask him how many sales representatives the company employs, how many books the company has produced in that category, and how many copies have been sold of each title. The answers to these questions—and to any other questions that occur to you during your conversa-

tion—will indicate how aggressively the company will market your book, and how much success it has enjoyed in the appropriate marketplace.

☐ Ask to speak to two or three authors who have published their books with this company. If the publishing company is reputable, your publisher will gladly give you the names and numbers of some of his authors. You'll then be able to ask these authors about their experiences with the company. Has the publisher made good on his verbal agreements? Has the author's book been effectively marketed? Was the editing of good quality? Have the royalties been paid on time? Although the publisher will probably choose those authors with whom he feels he has the best relationship, the authors will nevertheless provide you with helpful insights. (Some of these insights might surprise the publisher if he heard them!) And, of course, if the publisher refuses to put you in touch with his authors, you'll have a pretty good idea of how he's treating them.

Throughout negotiations, always keep in mind those terms that you would only prefer to have changed, and those terms that you feel *must* be changed. This will help you make wise use of your time, energy, and influence.

IF MORE THAN ONE COMPANY OFFERS YOU A CONTRACT

If you've followed the Square One System and sent a well-written submission to appropriate publishers, you very well could be offered contracts by more than one company. If so, you are in an excellent position to compare the two agreements and determine which best suits your goals.

The best strategy is to compare the terms line by line to see if one contract is more attractive than the other. Then make a list of changes you want from each, and present your requests to the respective publishers. If publisher number one agrees to some of your modifications, and publisher number two agrees to all of them, most likely, your first response will be to sign with the second publisher. But before you do that, remember the personal criteria you established in Chapter 4. It could be that publisher number one better meets those criteria. If this is more important to you than the other issues under negotiation, you should go with publisher number one.

Of course, you don't have to make it a secret that another publisher is interested in your book. You could even step up the negotiations by informing publisher number one that another company is offering more generous terms. This could motivate the first publisher to make some of the requested changes to your contract. But, again, you shouldn't necessarily choose the company that offers the largest advance or the highest percentage of subsidiary rights fees. Always look beyond the terms of the publishing agreement and try to determine which company would, overall, provide you with the most satisfying and profitable relationship.

> If you are lucky enough to be offered contracts by more than one company, start by comparing the agreements line by line to see if one is more attractive than the other. Then make a list of the changes you want from each, and present your requests to the respective publishers.

CONCLUSION

In its most basic form, a contract spells out your rights and responsibilities as an author, and the company's rights and responsibilities as the publisher of your work. Hopefully, this chapter has provided you with an understanding of your responsibilities, and will help you negotiate for those rights that are most important to you.

Now the real work will begin as your manuscript is polished and shaped into a finished book. Because most contracts detail your continued participation in the creation of your "child," you'll be part of this rewarding process. The result should be a beautiful volume of which both you and your publisher will be proud, as well as one that will delight young readers everywhere.

CHAPTER 8

When It Doesn't Happen

I have received so many rejection letters over the years and I no longer bother to keep count of them. And even after a writing career that has spanned two decades, each one has the power to smart. After sending out a submission package, the future sparkles with promise. It's almost impossible to stop yourself from imagining the hefty royalty checks, the fan mail, the appearances on day-time talk shows—maybe even a movie option. All that disappears the second you open your mailbox and spot your own SASE—a sure sign that the publisher isn't interested in your book. It's pretty hard not to take a publisher's rejection personally. And it's pretty hard not to feel bad.

What can you do to lift your spirits? First, think about all the now well-known children's authors who were rejected time after time before they got their first break. Judy Blume was once informed by an editor that she wasn't talented enough to write anything at all. Madeleine L'Engle faced more than twenty rejections before her classic *A Wrinkle in Time* was published. And author Donna Jo Napoli experienced fourteen years of rejection letters before she received her first contract. (See the inset on page 207 for excerpts from rejection letters received by other famous authors.) Almost every major modern-day author, in fact, has received his or her share of rejection letters. So you're in good company.

Second—and most important—take steps to accurately diagnose where the problem may lie. In earlier chapters, we discussed a few possible roadblocks to success. For instance, you know that by failing to target the right publishers, you can significantly decrease your

Theodor Seuss Geisel, also known as Dr. Seuss, received twenty-seven rejections for *And to Think That I Saw It on Mulberry Street.* He was on his way home to burn the manuscript when he bumped into a friend who worked for Vanguard Press. The friend published the book—which immediately became a hit.

chance of finding an interested editor, and may even totally sabotage your efforts. And you know that a poor submission package can also prevent you from reaching your goal. Your topic, your timing, and your approach may also be "off."

If the task of diagnosing the problem, let alone fixing it, seems a bit overwhelming, take a deep breath and relax. This chapter was designed to help you analyze where the problem may exist, and then choose the course of action that is most likely to get your book into print. It will also provide you with some intriguing possibilities, including that of self-publication. In fact, you may be amazed by the options available to you—options that will allow you to reach your goal of seeing your work move from manuscript to printed book.

IDENTIFYING THE PROBLEM

Short of a concerted plot to stop you from getting your work published, there are only a few basic reasons why manuscripts get rejected: the topic, the approach, the timing, the choice of publishers, the submission package, or some combination of these. Let's first briefly consider each of these possibilities so that you will be in a better position to pinpoint your problem. Later in the chapter, we'll look at what you can do to overcome these roadblocks.

From *Alice's Adventures in Wonderland* by Lewis Carroll

Illustration by John Tenniel

Your Topic

Your choice of topics can greatly influence your chances of getting published. If you have chosen a subject that has a very limited or difficult-to-reach audience, you may have created a project that is simply too hard to sell to a commercial press. On the other hand, if you have selected a topic that *everybody* is writing about, titles like yours may have already saturated the marketplace. Publishers may be reluctant to put out any more books on the subject—at this time, at least. Finally, if you have presented your topic in a manner that is unclear or that fails to demonstrate the project's marketability, you have definitely reduced your odds of being picked up.

Your Approach

Let's assume that the topic of your book is solid, with a good size

Something to Laugh About

It's easy to allow rejection letters to make you doubt your worth, as well as your ability to get your book into publication. To gain perspective, and to enjoy some much-needed laughter, spend an afternoon leafing through *Pushcart's Complete Rotten Reviews and Rejections*. This book includes hundreds of scathing comments directed at both adult and children's book authors whose works are now regarded with respect and, in some cases, with reverence. As you read the following remarks—culled from both rejection letters and reviews—think of the joy the reading public would have missed if these writers had meekly accepted the editors' comments as gospel instead of continuing their search for the right publisher.

Alice in Wonderland
Lewis Carroll, 1865
We fancy that any real child might be more puzzled than enchanted by this stiff, overwrought story.

And to Think That I Saw it on Mulberry Street
Dr. Seuss, 1937
. . . too different from other juveniles on the market to warrant its selling.

The Diary of Anne Frank
Anne Frank, 1952
The girl doesn't, it seems to me, have a special perception or feeling which would lift that book above the "curiosity" level.

The Adventures of Huckleberry Finn
Mark Twain, 1884
A gross trifling with every fine feeling . . . Mr. Clemens has no reliable sense of propriety.

Moby-Dick
Herman Melville, 1851
We regret to say that our united opinion is entirely against the book. . . . It is very long, rather old-fashioned, and in our opinion not deserving of the reputation which it seems to enjoy.

The Time Machine
H.G. Wells, 1895
It is not interesting enough for the general reader and not thorough enough for the scientific reader.

audience and a very reachable marketplace. Still, you are not getting any nibbles. The problem may center on the way you have decided to present or explore your topic—in other words, on your approach.

Let's say you've written a story about a sixteen-year-old girl with a drug problem. In your cover letter, you've identified this as a middle grade novel. The reality is that with a character of that age and a topic that's suitable for an older audience, it really should be labeled a young adult novel. Thus, your approach—to address middle grade readers—is a problem.

Or perhaps your picture book requires numerous cut-outs and moveable parts. While the publisher may like the story, the complicated format might be a problem, as it would require a sizeable investment of money on the part of the company.

Another problem related to approach may occur when, say, your book on "weird weather" assumes too much knowledge about weather on the part of the readers. Yes, your targeted audience—ten- to twelve-year-olds—would be interested in this topic. But they probably don't understand *normal* weather patterns, much less "weird" ones.

Timing

Kate DiCamillo's *Because of Winn-Dixie* (Candlewick Press) was rejected by every publisher to whom it was sent. But two years after DiCamillo had mailed the story out, an editor at Candlewick discovered the proposal in a pile of unread manuscripts and loved it. The book was named a Newbery Honor Book in 2001.

Over a decade ago, I wrote what was called a *problem novel*—a novel which deals with an issue that is pertinent to young adult readers. I did no market research, relying instead on the positive comments of friends and fellow writers, and, quite frankly, on the rush that comes from knowing you've written a strong manuscript. If I *had* done my homework and researched current trends, I would have learned that the young adult market was turning away from problem novels, and considered them passé. The result was a series of letters that rejected my book while complimenting my writing. One publisher did consider accepting my book for a while, but he, too, eventually decided that the time for this genre had come and gone.

The moral of the story? In writing, as in everything else, timing is crucial. Your proposal can be wonderful and you may submit it to the perfect house. But if your timing is off—if the genre is no longer popular, if the topic or approach is ahead of its time, or if the editor just signed an agreement for a similar project—you are not going to get that contract.

Your Choice of Publishers

Let's assume that you sent your proposal to appropriate houses— companies that produce the type of book you are writing, and that are willing to consider unsolicited manuscripts. Why hasn't your book been snapped up? If no other problem exists—if your approach, topic, and other elements are all what they should be—it may be that your package just hasn't clicked with the individual editors who have thus far received your submission. In other words, you haven't yet found the editor who will recognize the worth of your book.

On the other hand, you may have unintentionally targeted inappropriate publishers. For instance, although your topic may be perfect for small publishers that operate in a specific region of the country, you may have targeted only major New York houses because you want your book produced by a company with "a name." Sometimes you can take a lesson from Cinderella's stepsisters. They tried to force their feet into a glass slipper they knew wouldn't fit, hoping for a miracle. If your manuscript isn't right for a publisher, no amount of forcing will get it to fit.

Your Submission Package

Let us assume that your topic is fine, your timing is not a problem, your approach is flawless, and you carefully selected the publishing houses to which you mailed off your submission package. Nevertheless, either no one has asked for further materials, or one or more editors did request materials, but no one followed up with a contract.

Now it's time to take a step back and consider if the problem may be with your submission package. Most likely, if your manuscript is being held back by a problem found within the submission itself or within any follow-up materials you sent, you should be looking for at least one of two possibilities. Either the writing of the submission package or of the materials sent subsequently is lacking in necessary quality, or you have not identified the audience and marketplace for your book in a way that favorably impressed the editor. Let's look at each of these in turn.

Writing Quality

As discussed in Chapter 5, "Preparing the Package," your submission package not only provides a summary of your book, but also serves as a sample of your writing style and your ability to present information. A number of writing-related problems can turn an editor off, but the problems that are most likely to cause an editor to reject a proposal are poor grammar, lack of clarity, and lack of organization. Any of these difficulties signals the need for hours of rewriting by a capable editor. And in an industry in which the bottom line is all important, few if any publishers are interested in a manuscript that requires such an investment of time and money.

It took a year of submissions—and a number of rejections—before Bloomsbury Publishing offered a contract to J.K. Rowling for *Harry Potter and the Philosopher's Stone*—the original title of the first Harry Potter book.

WORDS FROM A PRO

Louise Borden

Author of *Fly High! The Story of Bessie Coleman*
(Margaret McElderry Publishers)

"Ten publishers rejected my book *Good Luck, Mrs. K.!* before it was accepted by Margaret McElderry Publishers. Usually I find that when something has been rejected, what I've really sent is more like a first draft and it needs to be worked on more. For most of my books, I revise at least twenty times before submitting it to publishers."

Too often, writers send out what is in effect their first draft. Any writer will tell you that it's difficult to determine when something is ready for submission, but for most successful authors, the rewriting stage takes longer than the creation of the first draft. The revision process is a necessity because as sterling as we all think our work is, chances are that it needs at least some polishing before it is presented to an editor. No matter how many times I looked at the manuscript for this book, there were still minor typos I caught later on—errors that I could almost swear had materialized after my last proofing. And there were sentences and whole paragraphs that needed further work.

If you didn't think that it was necessary to revise your submission package, or if you thought that a once-over was enough, consider the possibility that your package was sent out too soon.

Painting the Right Picture

If your submission package does not provide the editor with the information for which she is looking, there is little chance that your proposal is going to make her sit up and take notice. Perhaps your letter did not adequately identify your topic, your approach, your audience, or your marketplace. Or perhaps you didn't explain how the publisher might gain access to a hard-to-reach audience. You may be very aware of all of these factors, but simply have failed to point them out to the person on the receiving end of your package.

It's easy to understand how such omissions occur. Often, in our enthusiasm, we assume that the editor will immediately perceive all the wonders of our book—without being told. But the fact is that if you don't clearly provide the editor with the information she seeks, it's possible that no one will ever know just how great your book is.

Strategies for Pinpointing the Problem

You now know that there are a handful of problems that may be holding your project back. During your reading of the above discussions, you may have identified the problem. If you're still in the dark, though, there are a number of things you can do to pinpoint the flaws in your project.

Look for Clues in Your Rejection Letters

Although most rejections are frustratingly uninformative form letters, some editors do take the time to mention the reason for the rejection. Sometimes it's a line scrawled on a form letter; other times, it's a separate note.

If you receive such feedback, consider it a gift, and use it to correct any problems in your submission. (See the inset on page 212 for more details on this strategy.)

Enlist Some Help

If your rejection letters failed to provide any clues, consider showing your submission package to one or two people who you feel can be both discriminating and honest. Ask them for their opinions, and try to consider their comments with an open mind. You might want to provide them with a list of the pitfalls we've just discussed, and ask them if they believe that any of these problems may be holding your project back.

If you took the advice presented in Chapter 5, you have already shown your submission package to one person. This time, try to choose different people so that you can get a new perspective. As before, it would be helpful if your reviewers had solid English skills, as well as a knowledge of children's books. The best person would be a children's librarian or an elementary or secondary school teacher. If you do not already have a relationship with such a person, don't hesitate to visit your local library and introduce yourself to the children's librarian. Such a friendship may benefit you throughout your writing career.

If your chosen reviewers have not provided you with the answers you're searching for, you may want to look outside your circle of friends and acquaintances. Writers' groups and writers' workshops can be found throughout the United States. Through these groups, you may be able to find other writers who can look at your work objectively and offer valuable criticism. Similarly, writing

Anne of Green Gables by L.M. Montgomery was consistently rejected until a small house in England said they would give the author $500 to sign away the rights *or* pay her nine cents for each book sold. In 1908 she opted for the latter, and within the first six months, the book sold 26,000 copies.

How to Profit From Rejection

If you're lucky, at least one of the rejection letters you received was not a form letter, but actually mentioned the reason for the rejection. Perhaps an editor noted that the proposed book would be overwhelming in size for the suggested age group. Or perhaps after you had sent one or two chapters of your young adult crafts book to an interested editor, she informed you that the directions were unclear. This is not to suggest that the editor was necessarily correct in her evaluation. Every editor is a human being, after all, and if the inset on page 207 proves anything, it proves that editors can be dead wrong. However, if a busy editor has taken the time to note her impression of your project, it would be foolish not to take a long, hard look at your materials. Then, if the editor's criticism does make sense to you, by all means make any necessary revisions and send the revised package back to her, along with a personal note of your own.

If you decide not to make the changes that the editor has suggested—or if the rejection was due to a factor beyond your control, such as the editor's recent acquisition of a similar book—you should nevertheless send a note thanking her for her interest and expressing hope that your next submission will better suit her needs. It's always smart to be as polite and courteous as possible. As I've said before, editors move around from house to house all the time, so you never know when you'll run into that editor again.

If none of the editors shared her thoughts with you, you may be tempted to call some of them up and ask the reason for their rejections. While this may seem like a simple, commonsense approach, as I explained in Chapter 6, your calls are not likely to yield helpful answers. Most acquisitions editors sift through so many queries on a daily basis that they will probably not be able to even remember your proposal, much less offer useful comments and suggestions. On the other hand, if an editor was sufficiently impressed by your submission package to request further materials, and if she sent a rejection letter only after reviewing those materials, it would make sense to give her a call, as she may now be both willing and able to provide you with the feedback that you seek.

courses can put you in touch with other writers and, perhaps more important, with instructors who are both able and willing to critique your work. Objective advice such as this may be exactly what you need to pinpoint problems in both your proposal and your actual manuscript. (More information on these resources is provided later in the chapter.)

Find Out More About Your Category

If the cause of your problem still eludes you, you may want to carefully examine published books that are in the same category as yours, be it an early picture book or a young adult mystery. Look at books that are similar to yours in topic and genre, and pay special attention to the more popular titles. Your goal is to note the difference between your own book and other books in the same category. Compare the vocabulary used in books for that age group. Depending on the type of book you've written, also compare topic coverage; special features such as illustrations, tables, and boxed insets; chapter length; dialogue; and other aspects of your work. If you find marked differences—if the characters in your book are not as well developed as those in other novels of that type, or if your nonfiction book is far more technical and detailed than other books of its kind—you may have located the source of your problem.

When investigating possible problems with your project, it often pays to compare your book with published works in the same category. If you find marked differences between the two—if the vocabulary used in your book is far more sophisticated than that used in similar books, for instance—you may have found your problem.

If your search yields no published book that is similar to yours, that alone may be the problem. As I have said time and time again, editors may be interested in a unique approach to an old idea, but for the most part, they want books designed for an existing category and an eager audience. On the other hand, your search may have turned up dozens and dozens of similar books. You now know that you've chosen a subject or genre of interest. However, the glut of competing books may mean that the market is already saturated with books like yours. That, too, is not good.

How Much Are You Willing to Change?

I once heard children's book author Johanna Hurwitz tell her audience that the plot twists which you like the best because they reflect true-life experiences are always the first parts of the book the editor deletes, citing implausibility. She discussed how difficult it can be to accept the editor's changes, because you know that the events in question actually occurred. However, Ms. Hurwitz pointed out that if you can't convince your editor of the truth of an event, it is unlikely that you'll be able to convince your young reader.

Just as it might someday be necessary to revise your work so that it is acceptable to your editor, it may now be necessary to make changes to get that first contract. And these changes can be difficult—even painful—to make.

Before I move on to suggest ways of remedying any problem found, I want to point out that it is not necessarily in your best interest to do anything and everything to get your book into publication. Perhaps you have experienced success in the classroom by using a revolutionary approach to your topic. If that is the case, you certainly would not meet your personal goals by catering to popular opinion. But you should seriously question if the uniqueness of your book is a necessary and essential component of the work, or if it is an expendable feature that may be keeping you from getting published.

As just mentioned, editors are not looking for something that has never been done before. They are looking for a book that fits into an existing category, that has an existing and accessible audience, and that meets the needs of that audience in established ways. Your book may prove to be the exception—a middle grade work that covers topics so sophisticated that they usually appear only in young adult titles, but that nevertheless appeals to its intended readers. Chances are, though, that if you insist on a truly unique approach, you will greatly decrease your odds of finding an editor who is willing to champion your project.

SOLVING THE PROBLEM

Hopefully, you have now identified the problem that is potentially standing between you and a publishing contract. Your next step is to revise your materials in a way that will make your project more attractive to the targeted publishers. Depending on the nature of the problem, on your skills, and on the time you're able to devote to your proposal, you may be able to solve any problems alone, or you may want to enlist the help of others.

Going It Alone

Regardless of your writing skills and experience, you'll probably be able to make many types of changes on your own, without the help of either a more experienced writer or further training. Let's look at some of the problems discussed earlier in this chapter to see what action you can take to clear the path to success.

Topic

The solution to a topic-related problem will depend on the exact difficulty caused by your topic. If, for instance, you feel that your subject may be limiting your audience, and therefore may not be considered sufficiently profitable for a commercial press, consider refocusing on the nonprofits—organization or foundation presses. These houses are more likely to accept a book that has a relatively small audience.

If there appear to be too many books on your subject, try waiting six months or even longer, and resubmitting your proposal to the publishers on your original list. As time passes, many of the other books on the subject will disappear from the marketplace, possibly leaving room for yours. (For more about this strategy, see "Timing" on page 216.)

Finally, reread your cover letter. Is the topic of your book clearly spelled out? Have you avoided making your topic seem outlandish? Have you provided enough details about the book's audience to show that the book would, indeed, be marketable? By demonstrating that your book has an existing and accessible audience, you may stimulate interest in your project.

Approach

If you have decided that the flaw in your proposal lies in your approach to the topic, you may very well be able to rework your cover or query letter, table of contents, overview, and any sample chapters so that they reflect a new and more marketable approach.

For a moment, let's return to the middle grade novel about a sixteen-year-old-girl with a drug problem. (See page 207.) If you have determined that this book should really be geared for the young adult market, you could easily revise your cover letter to specify your new audience. If necessary, you should also revise your sample chapters to reflect the more sophisticated vocabulary of older readers.

Remember the picture book that required so many cut-outs and moveable parts that the production costs were prohibitive? Try to determine whether your story can stand alone, without all the bells and whistles. If the story is a strong one, rework your cover letter to focus on the narrative, and include only a line stating that you'd be

If you believe that the problem standing between you and a publishing contract lies in your approach to the topic, you may very well be able to rework your cover or query letter, table of contents, overview, and any sample chapters so that they reflect a new and more marketable approach.

happy to discuss creative ideas for the design of the book if the publisher feels that this would be appropriate.

Finally, think back to the book on weird weather. If you have concluded that your book should provide more fundamental information, add a first chapter that discusses basic weather patterns and explains how meteorologists track weather systems. This will give your readers the background they need to understand abnormal weather events.

There are many more ways to change your approach. Sometimes, you may have to pull your book apart and put it back together in a new way. Picture book writer Louise Borden—author of *Sea Clocks* and *The Little Ships*—prints out pages of her manuscript, lays them out on the floor, and moves them physically from one spot to another, each time rereading the lines in their new order to see how the story works. Don't be afraid to tinker with your creation—putting the action-packed middle chapters at the beginning of the book, for instance—until your story is the best it can be.

Finally, if you have written a nonfiction book and you suspect that your approach is the problem, but you're not sure what type of approach would be a better choice, consider adding a line to your query letter stating that you are amenable to changing the way in which you present your material. Of course, this is a good option only if you are not married to your book as it now stands, but are truly willing to make any revisions necessary to get it into print. And, as already indicated, this would be appropriate only with nonfiction books, in which case, editors will expect to make their mark anyway. If you have created a work of fiction, an offer to change your approach would immediately signal a lack of confidence in your own story, which would probably prejudice the editor against your proposal.

> Computers make it easy to experiment with different ways of presenting material. Simply save your original document and create a new document, which you can "play" with all you want until you find the best approach possible. If you ultimately conclude that your first approach was best, you'll still have the original document intact.

Timing

Timing is a unique problem in that you cannot solve it by changing your table of contents, reworking your cover letter, or taking a new approach, because the problem isn't in the proposal or the project. What you *can* do is adopt one of the strategies suggested earlier, under "Topic." Simply wait six months, and send out another set of submission packages to all of the publishers on your original list. You can begin your cover letter by stating that this is a resubmission, and that you hope the editor will reconsider your project in light of changing editorial needs.

Does this strategy work? Based on experience, resubmissions do hit their marks—not always, but enough times to make this a worthwhile option. Within six months, a company's ownership can change hands, editors may be replaced, editorial programs can change, new topics can catch on—dozens of things can happen to turn your project into a strong candidate for publication. Resubmitting your material will keep bad timing down to a minimum.

Your Choice of Publishers

If your problem is related to your choice of publishers, there are a couple of solutions you should consider. If you feel that the publishers on your original list were, in fact, appropriate, keep in mind that you have probably sent out your proposal to only about thirty publishers, while there are *thousands* of book publishers in the United States, with new ones cropping up all the time. That's why within Chapter 6, I suggest that if you don't find an interested editor among those on your first list, you put together another list of companies. If you haven't already done so, give this strategy a try. This time, consider expanding your list to include companies that may in some general way touch on your book's topic, but do not seem to cover the topic specifically. By basing your selection on more liberal criteria, you may be able to find as many as a *hundred additional publishers* who may show interest in your book.

After you have put together your new list of publishers, go back to Chapter 6 and use the Square One System to send out submission packages to these new companies. Perhaps your new list contains an editor—and, remember, it only takes one!—who will appreciate your project and personally guide it through the editorial process, all the way to publication.

What if you suspect that you did not, in fact, select the best publishing houses for your original list? Chapter 3, "The Business of Publishing," and Chapter 4, "Choosing the Right Publisher," will guide you to the most appropriate companies for your project. This time around, though, you may have to be a little more careful or a bit more realistic in your selection, and carefully consider each company before adding it to your list.

Every year, new publishing companies open, and older houses establish new imprints. That's why it often makes sense to check the most current editions of resources such as *Children's Writer's & Illustrator's Market*, and make up a new list of potential publishers for your project. All you need is one interested editor to get your book from the desk drawer to the bookstore.

Your Submission Package

Depending on your skills, you may be able to solve various problems with your submission package once these problems have been identified. For instance, although you may not initially have recognized that your writing contained vocabulary that was too sophisticated— or not sophisticated enough—for the targeted age group, now that you have found the problem, you may be more than capable of reworking your sample chapters using more appropriate language. And once you realize that your cover letter or overview fails to clearly describe your topic, audience, or approach, you may be able to easily integrate the missing information in your package. However, if these tasks are currently beyond your reach, if you suspect that your grammar or general writing skills are weak, or if you are unable to invest the time needed to bring your proposal and manuscript up to par, you may benefit from outside help. The following discussion will guide you to a variety of resources that may be able to provide the help and support that you need.

Finding Training, Support, and Other Assistance

It can be frustrating to find that despite your passion for writing— and, possibly, despite a wealth of wonderful ideas—you lack the expertise necessary to revamp your submission package and/or your manuscript. Be assured that some skills come with time and practice. As you exercise your writing "muscles" by writing and rewriting, and as you immerse yourself in the world of children's literature, your skills will become stronger. But everyone can use some support, especially when they're first starting out. Fortunately, there are many resources available to the writer in need. Some are designed to get your skills up to speed, while others involve finding an individual who is capable of performing the rewrite for you.

Writing Classes, Groups, Conferences, and Workshops

Earlier in the chapter, I mentioned how writing courses, writers' groups, and writers' workshops can put you in touch with people who have the judgment needed to critique your submission package. These same groups and courses can also help you hone your writing skills.

If you have determined that your grammar skills are in need of improvement, a grammar course at a local college will be your best bet. These courses, which generally take you step by step through a grammar workbook, cover a variety of important topics such as parallelism, tense, and verb and noun agreement—areas that baffle many writers. Just as important, most teachers are happy to address any specific questions that you have, and may even be willing to read through your proposal and offer constructive criticism. Night courses are usually available, and some colleges have continuing education programs designed specifically for adults who want to improve their skills.

If you wish to develop your ability to organize material and to express yourself clearly in writing, you should consider taking a writing course, also available at most colleges. In a good writing class, you will learn to arrange words to form a structured whole. Your writing will then be submitted for criticism to your teacher and, possibly, your classmates. Afterwards, you will rewrite your work, taking any comments and suggestions into account. You may also be asked to offer constructive criticism of your fellow students' writing—a process that will help you sharpen your ability to identify strengths and weaknesses. Although some of the focus of a traditional writing class may be on elements of fiction such as dialogue and plot, you will also learn about structure, transition, and other topics relevant to nonfiction writing. Contact those colleges and adult study programs near you and see what they have to offer. And keep in mind that, like any instruction, a writing class will give you only as much as you put in, so be prepared to work hard if you are serious about improving your skills.

Writing can be a lonely business, and even published authors sometimes seek out writers' groups for the camaraderie they offer. Newer writers find that involvement in a writers' group can provide the support of people who have objectives similar to their own, and

Once you overcome any initial shyness, you will probably find that the "sharing" portion of your writing class—where classmates critique one another's work—is the most enjoyable as well as the most helpful. Very soon, you will be able to identify not only your fellow students' strengths and weaknesses, but also your own.

are eager to share writings, tips, and encouragement. To find a local group that is being formed or is trying to fill a chair, check advertisements in local newspapers; scan school bulletins and writers' websites; and read coffee house, bookstore, and library posting boards. Allow yourself to be picky, and don't hesitate to leave a group that you feel isn't giving you the help and support you want. For a writing group to be productive, the members have to get along well, trust one another, care about one another, and be compatible in intelligence and focus. It may take some time to find a group that can provide you with the constructive criticism you need.

Yet another option is to join an online writing group. These groups don't foster the companionship and trust that "in-person" meetings might, but if you don't have the time or opportunity to attend such a gathering, an online group is a good alternative. (See pages 260 to 261 of the Resource List for some helpful sites.)

You might also wish to consider attending writers' conferences and workshops. Depending on their focus and format, these gatherings can provide you with advice on writing through workshops, discussions, and one-on-one tutorials; insights into the publishing world; and encouragement from both peers and professionals, including book editors, literary agents, and published authors. Some writers have even been able to forge useful relationships with editors and agents at such events. If this sounds appealing, you'll probably want to attend gatherings sponsored by the Society of Children's Book Writers and Illustrators (SCBWI). Every year, the SCBWI organizes two international conferences—one in Los Angeles and one in New York City—as well as many local events. Well worth the price of admission, SCBWI conventions will enable you to garner tips from editors, hear inspirational speeches from published authors, and chat with other children's book writers.

If you are looking for a local workshop or conference, flip through regional magazines and newspapers, and contact your local and state arts councils; your Town Hall; and your local schools, libraries, and

WORDS FROM A PRO

Johanna Hurwitz
Author of *Elisa in the Middle* (Puffin Books)

"The best advice I can give is that new writers in the children's book field join the Society of Children's Book Writers and Illustrators (SCBWI). One need not publish to be a member, but membership brings a bi-monthly bulletin with advice, names of new editors who are willing to read unsolicited manuscripts, and dates and locations of conferences. Often by attending a day-long conference, one can meet an editor or agent. This does not guarantee acceptance, but it's a start."

community centers. For instance, YMCAs across the country sponsor YMCA National Writer's Voice Centers. These centers host a variety of events, including workshops and writing camps.

Perhaps you would like to combine your training with a trip to another part of the country. A number of gatherings—including SCBWI-sponsored events—are listed in the *Children's Writer's & Illustrator's Market* and the *Literary Market Place (LMP)*, each of which devotes an entire section to writers' conferences and workshops. Also look through the ads and events listings in magazines such as *Writer's Digest* and *The Writer,* as well as the newsletter *Children's Book Insider,* which sponsors "Author Boot Camps" throughout each year. And, of course, the Internet can provide you with listings of numerous writers' gatherings. Simply use the search engine of your choice to look for "writers conferences."

Working With a Ghostwriter

If for any reason you feel that you cannot rework your submission package and/or your manuscript as necessary, you have another great option—a ghostwriter. A ghostwriter can organize your ideas, thoughts, and writings into a readable book. You will provide the knowledge of the subject or the ideas for the characters and story line, and your ghostwriter will provide the writing. A talented ghostwriter can even "mimic" your writing voice. Your name will still appear alone as author of the book, as the ghostwriter will not be credited as an author. She will, however, be compensated through a flat fee and/ or a percentage of the royalties, depending on your arrangement.

Most ghostwriters require an advance before they begin work on a project. Some, however, will allow you to delay payment until you have a signed contract in hand.

Where can you find a competent ghostwriter? Begin by talking to the people around you. Very possibly, one of them knows an experienced ghost. Writers' workshops and conferences are other good places to find candidates for the job. (Don't forget that the teachers of most writing courses are themselves writers, and may be interested in your project!) The "Editorial Services" section of the *LMP* lists a number of companies that provide ghostwriting. Finally, magazines like *The Writer* and *Writer's Digest* contain numerous advertisements of people who are willing to edit or rewrite your manuscript.

Whether a ghost has been highly recommended by a friend or was located through an ad, you'll want to do your homework and make sure that she is a skilled writer. Ask the ghost about her back-

Did you know that some of the most beloved juvenile fiction in America was written by ghostwriters? The Bobbsey Twins, Tom Swift, Hardy Boys, and Nancy Drew series were all penned by groups of hand-picked ghostwriters employed by the Stratemeyer Syndicate— an enterprise created by writer Edward Stratemeyer.

ground. What kinds of books has she written? Has she been published? Ask to see some of her work, and read it critically. If in doubt, ask other people to read it, too. You want to make sure not only that she can write, but also that she can write books in your category, whether that category is young adult fiction or middle grade nonfiction. Finally, make sure that this is a person with whom you can work. Collaboration can be a positive experience. It can also be instructive. Your own writing may improve as you see what your ghost does with your material. But collaboration can also be a nightmare if you don't choose your writer carefully. You and your ghost should be able to work well together.

Collaborating With a Coauthor

If you need help in the writing or rewriting of your submission package and manuscript, another good option may be a coauthor. What's the difference between a ghostwriter and a coauthor? Both are collaborators, but a ghostwriter is not credited as an author, while a coauthor is. Your coauthor may get equal billing, or may have a byline such as "as told to" or "with." And, of course, your coauthor will get a share of the royalties.

The working arrangements of coauthors vary widely according to the skills of the two people involved. Sometimes, each coauthor writes different sections of the book or even every other chapter. Sometimes, one does the research and provides the information, while the other does the lion's share of the writing. And sometimes, one person does the bulk of the writing and the other edits each section as it's completed.

If you don't already know someone with whom you feel you can collaborate, you may be able to find a competent coauthor just as you would find a ghostwriter—through workshops, conferences, recommendations, and ads. Again, before signing this person on, make sure that she has the necessary skills and that the two of you can get along. Many a project has been destroyed by the coauthors' inability to work together.

Using an Editorial Service

If you feel that your submission package and/or manuscript needs help, but you do not choose to work with a ghostwriter or coauthor, you may want to contact an editorial service. In exchange for a flat fee, and depending on your needs, a good editorial service can correct syntax, grammar, usage, style, and punctuation; help you with plot, pacing, characterization, and dialogue; and provide helpful feedback and suggestions. Unlike a coauthor, an editorial service is not, of course, credited as an author.

Editorial services are easy to find. The "Editorial Services" section of the *LMP*, mentioned earlier, is one good source, as are ads in periodicals such as *The Writer* and *Writer's Digest*. Another option is to simply type "editorial services" into your favorite Internet search engine. Note that many of these services offer free sample edits and critiques, which will give you a chance to determine if that service is the right one for you and your book.

OTHER OPTIONS

Perhaps, despite your best efforts to rework material, your book has not been published. Or perhaps you feel that it would not be in your best interest to change your work to meet the needs of a commercial publisher. Not every author wants or needs to get her work edited and produced by a standard commercial press. Maybe you simply want to get your book into print. As you will soon see, this is still a very realizable goal.

Don't despair if despite your best efforts, no publisher has offered you a contract. There are many ways in which you can make your book available to potential readers.

Vanity Presses

Vanity publishing has been around since the printing press was created. Nowadays, you see ads for these presses everywhere, from news magazines to mailings. Using phrases like "Looking for Children's Authors to Publish" and "Get Your Book Published," these ads can make your heart skip a beat. But remember that although a vanity publisher will get your book into print, it will do so only for a fee.

A vanity press—also called an author-subsidized publisher, subsidy publisher, author-investment publisher, or cooperative publisher—requires the author to pay for the cost of production and distribution. Usually the fees charged by a vanity press are high. For the 5,000-copy printing that is often considered a minimum run by these presses, the publisher may charge as much as $35,000, and sometimes more! For this fee, the company will typeset, print, and bind your book, and may even edit it. Generally, the press will also warehouse half of the print run; you will have to store the rest. Some vanity presses may offer to market your book. Most will send copies of your book to reviewers.

What's wrong with this picture? Perhaps nothing. However, you should be aware that vanity presses make their money through the fees they charge their authors, and not from the income made via book sales. Therefore, they have no great commitment either to produce a quality product or to market that product. As a result, many vanity presses claim to edit manuscripts, but in reality, do no editing at all or perform only the most superficial of edits. According to *Writer's Digest* magazine, most also do not deliver the promotion they promise.

Because of the well-known low standards of vanity publishers, having your book produced by such a company can negatively affect your credibility as an author. The accepted belief of the book publishing, book reviewing, and bookselling industries is that vanity presses will publish any book by anyone, without regard to quality. Therefore, even if your book is well written, it may be perceived as being substandard just because it was produced by a vanity publisher. As the editor of a parenting magazine, I've received my share of vanity published books. Since my job is to recommend truly good publications, I can't in good conscience tell parents to share with their child a book that hasn't been properly edited and, when appropriate, fact-checked. And I am not alone in feeling this way. When vanity produced books do get sent to reviewers, they are almost never reviewed. In addition, most bookstores won't carry titles produced by a vanity press, which is one reason why vanity press books rarely return even a fourth of the author's investment. Moreover, if you later send the printed book to a regular publisher in hopes of having it acquired, the editor won't seriously consider the title.

Considering the poor track record of vanity presses as a whole, as well as their negative image in the publishing world, should vanity presses ever be considered a viable option? If your goal is to simply get your book into print, and if you have the necessary money *and* the necessary storage space, a vanity press might be a good choice, as it will take the entire production process off your hands. Approach these presses with your eyes open, though, and investigate each company thoroughly. First, ask to see the company's existing books to determine if the quality is up to your standards. Then ask to see its catalogues and brochures so that you can find out how—and if!—your book will be marketed. Perhaps most important, ask for the names and numbers of some of the company's authors, and question these authors closely to see if the press actually provides the advertised services.

The *Children's Writer's & Illustrator's Market* and the *LMP* do not list vanity presses. However, you can find ads for these presses in magazines such as *The Writer* and *Writer's Digest.* Do not look for the words "vanity press," as this term is never used in ads. Instead, find a publisher who directs his ad "To the author . . ." or who states that "Manuscripts of all types are wanted . . . ." In other cases, a vanity press may advertise a "subsidy publishing program," or one that offers to "edit, design, illustrate, print, and store your book" regardless of the genre, and all for "easy installment payments." Another avenue of research is the Internet. Simply perform a search for "subsidy presses." If a vanity press is what you're looking for, you should be able to find one with very little trouble.

Self-Publication

Although the uninitiated often think that *self-publishing* and *vanity publishing* are one and the same, in truth, there's a big difference between the two. While a vanity house takes care of the whole publication process—albeit, for a hefty fee—in a self-publishing program, you literally do everything yourself. You edit the book or hire someone else to do the editing for you; design the layout and either typeset the text or hire a typesetter to do so; proofread and correct the copy; design the cover or arrange to have it professionally designed; arrange to have the book printed and bound; warehouse the finished book; and even do your own marketing and publicity. You then sell your book to individuals, bookstores, libraries, or other outlets. Finally, you do your own billing and collections.

While this may sound overwhelming, history has shown that self-publishing is a great option for an author who wants to get her book into print; who either can't find an interested publisher or

Although self-publishing involves a lot of effort, it is a great option for the writer who can't find an interested publisher, isn't amenable to making the changes requested by a commercial publishing house, or simply has an entrepreneurial spirit.

Before Beatrix Potter used her savings to self-publish *The Tales of Peter Rabbit*, the book was rejected by a number of British publishers, one of whom is said to have commented that "it smelled like rotting carrots." Once in print, though, the book sold so well that a publisher who had originally rejected the manuscript offered Ms. Potter a contract. Within a year, 50,000 copies were in the hands of eager readers.

refuses to make the changes requested by a commercial publishing house; and who has an entrepreneurial spirit. Why do most people prefer it to vanity publishing? First, self-publishing is an old and honorable practice. William Blake, Washington Irving, Walt Whitman, Mark Twain, and Beatrix Potter were all self-publishers. So self-publishing does not involve the stigma associated with vanity publication. This means that once your book is in print, you will have a good chance of getting it into bookstores; of getting it reviewed; and—if you can eventually show a solid record of sales success—of having it acquired by an established publishing house. In fact, since the late 1990s, when savvy authors began to successfully market their books on the Internet, several dozen self-published novels have been picked up by major publishing houses.

Second, self-publishing is usually much less expensive than publication through a vanity press. Thanks to computers, laser printers, and publishing software, authors can get their books and promotional pieces ready for printing without the numerous costly production steps that used to be necessary. Then, many small-run printers will print as few as 300 copies of the book—a far cry from the 5,000-book run demanded by many vanity presses. Naturally, prices change all the time, and your own costs will depend partly on the manufacturers with whom you deal. But, in general, authors who shop for the best prices can save thousands of dollars by choosing self-publication over vanity publication.

If you are interested in self-publishing but are intimidated by the idea of seeking out cover designers and printers, you might want to consider print-on-demand publishers. Found online, these companies often offer a variety of services, from copyediting to cover design to marketing. You can choose all of the offered services, or you can choose just a few. Most important, the companies keep an electronic version of your book on file, and print and bind copies of the book as needed for a relatively small fee—from less than $100 to about $2,000. Some even offer a special four-color picture book service. You retain the copyright, receive a certain number of bound copies, and earn a royalty rate of about 25 percent of the retail price on sales. Just remember that if you opt only for printing and binding, you will still be responsible for other aspects of your new business, such as marketing. Also keep in mind that you will be bound by the terms of your online agreement, so before you hit "send," you'll want to make sure that you're getting only the services you want. To find these services, simply perform an Internet search for "print on demand," and a number of websites will pop up.

Of course, self-publishing is not right for everyone. As stated earlier, you do need entrepreneurial zeal and some business savvy. Unless you use a print-on-demand service, you will have to find an affordable and reliable short-run printer. You will probably also have to find someone to design the cover of your book. Then, unless you are producing your work only for friends and family, you will have to arrange for your book's distribution; market and publicize your book; and set yourself up as a business—either a sole proprietorship, a partnership, or a corporation. (To further examine if self-publishing is right for you, see the inset on page 228.)

If you are interested in publishing your own book, it is essential to thoroughly investigate the self-publishing option before you make any commitments. A number of books can familiarize you with self-publishing and provide you with valuable tips. For starters, take a look at *The Self-Publishing Manual* by Dan Poynter, which is regarded as a leader in the field. Another excellent resource is that bible of the publishing world, the *LMP*. The "Book Manufacturing Section" of the *LMP* includes listings of typing and word-processing services, art services, and printing and binding services. Many of the printers specialize in short-run book manufacturing, and the majority of entries state the company's minimum run, which in some cases is as small as 300 books. And because your job as a self-publisher doesn't end when your book is in print, you'll want to examine Susan Salzman Raab's *An Author's Guide to Children's Book Promotion*, which will fill you in on what you'll have to do to promote your book.

You can learn a great deal about producing, marketing, and selling your book by joining one or two trade groups: the Publisher's Marketing Association (PMA) or the Small Publishers Association of North America (SPAN). Founded in 1983, PMA has a membership of 3,400-plus United States and international publishers—including many self-publishers. Created in 1996, SPAN has a membership of over 1,000 publishers. And, again, this includes many self-publishers.

Through their individual newsletters, publications, and services, the PMA and SPAN can guide you to reputable typesetters, printers, editors, and more; inform you of worthwhile publishing fairs, seminars, and workshops; and otherwise provide you with the informa-

The most famous children's book to be self-published in recent years is the fantasy novel *Eragon*, written by Christopher Paolini when he was still in his teens. His family edited the 500-page manuscript, produced the book through a print-on-demand operation they set up at home, and then marketed the title. When novelist Carl Hiaasen read *Eragon*, he immediately contacted his publisher, Alfred A. Knopf. The result was a three-book deal for a reported advance of $400,000, and an instant bestseller when *Eragon* was released in 2003.

tion you need to be a successful player in the publishing world. (See the Resource List for further details.)

Electronic Publishing

When most children's book writers dream of getting their works into publication, they think of physical books—books that will appear in displays at their local bookstore or, at the very least, can be presented to young friends and family members. But if you can revise your notion of a book to include works that exist as electronic publications, you will find that another option is available to you. You can see your work published as an e-book—a book that can be read on a computer screen or downloaded to your printer. Just keep in mind that while the world of e-publishing is growing by leaps and bounds,

---

Is Self-Publishing Right for You?

If you have been unable to find an established publisher for your book, or if you are too independent-minded to cater to the demands of a commercial publishing house, self-publishing may help you realize your dream of seeing your book in print. But as discussed on page 227, self-publishing isn't for everyone. When you commit yourself to self-publishing a book, you're really starting your own business. To see if you have what it takes, ask yourself the following questions:

☐ Is the publication of my book of such importance to me that I'm willing to invest both thousands of dollars and countless hours of time?

☐ Am I willing to accept the fact that I may never again see the money I invest?

☐ Am I willing to investigate typesetters, printers, and other manufacturers and services to find companies that can give me what I need for a reasonable price?

☐ Am I thick-skinned enough to face the possibility that the media may ignore or criticize my book?

☐ Will I really do the homework necessary to learn about book distribution, publicity, and marketing?

☐ Am I thick-skinned enough to face the possibility that bookstores may refuse to carry my book?

☐ Once my book is published, will I really spend the hours necessary to distribute, publicize, and market my book?

☐ Do I have the motivation and self-confidence it takes to continue to promote my book despite any rejections and setbacks?

It's not easy, but if you answered "yes" to most of these questions, self-publishing may be just what you're looking for.

and definitely offers a seductive alternative, it is a bit more complicated than you might think.

How Do E-Publishers Operate?

In a nutshell, e-publishers convert existing bound books or unpublished original works into electronic formats that can be downloaded by Internet users. The e-publishers then sell these e-books from their websites or through other Internet sites. Often, e-publishers specialize in a certain type of book. Some concentrate their efforts on securing the electronic rights of books that have already been published as printed works. Some focus on out-of-print titles. And some are most interested in original works.

Different from print-on-demand presses, which store books electronically but ultimately produce a bound book, e-publishers produce an electronic version of a book that consumers can read on-screen or run out on home printers.

Many parents, teachers, and librarians are still reluctant to embrace the e-book. Parents in particular, who are constantly told by educators and researchers that their children need to spend less time in front of the computer, are often unimpressed by books that must be read on a computer screen—even if the books are classics. And while you often can print out a copy of an electronic book, you won't, of course, end up with a neatly bound book, but with a pile of paper. For those who like to have bookshelves lined with favorite volumes, the electronic book holds little appeal.

Regardless, many publishers believe that it's just a matter of time before the public accepts the e-book. Emerging technology, like small handheld computers, are making it easier to curl up in bed with an electronic book. And children today are far more savvy about computers than their parents are. Born and raised on computer games, Internet searches, and e-mail, many children are likely to find e-books a sensible approach to reading. Moreover, as technology develops, e-publishers are adding a number of exciting features to electronic books, designed to appeal to kids. "Enhanced" e-books range from custom books in which a child's name appears; to electronic pop-up books; to e-books with spoken text, music, and animation. Even though the technology is expensive, some school districts have already put it to use in the classroom.

Now you have a better idea of the world of e-publishing. But what does this mean to you, the hopeful children's book writer? In order to understand your options, you must recognize that while some e-publishers operate just like traditional publishers, reviewing,

Electronic books can be read on desktop computers, laptop computers, handheld personal digital assistants (PDAs), or any device that is specifically designed for reading electronic documents. Some of these devices require the installation of special software before you can read the document on your screen.

editing, and producing books, and underwriting their own costs, the majority are vanity e-publishers—although they don't refer to themselves as such. A quick search of the Internet highlights several companies that will sign you up, convert your manuscript into the appropriate electronic format, and provide a place on their site for your book to be reviewed and sold. Most pay a royalty on works sold. Some charge you a monthly fee to maintain your book, usually for a minimum of one year. Others charge all the traditional costs of print vanity publishers, from a $50 set-up fee to $1,000 line-by-line editing fees. These companies may show a profit, but since the download fee for most books is about $4.95—and so far, readers aren't swarming to these sites—profits generally come from selling the use of their sites to authors.

As you might expect, those e-publishers that operate like traditional publishing houses should be considered a solid option. As a general rule, they pay little if any money in advances. However, because they don't have to invest in storage and inventory or worry about returns, they do pay good royalty percentages—from 24 to 75 percent of the retail price. If this type of e-company sounds like a good alternative to you, just be sure to determine the kind of e-publisher you're dealing with before making any submissions.

Now we turn to the vanity e-publisher. If your goal is simply to make your book available to others, this is a reasonable option. It's cheaper than working with a regular vanity press, and if you have the money, you could see your book online in less than a month's time. (Most of these companies "publish" within a week of receiving your manuscript—and check or credit card information.) Once your book is available, you could consider approaching traditional publishing houses and telling them that your book has been picked up by an e-publisher. But if they recognize that it's a vanity operation, this will probably work against you.

Where to Find an E-Publisher

If you're interested in making your book available in electronic form, your first step, of course, is to locate some e-publishers. The most obvious approach is to perform an Internet search for "e-book publishers." But a more efficient strategy is to visit the website of the Electronic Book Web (EBW), which offers a good deal of information about e-books and e-book producers. Click on "Publishers," and you'll find an alphabetical listing of publishing companies in the form of links that will take you directly to each website. (See the Resource List for further information.)

However you compile your list of e-publishers, you'll want to visit each company's website and review it critically, noting the relative ease with which you can navigate the site and locate submission and ordering information. If a publisher appeals to you, order a book from the company and see how it handles the order. Was your order confirmed? Was it filled promptly? Was the book—whether downloaded or on disk—easy to read? Your answers will tell you a great deal about the company's operation and about the ease with which readers will be able to access your work.

Of course, you'll want to check the formats in which the books are made available by each e-publisher. Some can be downloaded, and some are produced on disks. And some, but not all, companies make their books available through online bookstores. Obviously, there are a variety of factors—including the contract—that may make one company more appealing than another.

Once you choose a publisher, you'll find that the submissions process used in e-publishing is similar to that used in traditional publishing houses. You'll probably be asked to submit a cover letter, an outline, an overview, and a few sample chapters. As indicated earlier, some publishers are likely to accept your manuscript regardless of its subject matter or quality, while others will be more selective. With a little luck, your book will soon be made more available to its potential audience—and you'll join the growing ranks of e-authors.

A NEW BOOK

If vanity publishing sounds too risky, self-publishing requires more time and money than you care to invest, and e-publishing is a bit too high-tech for your taste, there is yet another way in which you can enter the world of publishing—a way that you have probably not yet considered. Many an author has simply put aside her first manuscript and begun a new one. While this might make you feel as if you are abandoning your original project, it's actually a very good idea. Why? For starters, this time you can carefully select a genre and/or topic that has proven to be marketable. In addition, if you choose to work

If you decide to make your book available in electronic form, be sure to investigate each potential e-publisher just as you would investigate a conventional publishing house. As a first step, visit each company's website and review it critically, noting the relative ease with which you can navigate the site.

There may be an added bonus to starting an entirely new project. If the second book is accepted for publication, doors will start opening for you, and you may have a greater chance of getting your *first* book published.

in the realm of nonfiction—an area in which publishers usually don't ask for a full manuscript as part of the submission—you can make less of an investment in time and money by initially writing only a submission package instead of the full book that you may have prepared for your first project. The unexpected bonus of this new enterprise may be that if your second book is accepted by a publisher and does well in the marketplace, doors will open to you, and you will have a greater chance of getting your *first* book into publication!

How can you choose a marketable project? While there isn't any guaranteed-to-sell topic or genre for children, there are ways to increase your odds of producing a winner. First, consider the category of books in which you have an interest. (See Chapter 2 if you have any questions about categories.) Baby books? Easy reader nonfiction? Young adult fiction? Research the books that sell well and garner good reviews in that category. In fact, locate the books and review them yourself, comparing bestsellers with books that don't appear to move off the shelves. Can you tell what makes one more popular than the other? If you can, you have taken an important step towards success.

Also ask your local children's librarian about the topics and genres in which children seem to have the most interest. Librarians can even tell you about any new national and state education requirements that will make certain types of books in particular demand. Also scan magazines like *Writer's Digest,* as well as newsletters from writers' organizations like the Society of Children's Book Writers and Illustrators, as from time to time, these publications list topics that librarians nationwide would like to see writers address. Be sure to attend writers' conferences and workshops like those mentioned previously in this chapter, as well, as these are great places to learn what editors are looking for. Above all, listen to and watch children, not only for hot trends that momentarily capture their attention, but also for the issues that are always of concern to them. For instance, there will always be a need for books that help children cope with annoying siblings, peer issues, and "first times"—going to school for the first time, going on a first date, etc. If you've decided that you truly want to be a children's book author, immerse yourself in that world. Sooner or later, you're sure to find a topic that will inspire you to launch a new project.

Once you select a new topic, don't forget to determine if your book will have a sizeable readership by doing the work discussed in

Chapter 2, "How Big Is Your Audience." Then return to Chapter 4 for a refresher course on targeting the most appropriate publishers, and refer to Chapter 5 for information on writing a strong submission package. If you've researched your topic and you know it has an audience, chances are that your new project will find a home.

EXPLORING OTHER LITERARY MARKETS

Your dream is to see your book in print, and so far, you have probably kept that goal clearly in sight and moved directly towards it. But if you've had trouble reaching your goal in this manner, you may want to try a different approach—a seeming detour that might eventually help you realize your dream. By writing for a children's magazine, competing in a writing contest, or working for a book packager, you may be able to hone your writing skills, test out topic ideas, and acquire credentials that will allow you to succeed in the world of children's book publishing.

Writing for Children's Magazines

One of the best ways to enter the world of children's writing is to have a story printed in a children's magazine. As already mentioned, doing so will help you develop your skills and also build writing credentials and name recognition, which can then be used as an entrée into the book publishing world. At the very least, you will be able to include your magazine credit in the cover letter of your next submission package. Just as important, children's book editors read children's magazines in part to learn of new talent. In fact, children's writer Sharon Creech was first discovered by a book publisher when her short story "Absolutely Normal Chaos" appeared in *Highlights* magazine. *Absolutely Normal Chaos* became her first project with that publisher, and its sequel, *Walk Two Moons*, won a Newbery Medal.

You'll be able to find a complete listing of children's magazines in the "Magazines" section of *Children's Writer's & Illustrator's Market*. Publications like *Babybug, Click, Cricket, Ladybug, Spider*, and *New Moon* each reach different age groups, so you'll have to research these magazines just as you would research book publishers. As you perform your research, you'll find that some periodicals accept work only from children, others don't take unsolicited work, some want

> Even if your ultimate goal is to become a children's book author, consider writing for a children's magazine. This is one of the best ways to enter the world of juvenile literature.

If you subscribe to the
Children's Book Insider
newsletter, look for their
monthly updates on new
children's magazines, as
well as tips on what's
hot and what's not.

only nonfiction, etc. Similarly, some magazines wish to receive only a query letter, while others want a complete manuscript. To avoid wasting time and money—both yours and theirs—you'll want to send each company only what it requests.

Once you've identified one or more magazines that seem to match your needs and interests, visit your local library and ask the children's librarian to pull out issues for at least the past year. This will enable you to study the magazine's format and writing style and to view the topics that have been covered in the recent past. This is important, as magazine editors will reject any story or article that sounds like one they've published in the last year or so. Your research will also help you detect themes. For instance, most children's magazines are season- and holiday-oriented, meaning that they publish stories and poems that highlight specific times of the year. You will fill the editor's needs if you find a new approach to a recurring theme, such as Halloween or the start of the school year.

Once you're sure that the magazine will work for your story, contact the company for its writer's guidelines. Then prepare your submission package according to these guidelines, strictly following word count specifications. Remember that magazines have limited space, so when they ask for 750 words, they mean what they say. You can go over by 25 words or so, but if you hand in a 900-word story, you can pretty much count on receiving a rejection letter. Remember, too, that magazine editors have to plan issues at least three months in advance, so if you're submitting seasonal material, you'll want to send it in well ahead of time.

There's no doubt that article writing is different from book writing, so it makes sense to do some research before you give it a try. The Resource List on page 249 suggests some great books that can help you get started.

Competing in Writing Contests

Publication is not the only means through which your work can be recognized. Contests are a great way to win notice in the industry and, if you're lucky, to pave the way for a book contract, as well.

You will be able to find an extensive list of contests in the "Contests, Awards & Grants" section of the *Children's Writer's & Illustrator's Market*. When you notice a contest that appeals to you, be sure to download or send for the rules and to follow them carefully, pay-ing special attention to the deadline. Editors receive too many entries to even consider those submissions that arrive after the due date. Also note whether you will retain the rights to your story in the event that you win. If the rights will not remain with you, consider skip-ping that competition. Why? Once you sign over your rights, the story will not be yours, so if a book publisher were to see your story and offer you a contract, you would not be able to sell your work.

Some contests, like the Delacorte Press Contest for a First Young Adult Novel and the Marguerite de Angeli Contest, offer not only a cash award but also a book contract, complete with advance. Open to United States and Canadian writers who haven't previously pub-lished a novel in that particular category, these contests may be your ticket to publication.

Finally, try to enjoy the competition and not be too disappointed if you don't win. Remember that most contests receive several hun-dred submissions at once, so that rejection doesn't mean that your manuscript isn't of value. As you now know, there are many ways in which you can get your children's stories read and appreciated.

Working for a Book Packager

A book packager is a type of middleman between writers and pub-lishers. Sometimes, publishers approach book packagers with ideas for projects that they want developed. Sometimes, book packagers approach publishers with ideas of their own. Usually, the book pack-ager will write, edit, illustrate, and design a book or series of books, and send the print-ready project to the publisher. The publisher will then send the "package" to the printer, add it to the company's list, and distribute it along with the company's own titles. Many young adult romance and mystery series are created in this way, although they all carry the name of the publisher—not the book packager.

What does this have to do with you, a writer of children's books? Book packaging presents a wonderful opportunity to new writers who want a chance to develop their skills. Often, a packager will cre-ate an outline for a book, and then search for someone to do the actu-al research and writing. Talented writers are always needed to produce books on demand. In return, writers are usually paid on a work-for-hire basis. In other words, they get a flat fee, with no royal-

Many young adult romance and mystery series are created by book packagers. If you are interested in writing this type of book, book packaging may be able to provide you with the opportunity you need to develop your skills and break into the world of children's publishing.

ties, and they do not own the copyright to the book. Usually, the writer's name does not appear on the book.

To find book packagers, look in the "Book Producers" section of the *LMP*. Once you identify one or more packagers for whom you'd like to work, send each one a resumé and a writing sample, listing your writing credentials—published stories and articles, for instance—if you have them. In return, the packager will probably send you an "audition"; that is, the company will ask you to write a sample chapter so that it follows a supplied outline.

Please recognize that it's not as simple as it sounds to write a book based on a scene-by-scene outline. If, for instance, you are creating a work that's part of a fiction series—which is often the case—you will have to match the writing style of all the books that came before yours, even down to capturing the "voices" of the various characters. Nonfiction is usually easier, as no characters are involved. If you have the necessary skills, though, a packager can provide you with a foot in the door of the publishing world, unparalleled experience in writing different types of material, and, of course, compensation for your work.

CONCLUSION

You've now come to the end of this chapter, and perhaps you are still not sure what the problem is and what you want to do about it. Is it you? Is it them? Is it the project? Should you revamp your old proposal or start an entirely new book? If your path is not clear at this point, I strongly suggest that you put the project aside and forget about it for a month—or longer if necessary. Once you've had time to relax and gain some perspective, return to this chapter and reread it. You may discover that it holds an option which will work perfectly for you.

On the other hand, you may now be truly excited about the possibilities that this chapter has put before you. If that's the case, don't be afraid to go for your dream. Believe in yourself and, perhaps most important, keep working. I hope that this chapter will help you as you move towards your goal.

CONCLUSION

I've been writing professionally since I was a freshman in college over twenty years ago. But I had decided to be a writer long before then. I was just six, in fact, when I began to read adventure books, and realized that I could create stories as well as read them. From that point on, I never veered from my course of becoming a writer. When I make author visits to schools, I always tell the children I was about their age when I decided what I wanted to be when I grew up. But I also tell them that they don't have to choose their career for a long time. In fact, many writers start out doing something completely different and discover the joy of writing somewhere down the road. I always emphasize that if you believe in yourself and work hard to reach your goals, your dreams will come true. I don't think we're ever too old to hear these words.

I absolutely believe that you can get your children's book into publication. The very fact that you've come to the end of this book shows that you have the drive you need to reach your goal. But, as you now know, there are no shortcuts to success. Hard work and dedication are needed to turn your dream into a reality. The rewards, however, are well worth the work. I strongly urge you to enjoy every moment of the process, from the time an idea first seizes you while you're standing in line at the supermarket or driving down the road. Even the anticipation of preparing submission packets and flipping through the daily mail delivery can be enjoyable. Then one day, when an editor calls and expresses an interest in your book, you'll feel an almost unbeatable thrill—unbeatable, that is, until the day you see your name in print on the cover of your book.

In Chapter 1, I talked about Rule #1: Sometimes, you just get lucky. Sure, sometimes luck can play an important role in getting your book accepted by a publisher. But to a great degree, I believe we make our own luck. You can make your own luck by setting up a course of action and following it with intelligence and perseverance.

I'd like to share a secret. As a writer for over two decades, I have seen dozens of my creations go from manuscript to published book. And I *still* get a kick out of seeing my name on a book cover! In the not-too-distant future, I hope that you experience the joy of seeing your own children's book in print.

One last thought: Even though this book has been edited and printed, it is a work in progress, and will be revised and updated over time as the world of children's book publishing changes. To make sure we meet your needs, we would like to know what you think. Therefore, should you like to offer any comments or suggestions, please write to the following address:

Att: Liza N. Burby
Square One Publishers
115 Herricks Road
Garden City Park, NY 11040

GLOSSARY

All words that appear in *italic type* are defined within the glossary.

acquisitions editor. The person in a publishing house who has the job of acquiring new books. This person may not have the actual title of acquisitions editor, but instead be the *editor-in-chief,* senior editor, associate editor, *executive editor,* submissions editor, or *publisher.*

action and adventure. A *genre* of *fiction* characterized by exciting physical acts—daring feats, fights, and chases.

advance. Money paid to the author in advance of publication, once the book is under contract. Sometimes called "advance against royalties," the advance is actually a prepaid portion of the money that will be earned from future *royalties* and *subsidiary rights* sales. Authors don't receive any additional payments until the royalty earnings have surpassed the amount of the advance.

annotated table of contents. A part of the *submission package* in which the author lists chapter titles along with brief descriptive information about each chapter.

audience. The targeted readers for your work. In children's books, this usually refers to the age level (e.g., toddlers) or reading level (e.g., easy readers).

author-investment publisher. See *vanity press.*

author's copies. Copies of the author's work given to him or her free of charge directly after publication. The number of author's copies is generally stated in the publishing contract.

author-subsidized publisher. See *vanity press.*

autobiography. A *nonfiction* account of a person's life written by that person.

baby books. The category of books created specifically for infants and young toddlers, from newborn to twelve months of age. These books may be regular paper books or may be printed on cloth, cardboard, or plastic.

backlist. *Titles* that were produced by a publisher in previous seasons, but that are still in print and available from the company. See also *complete list; frontlist; seasonal list.*

bestseller. Traditionally, any book that has sold over 50,000 copies in one year.

biography. A *nonfiction* account of a person's life written by another person.

board book. A book made of thick, durable cardboard, intended for babies.

book packager. A company that writes, edits, illustrates, and designs a book or series of books, and then sends the print-ready project to the publisher.

Caldecott Medal. A medal created in 1938 to honor the illustrator of the most distinguished American picture book of the year. This award was named in honor of nineteenth-century English illustrator Randolph Caldecott, and is presented annually by the Association for Library Service to Children, a division of the American Library Association.

category. A division of books into which a work falls because of its subject matter and intended audience. The Square One Book Classification System for children's books is specifically based on the needs of editors. It is comprised of twelve categories, including *baby books, toddler books,* *early picture books, picture books for older readers, easy readers, chapter books, middle grade books, young adult books, hi-lo books, juvenile series books, elementary and secondary school textbooks,* and *religious books.*

chapbooks. Small penny books that were generally printed on one large sheet of paper, which was then folded into a book of sixteen to sixty-four pages. First made available in the early 1500s, these books, which presented *legends* and *fairy tales,* were produced for adults but enjoyed by children as well.

chapter books. The category of books designed for children who can read on their own—usually, children from age seven to age ten. Chapter books may be illustrated, but rely predominantly on text, which is organized into chapters.

complete list. All of a publisher's *titles,* old and new, that are still in print and available from the company. See also *backlist; frontlist; seasonal list.*

concept book. A book that—using illustrations and one- or two-word explanations—presents children with basic information on subjects like numbers, letters, colors, animals, and foods. These are usually *baby books* or *toddler books,* created to help children understand their world.

copy editor. The person in a publishing house who is responsible for making manuscript changes necessary for stylistic consistency; for correcting spelling, grammar, and typographical errors; and for fact checking.

copyright. The legal overall right granted to an author or publisher for ownership of a written work. Under this ownership comes a number of specific rights, including the exclusive rights to print, sell, distribute, and translate a literary work.

cover letter. A brief letter accompanying a manuscript written to the *acquisitions editor* in order to spark his or her interest in a project. See also *query letter.*

distributor. A company that inventories and sells the books of one or more publishers to bookstores, libraries, and nontraditional outlets on an exclusive or nonexclusive basis. Although the terms formerly meant different things, the words distributor, jobber, and wholesaler are now used interchangeably. See also *independent distributor.*

dummy book. A mock-up of a book that shows the placement of artwork and text.

early picture books. The category of books geared for children of three to five years of age— preschoolers and slightly older children. Early picture books tell simple stories through numerous illustrations and a small amount of text. They are also called storybooks.

easy readers. Often thought of as difficult to define because of their varying formats, these books are aimed at preschoolers through eight-year-olds, depending on their reading skills. The purpose is to provide emerging readers with simple chapter books that they can read on their own. Often, reading clues such as rhyming patterns are used, sentences are kept simple, and illustrations appear on every page.

e-books. A book in electronic form that can be read on a personal computer or hand-held reader, or downloaded to a printer.

editor. The person in a publishing house who actually shapes a manuscript by making necessary changes to format, organization, coverage, focus, and reading level. See also *acquisitions editor; copy editor; editorial assistant; managing editor; sponsoring editor.*

editorial assistant. The person in a publishing house who helps the *editor* by making photocopies, filing, proofreading, indexing, and performing similar tasks. The editorial assistant may also review manuscripts in the *slush pile* to see if they may be appropriate for that particular publishing house.

editorial review copies. Non-royalty-bearing copies of a book that the marketing department of a publishing house sends to media outlets with the hope that they'll be positively reviewed.

editor-in-chief. The person in a publishing house who oversees acquisitions and editorial operations, and may set editorial goals. In some houses, the *publisher* may perform the functions of an editor-in-chief.

electronic publishing. The production and distribution of electronic versions of books—commonly known as *e-books*—to customers via the Internet. This is also called e-publishing

elementary and secondary school textbooks. See *el-hi books.*

el-hi books. The category of books designed for use as learning materials in elementary schools, intermediate schools, middle schools, and high schools.

e-mail submission. The sending of a *submission package* to an *editor* via e-mail. This is also called an electronic submission.

e-publishing. See *electronic publishing.*

ethnic stories. Fictional works that involve characters with a distinctive racial, national, cultural, or religious heritage as a means of promoting awareness of different peoples.

executive editor. The head of the editorial department who assigns projects and oversees the work of the *editors,* who are responsible for the actual shaping of manuscripts. In some companies, the executive editor works as an *acquisitions editor.*

fairy tales. Fanciful stories, usually intended for children, that tell of magical creatures and legendary deeds. Fairy tale characters can include giants, elves, dragons, talking animals, and other beings not found in real-life-experience fiction.

fantasy. A literary work that includes mythical creatures such as unicorns and dragons, and takes place in a magical world that does not obey the natural laws of our present world.

fiction. A literary work created by the imagination, rather than being based strictly on facts. Popular genres include but are not limited to *fantasy, historical fiction, horror, mystery, romance, science fiction, short stories,* and *Westerns.*

fingerplay. Verses accompanied by finger movements, such as the classic "Itsy Bitsy Spider." Some fingerplays are found in collections of *baby books.*

first serial rights. The rights to publish excerpts of a given work in a periodical such as a magazine or newspaper prior to its publication. See also *subsidiary rights.*

flat fee. A form of payment in which an author, illustrator, or photographer is paid a lump sum for his or her work, and receives no royalties. This arrangement is often called *work for hire.*

force majeure. An unexpected event that can't be controlled, such as a restriction imposed by governmental agencies, a labor dispute, or an unavailability of materials necessary for a book's manufacture. According to the standard publishing contract, the failure of the publisher to publish or reissue a work wouldn't be considered a breech of the agreement or give rise to termination if it were caused by events such as these because they're beyond the publisher's control.

foreign rights. The subsidiary right under copyright law that allows an author, agent, and/or publisher to sell the translation rights of a work to another publisher located in a foreign country. The right to sell the foreign language edition may apply to a specific country, a group of countries, or any country in which the foreign language is spoken, as specified in a foreign rights agreement. Authors' *royalties* on the sale of foreign rights are usually calculated according to a separate royalty scale.

foreign sales. Any international book sales that draw from the original publisher's inventory. Authors' *royalties* on the sale of foreign rights are usually calculated according to a separate royalty scale.

frontlist. *Titles* produced by a publisher within the last nine months. See also *backlist.*

galleys. Originally, long strips of typeset copy created from an edited manuscript. Today, this term may be used to refer to the first set of typeset pages. See also *proofs.*

genre. A type of fiction marked by a distinctive style, form, or content. Popular genres include but are not limited to *fantasy, historical fiction, horror, mystery, romance, science fiction, short stories,* and *Westerns.*

ghostwriter. A person who does the actual writing of a book, but isn't credited on the cover of the book or within its pages.

graphic novel. A story that is written and illustrated in comic-book style, but published in book form, in either a hardcover or paperback format. Despite their name, graphic novels—which fall into the *young adult* category—can be either *fiction* or *nonfiction*.

hardcover. A book that has a stiff cardboard cover over which is stretched a material such as cloth, treated paper, or some type of plastic. In most cases, a paper dust jacket is placed over the cover.

hi-lo books. The category of books designed for readers in the upper grades—middle school and beyond—who need help developing their reading skills, but want information that's age-appropriate. "Hi-lo" stands for "high-interest, low reading level."

historical fiction. A *genre* of *fiction* in which the story takes place in a historical setting, such as the Revolutionary War. While these books are often carefully researched, contain numerous factual details, and may even feature historical figures, the main characters and events are generally invented.

hornbook. A type of simple book, introduced in the 1400s, that consisted of a printed sheet of text glued onto a small wooden paddle and covered with a very thin protective sheet of cow's horn. Usually the text included the alphabet, numbers, and religious verses such as The Lord's Prayer, and was used to teach both children and adults to read.

horror. A *genre* of *fiction* that centers on terror or the evoking of intense fear or shock in the reader, usually through the use of suspense, gore, and unworldly creatures.

how-to book. A *nonfiction* book that provides readers with instruction in playing chess, building a birdhouse, gardening, putting on a play, etc.

humor. A *genre* of *fiction* that involves a deliberately witty or funny plot.

ID. See *independent distributor.*

independent distributor. Commonly referred to as an ID, a company that inventories and sells the *mass market paperback* books of publishers to high-traffic retail outlets, like drugstore chains, supermarkets, discount chain stores, and airport bookshops. Unlike traditional distributors, IDs rip the covers off any unsold books, and provide the publishing company with a certified statement that a specific number of book covers have been stripped for credit against the publisher's invoice.

independent publisher. Any publishing house that is managed by its owners as opposed to being publicly held or part of a large publishing house or business entity.

in-house. Within a specific publishing house. Editors often refer to the "in-house style"—styles of punctuation, spelling, capitalization, hyphenation, etc.—followed within that particular publishing company.

International Standard Book Number. Commonly referred to as ISBN, a means of book identification used by publishing companies and by anyone who orders books from those companies. Every publisher buys a book of ISBNs—each of which contains that publisher's unique numerical prefix—and assigns one ISBN to each title. Once assigned, an ISBN refers to only that title—and to only a specific edition of that title.

ISBN. See *International Standard Book Number.*

juvenile series books. Series of *fiction* books for all age groups from *easy readers* through *young adult.* Every book in a series is a self-contained story, but all share the same format and main characters.

kill. To reject a manuscript proposal.

legend. A story handed down by tradition and popularly regarded as being true, but actually containing a mixture of fact and fiction.

licensing. The formal right to utilize the characters, likeness, or other aspects of a book in non-book products such as related cartoons, toys, comic books, or calendars.

lifestyles. A *genre* of *picture books* that teaches about different ways people live, such as country living.

lift-the-flap book. A type of interactive book designed with moveable windows under which is found a piece of art.

literary agent. A legal representative of an author who sells the author's work to a third party, such as a publisher, and receives a commission on all monies derived from the work.

managing editor. The person in a publishing house who oversees the timely coordination of different departments—such as the editorial department, art department, and typesetting department—to maintain a smooth production process and meet deadlines. The managing editor is sometimes called a production editor.

manga. A type of *graphic novel* that has a distinctive artistic style, including characters with huge eyes. In Japanese, "manga" means "comic."

market. The segment of the population considered buyers for a particular type of book; or a place or system through which books are sold to consumers, such as a bookstore.

marketplace. A place or system through which books are sold to consumers, such as a bookstore, library, or other book outlet.

mass market outlet. A book outlet found in high-traffic areas such as airport stores, newsstands, drugstores, discount retailers, and supermarket chains. These outlets can reach the "mass" audience rather than the general bookstore's trade audience.

mass market paperback. A $4\frac{1}{2}$-by-7-inch paperback. Often displayed in book racks, these paperbacks sometimes are reprints of a hardcover edition, and sometimes are published in paperback form without a previous hardback printing. Although occasionally sold in bookstores, mass market paperbacks are primarily designed for sale in high-traffic areas such as newsstands, drugstores, and supermarket chains.

middle grade books. The category of books designed for the eight-to-twelve-year-old, who is reading completely on his or her own. Middle grade plots are complicated and include subplots, as well as both primary and secondary characters.

multiple submission. See *simultaneous submission*.

mystery. A *genre* of *fiction* that tells the story of a puzzling crime—usually a murder.

myth. A traditional or legendary story that involves gods and heroes, and serves to explain a cultural practice or natural phenomenon.

net price. The price actually charged by the publisher to any of the customers to whom it sells directly. This can include any book resaler or direct-to-consumer sale. The prices charged by the publisher may be the same as the *retail price*, or may be lower based on an established discount schedule. The cost of shipping the book isn't calculated as part of the net price. See also *retail price; wholesale price*.

Newbery Medal. A medal created in 1922 to honor the author of the most distinguished contribution to American literature for children of the year. The award was named in honor of eighteenth-century English bookseller and publisher John Newbery, and is presented annually by the Association for Library Service to Children, a division of the American Library Association.

niche market. A well-defined *audience* or *marketplace* that has a specialized interest.

niche publisher. A publishing house that produces books in one or more specialized areas.

nonfiction. A work based on fact, and designed to convey information, present instructions for activities or experiments, or recount historical events with little or no embellishment. Nonfiction books can cover a wide range of topics, from action and architecture to technology and transportation.

novel. A lengthy work of prose *fiction* in which the plot unfolds through the actions, thoughts, and speech of the characters.

novelty books. Any book that is interactive, including *pop-up books*, *lift-the-flap books*, and books that make sounds or offer different scents or textures.

option clause. A clause in a contract that gives the publisher an option to acquire the author's next book before the project is offered to another publisher.

out of print. A term describing a *title* that is no longer available from a publisher. Most publishing contracts define the circumstances under which a book will be taken out of print, as well as what will be done with the remaining copies of the book.

overview. The part of the *submission package* in which the author briefly explains the scope and

thrust of a proposed work of *nonfiction*, and clarifies his point of view.

page proofs. See *proofs*.

photo essay. A new *picture book* format, influenced by television, that uses simple text and dramatic photos to explore a variety of topics, especially nature subjects.

picture book. A children's book that has pictures on every page, and tells its story largely though its illustrations.

picture books for older readers. The category of books designed for children of ages six to ten. Like *early picture books*, these works tell their stories largely through illustrations. However, they deal with more complex subject matter.

pop-up books. A *novelty book* designed so that portions of the page pop up for a three-dimensional effect.

print-on-demand publisher. An online publisher that keeps an electronic version of a book on file, and prints and bind copies of the book as needed.

print run. The number of books printed when a book goes to press.

problem novel. A *young adult book* in which the main character deals with drug use, sex, or another issue that is pertinent to readers of that age.

production editor. See *managing editor.*

proofs. Typeset pages created from an edited manuscript. Also called page proofs, they are given to the author and editor to be proofread—that is, to be read for the purpose of finding and correcting typographical errors and other problems.

publisher. The person in a publishing house who

oversees every aspect of operation of all of the company's departments, including editorial, art, marketing, sales, etc. In some houses, the publisher may also perform the functions of an *editor-in-chief*. Also, a business entity that edits, produces, markets, and otherwise makes available printed and/or electronic material.

quality paperback. See *trade paperback*.

query letter. A letter sent to an *acquisitions editor* to determine if he or she is interested in receiving the manuscript for a proposed book. See also *cover letter*.

query package. See *submission package*.

rack-size paperback. See *mass market paperback*.

religious books. Books that are designed to pass on information specific to a given faith or to instill moral values important to a given religion. Religious books may be written for any age group, and therefore may fall into any of the children's book categories, from baby books and easy readers to juvenile series and young adult books.

remaindered books. Books sold by the publisher to a discounter for a price that is slightly above or below the manufacturing cost. Books are often remaindered after their sales fall off.

retail price. The full price of a book as marked on the book itself and/or as listed in a consumer catalogue and/or other consumer-oriented promotional literature. This is usually different from the *net price*, and is always different from the *wholesale price*.

right of first refusal. The right of a publisher to acquire or reject a previously contracted author's next work before it is offered to another publisher. See also *option clause*.

romance. A *genre* of *fiction* in which the main plot focuses on two people falling in love and struggling to make the relationship work, and the ending is emotionally satisfying and optimistic. Many types of romances are popular, ranging from historical romances set in other times to contemporary stories with modern themes.

royalties. The money received by an author based upon the sales of his or her book. The publishing contract specifies the royalty percentage for each form of the book being produced; shows whether it's based on the *retail price* or *net price*; and details how the royalty is divided among two or more authors.

SASE. A self-addressed, stamped envelope. Every *submission package* should include a SASE.

science fiction. A *genre* of *fiction* that draws imaginatively on scientific knowledge and speculation, and takes place at a future time, in imaginary worlds and planets.

season. A specified time of the year in which a publisher presents a new group of *titles* for sale. Most children's publishers have two seasons: spring and fall.

seasonal list. A publisher's new spring or fall *titles*. See also *backlist; frontlist; complete list*.

second serial rights. The rights to republish parts of a given work in a periodical such as a magazine or newspaper after its first publication. See also *subsidiary rights*.

self-help books. Popular psychology, inspirational, and other books designed to improve the inner person.

self-publishing. A publishing option in which the author arranges and pays for every stage of the publishing process, from editing to typesetting to printing and binding, and often sets up a business to take care of the promotion, distribution, and sales of his or her book.

short story. A short work of prose *fiction,* usually containing less than 10,000 words.

simultaneous submission. The practice of sending a proposal to several different publishers at one time. This practice is also called multiple submission.

slush pile. Traditionally, the stack of *unsolicited manuscripts* that are usually read by an *editorial assistant* instead of an *editor,* and—in the case of many large publishing companies—are generally returned to the author unread.

special sales. The sale of books on a deep discount, on a nonreturnable basis, to a *marketplace* that doesn't interfere with bookstores, libraries, and book clubs. An example is the sale of a book to a cereal company, which then packs a copy of the book with each box of cereal as a special promotion.

sponsoring editor. A person in a publishing house who is responsible for guiding or overseeing a manuscript through the various phases of production.

storybooks. See *early picture books.*

submission package. A book proposal that is designed to summarize a proposed book and pique an editor's interest in the project. Depending on the preferences of the publishing house, this package can include any of a number of components, including a *cover letter, annotated table of contents, overview, synopsis,* and sample chapters. In the case of a *picture book,* the entire manuscript is included. A submission package is also called a query package.

subsidiary rights. Those rights derived from the literary work other than the primary right to publish the work. Subsidiary rights may include periodical or newspaper publications; condensations or abridgements; book club publications; foreign-language publications; English-language publications not covered in the "Rights" section of the contract; reprint editions; motion picture, television, radio, and stage interpretations; audio recordings; electronic recordings; public reading rights; Braille, large-type, and other editions for the handicapped; and merchandising/commercial uses, in which a portion of the book or its characters are used to make non-book products such as posters, calendars, greeting cards, coloring books, and toys.

subsidy publisher. See *vanity press.*

synopsis. A part of the *submission package* in which the author summarizes either a work of *fiction* or the story line of a *nonfiction* work such as a *biography.*

tearsheet. An actual sample of a writer's or artist's work "torn" from published material.

title. The formal name of a book; or a written work that will be or has already been published.

toddler books. The category of books designed for children from one to three years of age. These books may be regular paper books or may use a number of novelty formats such as *pop-up* and *lift-the-flap.* Generally, toddler books present simple stories that reflect scenes from a child's everyday life, such as bath time or mealtime.

trade book. A book designed for the general reader, and primarily sold in bookstores. Trade books include hardcover books and full-sized ($5\frac{1}{2}$-by-$8\frac{1}{2}$-inch or larger) paperbacks known as *trade paperbacks.*

trade paperback. A 5½-by-8½-inch or larger softcover book sometimes referred to as a quality paperback. Unlike *mass market paperbacks*, which are often sold in drugstores and other nontraditional outlets, trade paperbacks are usually sold in bookstores.

trade show. An event designed to enable publishers, booksellers, writers, and other people in the book industry to network, sell rights, and conduct business. Good trade shows for children's book writers include BookExpo America (BEA), BookExpo Canada, and the Bologna Children's Book Fair.

trademark. A word, name, or symbol that identifies a literary character or concept, and prevents another party from using that character or concept without the written consent of the trademark owner.

trim size. The outer dimensions of a finished book.

unagented manuscript. A manuscript that isn't represented by a *literary agent*.

unsolicited manuscript. A manuscript that an *editor* hasn't specifically asked to see.

vanity press. A publisher that requires the author to pay a fee for the cost of production and distribution. Also called a subsidy publisher, author-subsidized publisher, author-investment publisher, and cooperative publisher, a vanity press typically offers editorial and marketing services, as well as unusually large royalty payments.

warranty. A legal assurance by the author—stipulated in a publishing agreement—that he or she is the sole proprietor of the work, and that the work doesn't contain any material that is libelous or that violates any right of privacy.

Western. A *genre* of *fiction* in which the action is set in the old American West, usually between the mid-1800s and the early 1900s.

wholesale price. The price of a book that has been discounted based upon the publisher's established discount schedule, and is sold to only a recognized resaler of the *title*. See also *net price; retail price.*

wholesaler. See *distributor.*

work for hire. An arrangement whereby an author, illustrator, or photographer is paid a lump sum for his or her work, and receives no royalties. The publisher owns all rights to the work, including the copyright.

writer's guidelines. The specific submission requirements of an individual publishing house. The writer's guidelines specify the *categories* and *genres* that the publisher will and won't accept, as well as the means by which the company wants to be contacted and the materials it wishes to receive.

young adult books. The category of books designed for readers of age twelve and over—preteens and teenagers—who are not yet ready for adult books, but can handle more sophisticated topics, complex plots, and numerous characters.

Resource List

Many excellent books and periodicals offer insights into the world of publishing; provide helpful guidelines for producing effective submission packages, improving your manuscript, developing your writing skills, negotiating contract terms, self-publishing your work, and effectively marketing your book; and explore other subjects that may be of interest to you. In addition, a number of groups and organizations—including some that are accessible through the Internet—can offer aid and support. I depend on many of these resources when I write and submit my own children's books. However, the following list should be viewed only as a starting point. Don't hesitate to scout out resources on your own or with the help of your local children's or reference librarian.

BOOKS

Backes, Laura. *I've Written A Story . . . What Do I Do Now?* www.writeforkids.com, 2003.

This electronic book includes exclusive success checklists, step-by-step guides to make manuscripts tight and ready to go, submission techniques and secrets, tips for great query letters and plot synopses, and special tricks that can make a submission stand out from the slush pile. Information is also provided about agents, copyrights, and finances.

The Chicago Manual of Style. **Fifteenth Edition. Chicago: University of Chicago Press, 2003.**

Since 1906, this well-known resource has helped set editorial standards, providing systematic guidelines for editors, proofreaders, indexers, publishers—and writers. It's an important reference tool when you're unsure of where to place a comma, or whether or not you should spell out the number or use a numeral. The most recent edition reflects changes made in style, usage, procedure, and technology, with substantial sections on preparing manuscripts for electronic publishing, editing for online publications, and citing electronic sources. Be aware, however, that publishers often have their own in-house style, which may conflict with this manual.

Children's Writer's & Illustrator's Market. **Cincinnati: Writer's Digest Books, updated annually.**

In my experience, this is the best resource for children's book writers. It contains over 800 publishers, including independent houses, as well as a special section devoted to Canadian, UK, and Australian markets. While this resource offers fewer listings than the *LMP*, it is often more helpful for prospective authors, as its entries include the names of acquisitions editors, the percentage of titles that come from first-time authors, and other useful information. In addition, it contains listings of magazines that accept work for children, names of agents and art reps, clubs and organizations, conferences and workshops, contests, awards and grants, and online resources, as well as short articles of advice from editors and published authors. Although you'll find it in most libraries, you may want to buy this book as it's quite affordably priced.

The International Directory of Little Magazines & Small Presses. **Paradise, CA: Dustbooks, updated annually.**

Although not as easy to use as the *LMP* and *Children's Writer's & Illustrator's Market*, this directory lists over 5,000 small publishers and magazines. In addition to basic contact information, most entries offer payment rates, proposal requirements, and recent publications. Subject and regional indexes are also included.

Jones, Allan Frewin, and Lesley Pollinger. *Writing for Children and Getting Published.* **Chicago: NTC Publishing Group, 1996.**

For the writer who isn't sure how to get started, this book is a strong guide to the writing process, complete with tips about improving your language skills and deciding whether to write fiction or nonfiction. The authors present basics about developing plotline and finding your voice, complete with grammar lessons and writing exercises. They also explain how to present and submit work, how to deal with rejection, and how to handle acceptance. A special chapter addresses the needs of illustrators.

Karl, Jean E. *How to Write and Sell Children's Picture Books.* **Cincinnati: Writer's Digest Books, 1994.**

For any writer interested in selling a picture book, this title presents all the basics. The author helps you assess your abilities as a writer, tells you how to develop your own voice and style, explains how to choose the right genre, and guides you in writing both fiction and nonfiction, as well as poetry. Finally, the author explains how to get your book into print.

Kawa-Jump, Shirley. *How to Publish Your Articles.* **Garden City Park, NY: Square One Publishers, 2002.**

Based on a career of more than two decades, veteran freelance writer Shirley Kawa-Jump wrote this book to guide the novice writer through the maze of magazines, journals, newspapers, and e-zines to the ultimate goal of publication. The book reviews the nuts and bolts of the profession, from idea development, to research and writing, to contract negotiations. Most important, it provides a complete system of article submission geared to maximize the odds of getting an acceptance while avoiding those errors that can turn off an editor. The author even offers alternative ways of using writing skills to boost income.

Kirsch, Jonathan. *Kirsch's Guide to the Book Contract: For Authors, Publishers, Editors and Agents.* **Los Angeles, CA: Acrobat Books, 1999.**

Written by an intellectual property attorney and designed for use by authors, publishers, editors, and literary agents, this book begins with a model book contract. The contract's clauses are organized under topic headings—such as "Introductory Clauses" and "Grant of Rights"—each of which corresponds to a chapter of the guide. This format enables you to turn to the appropriate chapter for a detailed explanation of that portion of the contract. The author provides a wealth of tips for negotiating the deal, as well as cautions about contract elements that may prove problematic. Thorough and truly helpful, *Kirsch's Guide* is a must-have resource for the writer who is serious about participating in contract negotiations.

Kozak, Ellen M. *Every Writer's Guide to Copyright and Publishing Law.* **Third Edition. New York: Owl Books, 2004.**

This straightforward text doesn't overwhelm you with legal terminology, but simplifies confusing terms and issues that arise for new authors. Some subjects that will be of interest are U.S. copyright law, including e-copyrights; fair use; libel; work for hire; collaboration agreements; and contract information.

Lamott, Anne. *Bird by Bird: Some Instructions on Writing and Life.* **New York: Anchor Books, 1994.**

This book is required reading for English and writing teachers, and it should be for writers of all books regardless of their intended audience. In her humorous and poetic style, Lamott, a writing professor and published author, shares her personal experiences as a writer, while offering honest instructions on how to get started, from dealing with plot to handling writer's block. Read it for inspiration before sitting down to work on your own book. Or just enjoy Lamott's wit and wisdom.

Larsen, Michael. *How to Write a Book Proposal.* **Cincinnati: Writer's Digest Books, 1997.**

Written by a literary agent, *How to Write a Book Proposal* focuses on the nonfiction book, but is also a good guide for the fiction writer since it offers tips on how to prepare an introduction that conveys the book's purpose and audience, and guides the writer through proposal components like the sample chapters. Three sample proposals are included for review.

Lee, Betsy B. *A Basic Guide to Writing, Selling, and Promoting Children's Books: Plus Information About Self-Publishing.* **Learning Abilities Books, 2000.**

Created as a teaching and review text for writing classes, this electronic book guides the writer in writing, selling, and promoting stories for children. The author discusses different types of children's stories, as well as where and how each one should be sold. Basic principles of writing are explained, and a wide variety of resources are included.

Levin, Martin P. *Be Your Own Literary Agent: The Ultimate Insider's Guide to Getting Published.* **Berkeley, CA: Ten Speed Press, 1996.**

Levin provides clear step-by-step instructions for writing a successful book proposal, negotiating a contract, and otherwise acting as your own literary agent. Included is a wealth of model proposals, as well as a helpful glossary and a list of small publishers who, according to the author, are most likely to read and accept your book. But perhaps the most valuable feature is a section-by-section review of a sample literary contract.

Literary Market Place. **New Providence, NJ: R.R. Bowker, updated annually.**

Considered the bible of the publishing industry, the *LMP* is a comprehensive listing of American and Canadian publishers; literary agents; editorial services; trade associations and foundations; book trade courses; book reviewers; book clubs; manufacturers; and more. The *LMP's* high price makes it impractical for individual purchase, but it can be found in the reference section of any library. Although the scope and format of this resource makes it a bit unwieldy for children's book authors, it not only includes publishers not listed in *Children's Writer's & Illustrator's Market*, but also provides business-related information not found in the other resource.

Litowinsky, Olga. *It's a Bunny-Eat-Bunny World: A Writer's Guide to Surviving and Thriving in Today's Competitive Children's Book Market.* **New York: Walker & Company, 2001.**

This intriguing title comes from a former executive editor of children's books for Simon & Schuster and an author of several children's books. Litowinsky offers insider's information about the changing children's book publishing industry, and provides helpful tips for writing, editing, and marketing a children's book. Valuable suggestions are included for improving writing skills.

Lukens, Rebecca J. *A Critical Handbook of Children's Literature.* **Seventh Edition. Boston: Allyn & Bacon, 2003.**

A great book for anyone interested in children's literature, education, language arts, and/or educational media, this handbook covers the various genres, exploring plot, character, theme, setting, point of view, style, and tone. Chapters are included on rhymes, poetry, biography, and informational books, and listings of recommended readings are provided.

Malone, Eileen. *The Complete Guide to Writer's Groups, Conferences, and Workshops.* **New York: John Wiley & Sons, 1996.**

In addition to serving as a listing of organizations, resources, and educational programs for writers, this book also helps you first evaluate your needs, and then select the group or program that best satisfies them. Other topics include what you can get out of a writer's group, conference, or workshop; what is expected of a member of a writer's group; how you can give and take criticism; and how you can start your own writer's group.

Mogilner, Alijandra. *Children's Writer's Word Book.* Cincinnati: Writer's Digest Books, 1992.

If you're ever uncertain about the best word to use for the reading level you've chosen, look it up in this reference, which provides word lists for children from kindergarten through grade six, a thesaurus of listed words, reading levels of synonyms, and practical advice on word usage in children's writing.

Norton, Donna E. *Through the Eyes of a Child: An Introduction to Children's Literature.* Sixth Edition. Saddle River, NJ: Prentice Hall, 2002.

A widely-respected means of introducing future teachers to children's literature, this book is also a good reference for the children's book writer who wants to learn more about multicultural books, and who wishes to know what teachers look for in good literature. The author also covers the history of children's books.

Poynter, Dan. *The Self-Publishing Manual: How to Write, Print, and Sell Your Own Book.* Fourteenth Edition. Santa Barbara. CA: Para Publishing, 2003.

Considered to be the seminal text for anyone contemplating self-publishing, this is a complete guide to writing, publishing, and selling your own book. Included is a step-by-step system for producing a commercial book, as well as guidelines for getting your book quickly into print, information on setting up your own publishing company, and "secrets" of low-cost book promotion. Information is also offered on spinning off electronic editions.

Publishers' International ISBN Directory. Berlin, Germany: International ISBN Agency, updated annually.

Here is the most comprehensive listing of worldwide publishers—including, of course, publishers in English-speaking foreign countries. All in all, over 200 countries and more than 600,000 publishers are included in a format that allows you to find a publishing house by country or name. Like the *Literary Market Place*, though, this book has a prohibitively high price, so look for it in the reference section of a large public library rather than your local bookstore.

Pushcart's Complete Rotten Reviews and Rejections: A History of Insult, a Solace to Writers. Edited by Bill Henderson and Andre Bernard. Wainscott, NY: Pushcart Press, 1998.

This book is a great pick-me-up if you've ever received a rejection letter of your own, or if you just want a good laugh. The editors have compiled some of the nastiest comments received by well-known published authors, including Shakespeare, Melville, Twain, Updike, and Dickens. You'll probably be most interested in the comments about children's authors, but all are fun to read.

Raab, Susan Salzman. *An Author's Guide to Children's Book Promotion.* Chappaqua, NY: Raab Associates, 2001.

This self-published book guides children's book authors and illustrators in setting up appearances, getting a book distributed, working the school and library markets for potential sales, arranging special promotions in museums and community organizations, creating publicity packages, and building a website. A detailed directory includes key associations and organizations, children's book information sources, children's books clubs, wholesalers, book chains, and trade and educational publications. This is a great guide for writers who want to take an active role in the marketing of their book.

Seuling, Barbara. *How to Write a Children's Book and Get It Published.* New York: John Wiley & Sons, 1991.

This book details the five essential steps to publication: researching the current marketplace, developing story ideas, strengthening writing skills and improving work habits, submitting proposals and manuscripts to agents and publishers, and becoming part of the writing community. Also included is a chapter on writing plays for children, as well as one for the writer who is also an illustrator.

Shaw, Eva. *The Successful Writer's Guide to Publishing Magazine Articles.* Loveland, CO: Loveland Press, 1998.

In this book, writer, teacher, and lecturer Eva Shaw offers a systematic business approach to every aspect of the article-writing craft, from finding a topic to getting an article into print. Separate chapters are devoted to setting goals, querying, reading a magazine for which you want to write, doing meaningful research, and marketing yourself and your work.

Silvey, Anita. *The Essential Guide to Children's Books and Their Creators.* New York: Houghton Mifflin, 2002.

This comprehensive survey of children's books—from alphabet books to young adult novels—is set up like an encyclopedia. More than 475 entries focus on best-loved children's authors and illustrators, different genres, social and historical issues, and more. Authors and illustrators provide their personal insights into the trade, and a great Basic Reading List guides you to worthwhile children's literature.

Subject Guide to Children's Books in Print. New Providence, NJ: R.R. Bowker, updated annually.

Revised on a yearly basis, this reference guide lists more than 212,000 fiction and nonfiction children's books arranged under 8,900 subject headings. The *Subject Guide* is the easiest way for authors to compare their ideas for new books with what is already in print, and to pinpoint topics currently of interest to children, parents, and librarians.

Sutherland, Zena. *Children & Books.* New York: Addison-Wesley Publishing, 1996.

This textbook for students of children's literature provides a thorough history of the children's book publishing industry. Included are an exploration of theoretical approaches to writing for children, information about awards and censorship, and an extensive bibliography. If you want to know all there is to know about the history of kid's lit, this is the book for you.

Underdown, Harold D., and Lynne Rominger. *The Complete Idiot's Guide to Publishing Children's Books.* **Indianapolis, IN: Alpha Books, 2001.**

Arranged in the easy-to-read format of the *Idiot's Guides,* this book offers a lot of snappy snippets about the industry, touching briefly on everything from the history of children's book publishing to writing a children's book to promoting a book once it's in print. This is a good resource if you want a quick overview of the children's book publishing world.

Writers' & Artists' Yearbook. London, England: A & C Black, updated annually.

This best-selling guide to all areas of the media presents listings of publishers in the United States, the United Kingdom, Ireland, Australia, and New Zealand, including all contact information. Also included is advice on proofreading, marketing your book, acquiring an agent, and other topics of interest. As a plus, *Writers' and Artists' Yearbook* is affordably priced so that you can easily add it to your home reference library.

Wyndham, Lee. *Writing for Children & Teenagers.* **Cincinnati: Writer's Digest Books, 1989.**

A helpful guide for both the novice and the more experienced writer, this volume provides step-by-step instructions for writing, with practical advice about holding a child's attention, developing ideas, and using appropriate vocabulary for each age level. Information is also included on performing research, writing plays, contributing to magazines, writing mystery books, and working with packagers.

PERIODICALS

Bookbird

Ohio State University
School of Teaching and Learning
333 Arps Hall
1945 North High Street
Columbus, OH 43210
Phone: 614-292-8059
Website: www.ibby.org/Seiten/04_bookb.htm

Bookbird is the quarterly journal on international children's literature from the International Board on Books for Young People (IBBY). Articles regularly focus on topics such as "Sense of Place in Children's Literature" and "Autobiographical Writing About Childhood." Also included are author and illustrator profiles, book reviews and recommendations, and news of IBBY and regional projects and events.

Booklist

American Library Association
50 E. Huron
Chicago, IL 60611
Phone: 800-545-2433
Website: www.ala.org

For more than ninety years, this publication of the American Library Association has been the librarian's leading choice for reviews of the latest books and electronic media. Each year it reviews more than 2,500 children's titles—as well as 4,000 books for adults. *Booklist* also offers author interviews, bibliographies, book-related essays by well-known writers, and a selection of columns, including a wealth of information on industry trends.

Children's Book Insider

901 Columbia Road
Fort Collins, CO 80525
Phone: 970-495-0056 (questions)
        800-807-1916 (oders only)
Website: www.writeforkids.com

Children's Book Insider is a monthly ad-free publication for both aspiring and experienced writers of children's books. Each issue contains up-to-the-minute marketing information from publishers accepting manuscript submissions, how-to articles on all aspects of writing for children, interviews with top editors and authors, notices of contests and grants, and articles on the business side of publishing. *CBI* also provides quarterly updates of the listings in *Children's Writer's & Illustrator's Market,* as well as information on emerging technologies such as electronic books.

The Horn Book Magazine

56 Roland Street, Suite 200
Boston, MA 02129
Phone: 800-325-1170
        617-628-0225
Website: www.hbook.com

Both opinionated and authoritative, *The Horn Book Magazine* is for everyone who needs to know about children's literature. Each bimonthly issue contains reviews of the newest books available; articles and columns covering a range of related topics; a parent's page; and more. A special section "For Authors & Illustrators" provides extensive information on the world of children's book publishing. In conjunction with the *Boston Globe,* the magazine also selects books annually to win the Boston Globe-Horn Book Awards for outstanding children's literature, including fiction, nonfiction, and picture books.

The Lion and the Unicorn

The Johns Hopkins University Press,
    Journals Division
2715 North Charles Street
Baltimore, MD 21218-4363
Phone: 800-548-1784
Website: www.press.jhu.edu/journals/lion_and_
    the_unicorn

The Lion and the Unicorn is a peer-reviewed journal that critically examines children's literature. The journal's coverage includes the state of the publishing industry, comparative studies of significant books, the art of illustration, and popular culture.

Once Upon a Time

553 Winston Court
St. Paul, MN 55118
Phone: 651-457-6223
Website: www.onceuponatimemag.com

This thirty-two page quarterly magazine for and by children's writers and illustrators offers instructional, informative, supportive, and entertaining articles on writing for children. It accepts freelance submissions, as well.

Publisher's Weekly

360 Park Avenue South
New York, NY 10010
Phone: 800-278-2991
Website: www.publishersweekly.com

The most important journal within the book trade, *PW* is read by publishers, bookstore buyers, librarians, and other people in the industry. A window on the publishing world, it provides book reviews, profiles of best-selling authors, an insider's look at book and marketing trends, seasonal "Children's Announcements" to introduce upcoming titles, and a weekly "Children's Books" column, as well as lists of bestsellers.

School Library Journal

PO Box 16178
North Hollywood, CA 91615-6178
Phone: 800-595-1066
Website: www.schoollibraryjournal.com

School Library Journal, the print magazine, and *School Library Journal Online,* the website, serve librarians who work with young people in school and public libraries. Read the journal to learn more about the current world of children's literature, and to discover what librarians and teachers would like to see in print.

The Writer

Kalmbach Publishing Co.
21027 Crossroads Circle
P.O. Box 1612
Waukesha, WI 53187-1612
Phone: 800-533-6644
Website: www.writermag.com

Designed for the professional writer, this journal presents interviews with successful writers; lists of helpful books and other writing tools; notices of literary contests, workshops, and conferences; writing tips; and more.

Writer's Digest

F & W Publications, Inc.
4700 E. Galbraith Road
Cincinnati, OH 45236
Phone: 513-531-2222
Website: www.writersdigest.com

Produced by the publisher of *Children's Writer's & Illustrator's Market,* this easy-to-read magazine is filled with interviews of both adult and chil-

dren's authors, and with articles about improving your writing, working with editors, writing better proposals, and more. Included is a special section that guides you to writers' workshops, conferences, and classes; literary contests; professional editorial services and ghostwriters; and literary agents.

GROUPS AND ORGANIZATIONS

Association of Author's Representatives (AAR)

P.O. Box 237201
Ansonia Station
New York, NY 10003
Website: www.aar-online.org

The AAR was formed in 1991 through the merger of the Society of Authors' representatives and the Independent Literary Agents Association. Although designed to serve the needs of literary and dramatic agents, it also serves writers by providing a listing of member agents, as well as suggested topics that you can discuss with potential agents as a means of choosing the best person to represent you and your project.

The Author's Guild

31 East 28th Street, 10th Floor
New York, NY 10016-7923
Phone: 212-563-5904
Website: www.authorsguild.org

A professional organization for published writers, the Guild represents more than 8,000 authors. The Guild's legal staff reviews members' publishing and agency contracts, intervenes in publishing disputes, and hold seminars and symposia on issues of importance to writers. The Guild also lobbies at the national and local levels on behalf of all authors on issues such as copyright, taxation, and freedom of expression. Reports bring members up-to-date on subjects of immediate importance, and give them the information necessary to negotiate from a position of strength.

Children's Book Council (CBC)

12 W. 37th Street, 2nd Floor
New York, NY 10018-7480
Phone: 212-966-1990
Website: www.cbcbooks.org

The CBC is a nonprofit trade organization dedicated to encouraging literacy and the use and enjoyment of children's books. It is the official sponsor of Young People's Poetry Week and Children's Book Week, two national events that are aimed at educators and librarians, but are wonderful opportunities for author visits and book signings. The CBC's website offers invaluable information about industry trends, author and illustrator interviews, lists of children's book publishers, an annual industry calendar of events, notices of awards and prizes, and much more.

Publisher's Marketing Association (PMA)

627 Aviation Way
Manhattan Beach, CA 90266
Phone: 310-372-2732
Website: www.pma-online.org.

Founded in 1983, this trade association of independent publishers has a membership of over 3,000 United States and international publishers—including self-publishers. Through its newsletter, online chat group, and other publications

and services, the PMA can guide you to reputable typesetters, printers, editors, and more; inform you of worthwhile publishing fairs, seminars, and workshops; and otherwise provide you with the information you need to succeed as a self-publisher. Services are provided for members only.

Small Publishers Association of North American (SPAN)

PO Box 1306
Buena Vista, CO 81211
Phone: 719-395-5761
Website: www.spannet.org

Founded in 1996, SPAN's stated mission is "to advance the image and profits of independent publishers through education and marketing opportunities." SPAN offers its members—over 1,000 small presses and self-publishers—a range of resources and services, including an information-packed monthly newsletter; a variety of conferences and seminars on publicity and marketing; discounts on health insurance, shipping, office supplies, and industry publications; and a membership resource directory that will allow you to network with other SPAN members. Like the PMA, SPAN provides services for members only.

Society of Children's Book Writers and Illustrators (SCBWI)

8271 Beverly Boulevard
Los Angeles, CA 90048
Phone: 323-782-1010
Website: www.scbwi.org

An international organization with over 18,000 members, the SCBWI acts as a network for the exchange of knowledge between writers, illustrators, editors, publishers, agents, librarians, educators, booksellers, and others involved in literature for young people. The organization sponsors two annual International Conferences on Writing and Illustrating for Children, as well as dozens of regional conferences and events throughout the world. It also publishes a bi-monthly newsletter, provides many informational publications on the art and business of writing and selling, and offers manuscript and illustration exchanges for the purpose of receiving written critiques.

U.S. Copyright Office

Library of Congress
101 Independence Avenue, SE
Washington, DC 20559-6000
Phone: 202-707-3000
Website: www.lcweb.loc.gov/copyright/

If you're worried that a publishing company might steal your work, the U.S. Copyright Office can provide legal protection by copyrighting your manuscript. You can either order the necessary forms over the phone or download them from the website. Be sure to observe the fee information. The website also explains how to register your work, and provides information about licensing, patents, and trademarks.

U.S. Department of Education

400 Maryland Avenue, SW
Washington, DC 20202-0498
Phone: 800-USA-LEARN
Website: www.ed.gov

Contact this organizatin to find national, state, and local education resources, as well as information on early childhood, math and science, social studies, and reading and language requirements.

U.S. Patent and Trademark Office

General Information Services Division
Crystal Plaza 3, Room 2C02
P.O. Box 1450
Alexandria, VA 22313-1450
Phone: 800-786-9199
Website: www.uspto.gov

If you wish to protect a character or concept with a trademark, this is the organization to contact. Visit their website or give them a call to learn about licensing, trademarks, and more.

INTERNET SITES

American Booksellers Association (ABA)

Website: www.bookweb.org

A nonprofit trade association that represents independent bookstores in the United States, the ABA also hosts the annual ABA Convention in conjunction with BookExpo America each spring. Visit the association's website to find book industry research and statistics, and to learn about related organizations and events.

Book Marketing Update

Website: www.bookmarket.com/index.html

Designed for anyone who's "into book marketing, book promotion, free publicity, self-publishing, e-publishing, or print-on-demand," this site offers a list of children's book publishers, complete with editors' names as well as links that take you directly to the publishers' websites.

BookExpo America (BEA)

Website: www.bookexpoamerica.com

Visit this website to learn about BookExpo

America—an important annual event that can put you in touch with publishers, editors, agents, and other people in the world of book publishing. BookExpo is also a great place to learn about industry trends.

Child and Family Web Guide

Website: www.cfw.tufts.edu

The Web Guide evaluates, describes, and provides links to hundreds of sites containing child development research and practical advice. This is a valuable resource for the writer who wants to better understand the young characters about whom he or she is writing.

Children's Book Insider

Website: www.writeforkids.com

Rated by *Writers' Digest* as one of the 101 best websites for writers, this site was created by a former literary agent in 1990. Visit it for online excerpts of the monthly newsletter *Children's Book Insider;* a message board; articles about the industry; free e-books; links to other helpful sites; and more.

Children's Literature Web Guide

Website: www.ucalgary.ca/~dkbrown/

This site was created by a librarian at the University of Calgary to gather and categorize the growing number of Internet resources related to books for children and young adults. Use it to find commentary on children's books, lists of children's book awards, information on children's authors and illustrators, and much more.

The Drawing Board

Website: http://members.aol.com/thedrawing

This site for illustrators features interviews; an-swers frequently asked questions; and provides information on new markets, compiling a portfolio, and more. A "Book Talk" section alerts artists to new books that are of special interest to them.

Electronic Book Web (EBW)

Website: http://12.108.175.91/ebookweb/ publishers

Designed to serve the needs of the international e-book community, this site offers e-book news and a wide variety of resources, including an alphabetical listing of e-publishers in the form of links that will take you to each company's website.

The Purple Crayon

Website: www.underdown.org

Created by editorial consultant Harold D. Underdown, The Purple Crayon is recognized as one of the best sources of information about the children's publishing industry. In addition to offering editorial services for a fee, the site presents a wealth of articles on agents, book packagers, multiple submissions, and many other topics of interest to the children's book writer. Links are also provided to author websites.

SmartWriters.com

Website: www.smartwriters.com

Designed for "everyone who writes, reads, or teaches literature for kids," this website provides directories of writers and illustrators, children's book publishers, and paying magazine markets; offers information about conferences and contests; tells you how to build your own website; and more. And for those times when you need feedback, there's a chat room and a section called "Ask the Editor."

Society of Children's Book Writers & Illustrators

Website: www.scbwi.org

You have to become a member of SCBWI to participate in this discussion group, but it's well worth the effort, as membership will enable you to post your own questions, answer the questions of other writers, and join online critiquing groups that will provide you with feedback on your work. The site has both a writer's section and an illustrator's section.

Trade Show News Network

Website: www.tsnn.com

This is the leading online resource for the trade show and exhibition industry, with data on more than 15,000 trade shows and conferences, and more than 30,000 seminars. Look under "media-book publishing" for information on events that may be of interest to you.

Verla Kay's Website for Children's Writers & Illustrators

Website: www.verlakay.com

Visit this author's site for discussion boards and live chats, as well as daily writing exercises designed to sharpen your skills and get you started on the day's work. The message board enables you to read messages from other writers and illustrators, and post your own comments. During the live chat, writers and illustrators "talk" to one another in "real time."

Writing-World.Com

Website: www.writing-world.com/children

This site provides a comprehensive collection of articles about writing and illustrating for children, lists of books for writers, links to online resources, interviews with published authors, writing classes conducted by e-mail, notices of writing contests, lists of writing opportunities, and more.

Yahoo

Website: www.yahoo.com/business_and_ economy/shopping_and_services/publishers

It takes a while to type in the web address, but once you get there, you can click on "children's" and get a listing of more than one hundred children's book publishers, magazine publishers, and more.

ℐNDEX

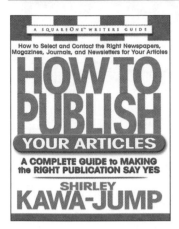

For every writer who hopes to break into print, getting that first article published is essential. Most new writers, however, find the process of getting an article published somewhat overwhelming. Freelance article writer Shirley Kawa-Jump has written an exceptional book designed to answer all the novice writer's common questions about getting articles into magazines, journals, and newspapers.

While some writers write for pleasure, others may want to start a career. And for some, frequent publication is simply a requirement of their chosen profession. Part One examines each of these possibilities, and then goes on to explore the available writers' markets and explain how they work. Part Two provides a complete system of article submission geared to maximize the writer's odds of getting an acceptance, while avoiding the common errors that can turn off an editor. Part Three looks at the possibility of building a career as a freelance article writer. It reviews the nuts and bolts of the profession—from idea development to contract negotiation. And it provides the writer with a realistic view of what could be a rewarding occupation.

$17.95 • 352 pages • 7.5 x 9-inch quality paperback • 2-Color • ISBN 0-7570-0016-9

Perhaps you began writing poetry as a means of private expression. Or perhaps your verse was meant to share your feelings with that special someone. But now your goals have changed, and you want to get your poetry into print.

How to Publish Your Poetry is a complete guide to breaking into the world of print poetry. The book begins by providing a window to the publishing world so that you can see the kinds of publications you should target. You will learn about great market resources for locating appropriate publishers, and you will learn the importance of defining your audience. Following this, the author helps you write a persuasive submissions package, and presents a proven step-by-step system for sending your package out—a system designed to maximize results. When the acceptance letters start rolling in, the author guides you in selecting the publications that will allow you to meet your personal goals. You will even learn of the resources that can help you further develop your special gift.

$15.95 • 192 pages • 7.5 x 9-inch quality paperback • 2-Color • ISBN 0-7570-0001-0

In today's topsy-turvy world of film production, getting a screenplay sold and produced is no easy task. To play the film game, you need to know the rules. *How to Sell Your Screenplay* not only lets you in on the rules, but also lets you in on the secrets of winning the game.

Written by two veteran screenwriters, *How to Sell Your Screenplay* was designed as a complete guide to getting your screenplay seen, read, and sold. The book begins by giving you an insider's understanding of how the business works. It then guides you in putting your script into the proper format so that you can make the best first impression. Later chapters introduce you to the "players," including agents, lawyers, producers, and more; guide you in preparing a perfect pitch; provide you with the proven Square One System for query submission; and aid you in getting the best contract possible. Throughout, tips from experts help you swim with the sharks without getting eaten by them.

$17.95 • 320 pages • 7.5 x 9-inch quality paperback • 2-Color • ISBN 0-7570-0002-9

John Grisham, Toni Morrison, Danielle Steele, Stephen King, and Anne Rice—all successful novelists whose new books immediately rise to the top of the bestsellers list. Yet there was a time when even they were struggling to sell their first stories. To help all those budding authors negotiate the difficult road ahead, literary manager Ken Atchity has written *How to Publish Your Novel*—a guide that provides the knowledge and strategies needed to get a work of fiction into print.

Part One begins with the basics—understanding the world of fiction publishing and how various types of fiction fit in. It also examines writers' motives for getting published. Part Two offers the practical guidance necessary to find a literary representative or publisher. It provides the information required to create an effective plan of action—from deciding whether to be agented or self-represented to developing a proposal package; from selecting a list of potential publishers to understanding a contract. Finally, Part Three offers sound advice on choosing a career as a writer, guiding you as you perfect your craft.

$18.95 • 284 pages • 7.5 x 9-inch quality paperback • 2-Color • ISBN 0-7570-0049-5

For nonprofit organizations, businesses, clubs, hobby groups, and professional societies, newsletters can provide a perfect way to educate, motivate, sell, and promote. Unfortunately, few newsletters realize their full potential. Now, newsletter expert Carol Luers Eyman has written a comprehensive guide and reference to creating, maintaining, and marketing an effective and cost-efficient newsletter.

How to Publish Your Newsletter is designed to steer editors, entrepreneurs, and volunteers through every phase of the newsletter publishing process. The author helps you set up shop, from the creation of a budget to the development of a capable staff and a realistic schedule. And she guides you through the writing and design of newsletter articles, including the use of photos and other graphics. Every aspect of the process, from planning to distribution, is carefully explored and explained, enabling you to launch your new newsletter—or improve your existing one—with both confidence and competence.

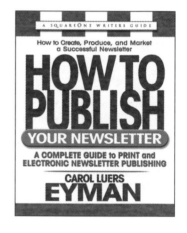

$19.95 • 268 pages • 7.5 x 9-inch quality paperback • 2-Color • ISBN 0-7570-0045-2

All writers dream of seeing their books in print. While some succeed, the fact is that most don't. Why? Most writers simply don't know what publishers are looking for. Or they didn't—until now. Written by a publisher with over twenty-five years of experience, this book helps you avoid the common pitfalls that foil most writers, and maximize your chance of getting your nonfiction book into publication.

How to Publish Your Nonfiction Book begins by helping you define your book's category, audience, and marketplace so that you know exactly where your book "fits in." You're then guided in choosing the best publishing companies for your book, and crafting a winning submission package. Then the Square One System tells you exactly how to submit your package to optimize success, while minimizing time, cost, and effort. A special section on contracts turns legal mumbo-jumbo into plain English, allowing you to be a savvy player in the contract game. Most important, this book will help you avoid the errors that so often prevent writers from reaching their goal.

$16.95 • 252 pages • 7.5 x 9-inch quality paperback • 2-Color • ISBN 0-7570-0000-2

For more information about our books, visit our website at www.squareonepublishers.com.